Writing National CINEMA

Interfaces: Studies in Visual Culture
Editors Mark J. Williams and Adrian W. B. Randolph,
Dartmouth College

This series, sponsored by Dartmouth College Press, develops and promotes the study of visual culture from a variety of critical and methodological perspectives. Its impetus derives from the increasing importance of visual signs in everyday life, and from the rapid expansion of what are termed "new media." The broad cultural and social dynamics attendant to these developments present new challenges and opportunities across and within the disciplines. These have resulted in a trans-disciplinary fascination with all things visual, from "high" to "low," and from esoteric to popular. This series brings together approaches to visual culture—broadly conceived—that assess these dynamics critically and that break new ground in understanding their effects and implications.

For a complete list of books that are available in the series, visit www.upne.com

Barbara Larson and Fae Brauer, eds., *The Art of Evolution: Darwin, Darwinisms, and Visual Culture*

Jeffrey Middents, *Writing National Cinema: Film Journals and Film Culture in Peru*

Michael Golec, *The Brillo Box Archive: Aesthetics, Design, and Art*

Rob Kroes, *Photographic Memories: Private Pictures, Public Images, and American History*

Jonathan Beller, *The Cinematic Mode of Production: Attention Economy and the Society of the Spectacle*

Ann B. Shteir and Bernard Lightman, eds., *Figuring It Out: Science, Gender, and Visual Culture*

Anna Munster, *Materializing New Media: Body, Image, and Interface in Information Aesthetics*

Luc Pauwels, ed., *Visual Cultures of Science: Rethinking Representational Practices in Knowledge Building and Science Communication*

Lisa Saltzman and Eric Rosenberg, eds., *Trauma and Visuality in Modernity*

Writing National CINEMA

Film Journals and Film Culture in Peru

JEFFREY MIDDENTS

DARTMOUTH COLLEGE PRESS
HANOVER, NEW HAMPSHIRE

PUBLISHED BY UNIVERSITY PRESS OF NEW ENGLAND
HANOVER AND LONDON

Dartmouth College Press
Published by University Press of New England,
One Court Street, Lebanon, NH 03766
www.upne.com

Printed in U.S.A.

5 4 3 2 1

Library of Congress Cataloging-in-Publication Data
Middents, Jeffrey.
Writing national cinema : film journals and film culture in Peru / Jeffrey Middents.
p. cm.—(Interfaces: studies in visual culture)
Includes bibliographical references and index.
ISBN 978-1-58465-776-7 (cloth : alk. paper)
1. Film criticism—Peru—History. 2. Motion pictures—Peru—History—20th century.
3. Motion pictures—Periodicals—History.
4. Peruvian periodicals—History—20th century. I. Title.
PN1995.M4875 2009
791.430985—dc22 2009015184

University Press of New England is a member of the Green Press Initiative. The paper used in this book meets their minimum requirement for recycled paper.

CONTENTS

ILLUSTRATIONS

ACKNOWLEDGMENTS

This project first came to light in 1998 and therefore there are many people to thank. First and foremost, I must warmly thank Carina Yervasi, Margarita de la Vega-Hurtado, Catherine Benamou, and Santiago Colás, who helped shepherd and steer this project while I was a graduate student at the University of Michigan. My colleagues at American University provided much-needed support, critique, and encouragement, especially Chuck Larson, Richard Sha, Marianne Noble, Keith Leonard, Erik Dussere, and Despina Kakoudaki. In addition, I thank Joan Catapano, Tamara Falicov, and Silvia Spitta for their extensive commentaries that proved essential to getting this project to fruition. My extended *colegas* in the Society of Cinema and Media Studies Latino/a Caucus opened my world to the myriad facets of Latin American cinema and showed me how all of our work intersects into the fantastic tapestry that makes up our discipline. I am especially grateful to those with whom I had the honor to present various portions of this work at SCMS conference panels in Washington, D.C., London, and Vancouver, as well as at an ACLA panel in Puebla, Mexico, and an ASA panel in Atlanta. My students at American University also deserve a round of applause, especially those in my summer 2006 seminar on short films and my spring 2007 honors colloquium on film criticism; these students (somewhat unwittingly) pushed me to define crucial points of my overall argument. Various friends in Ann Arbor, Monterey, and Washington, D.C., made getting through this project that much easier: a shout-out therefore to Marcy, the Zanzibar crew, Eric, Marit, Todd, Jen, Mike, and Meipo for keeping me sane all these years. Many people, too many to thank individually, were extremely supportive as the project headed to its final stages; nonetheless, Richard Pult and the folks at University Press of New England deserve an extra round of applause for the warm embrace they gave this project.

Most of the primary research on film journals was done on location in Lima, Peru, for which I am grateful to have received funding from both the University of Michigan and the College of Arts and Sciences at American University. In Lima, I am indebted to Norma Rivera, director of the Filmoteca de Lima (now housed at the Pontificia Universidad Católica del Perú), for allowing me unlimited access to the full collection of *Hablemos de cine* as well as for helping to secure permissions for the artwork in this volume: without her gracious help over the years, this project would certainly never have come to fruition. Many thanks also to the number of cinephiles and directors in Peru and elsewhere for granting the time for interviews, including Issac León Frías, Federico de Cárdenas, Ricardo Bedoya, Melvin Ledgard, Augusto Cabada, Francisco Lombardi, Federico García, Miguel Reynel, Desiderio Blanco, Augusto Tamayo, Marianne Eyde, Alberto Durant, Alvaro Velarde, Mario Cabos Castro, and Gabriel Quispe. My extended family in Lima, particularly Elsa and Jaime Ruiz-Huidobro, also deserve *un beso enorme*, along with the late Rosemary Singer. My parents, John and Alicia Middents, started me on this journey by dragging me to live in Lima in 1986 where I slowly learned Spanish and fell in love with what was already my second country. I can never thank them enough for their love, inspiration, and support.

Finally, as trite as it sounds, my deepest gratitude and love goes to the two people whose lives were completely taken up with mine in the process of writing the book, the two people to whom this book is truly dedicated: my wife, Angela Dadak, who put up with so much and who loved me nonetheless; and my son, Alexander, whose appearance in the midst of the writing process made it that much more important to complete.

Writing National CINEMA

INTRODUCTION

We must clearly differentiate between what is simply made to be commercial and what is considered art. Otherwise, "national cinema" will be another tall tale, another limeño fantasy, only one that will undoubtedly be greedy and commercially oriented.

—PERUVIAN FILM CRITIC JULIO ORTEGA, INTERVIEWED IN *HABLEMOS DE CINE* (AUGUST 1966)[1]

South American cinema was especially ripe for the confluence between critic and filmmaker in the mid-1960s, when a growing worldwide trend in cinephilia arrived at the time that filmmaking was becoming possible again (during World War II, cinematic efforts had been halted throughout the continent). In Peru, the emergence of an as yet undefined national cinematic tradition coincided with the coming of age of a group of equally young students at Universidad Católica in Lima. Tired of talking about thematic concerns — such as whether the story was interesting or whether perhaps the film signified something about the filmmaker's childhood — these young men often called out during postscreening discussions: "hablemos de *cine*" (let's talk about *cinema*!) To "talk about *cinema*," particularly in the mid-1960s, meant to privilege the formal structural elements intrinsic to cinema — the mise-en-scène — over all other aspects referenced by a particular film, which the young French critics at *Cahiers du Cinéma* made fashionable by subsequently making films that received wide international acclaim. In 1965, four *limeño*[2] university students, Isaac León Frías, Federico de Cárdenas, Juan Bullitta, and Carlos Rodríguez Larraín, transformed their battle cry into the name of what would become the first and most influential film publication in Peru and the longest-running independent film journal in Latin America: *Hablemos de cine*.

In addition to writing about the American and European movies that dominated local screens, Peruvian critics paid particular attention to the films produced locally, particularly as feature film production started in earnest in the late 1970s. Reading contemporary critical perspectives alongside the films traces the place of cultural writing within a national discourse, specifically contextualizing the historical trajectory of a developing cinema and the influence of the *hablemistas* on the aesthetic and narrative choices made by Peruvian filmmakers. *Hablemos de cine* enjoyed a twenty-year publication run, and the large majority of Peruvian filmmaking fell in quickly with the journal's overarching ideals of the primacy of traditional mise-en-scène used in genre pictures—even as filmmakers from Argentina, Bolivia, Brazil, Chile, and Cuba were garnering international attention precisely because of their more militant aesthetic. The journal's larger, if subtler, role in shaping Peruvian production may also be key to why Peruvian filmmaking remains largely unnoticed internationally even at the beginning of the twenty-first century. By embracing a commercial "Peruvian aesthetic" that was technically proficient and exportable, yet still lacked teeth, Peruvian national cinema remained a still-unrealized "*limeño* fantasy."

Film Criticism and National Cinema

Writing about national cinema is not so simple as writing about the films made in a particular country. To do so overlooks who sets the parameters of defining what is "national" and how cinema contributes to this definition; doing so also leaves out the influence debates on canonization have in the development of a national cinematic identity. The relationship between national identity and cinema remains important even in the twnety-first century with the rise of globalized economics and new media (as evidenced by the successful inclusion of terms of cultural exception with specific reference to audiovisual products in the General Agreement on Tariffs and Trade in the 1990s). Ideologically, connecting cinema to constructions of nationhood is relatvely simple. Benedict Anderson's assessment of the nation as "an imagined political community... both inherently limited and sovereign" specifically references the arbitrary notion that "the members of even the smallest nation will never know most of their fellow-members, meet them, or even hear of them, yet in the minds of each lives the *image* of their communion."[3] Film therefore not only reflects the values, morals, and ideologies of a particular culture but also encourages viewers who share a particular national identity to *recognize* those values. In providing the images in the first place to be recognized by local viewers, filmmakers also have the power to influence those viewers, as

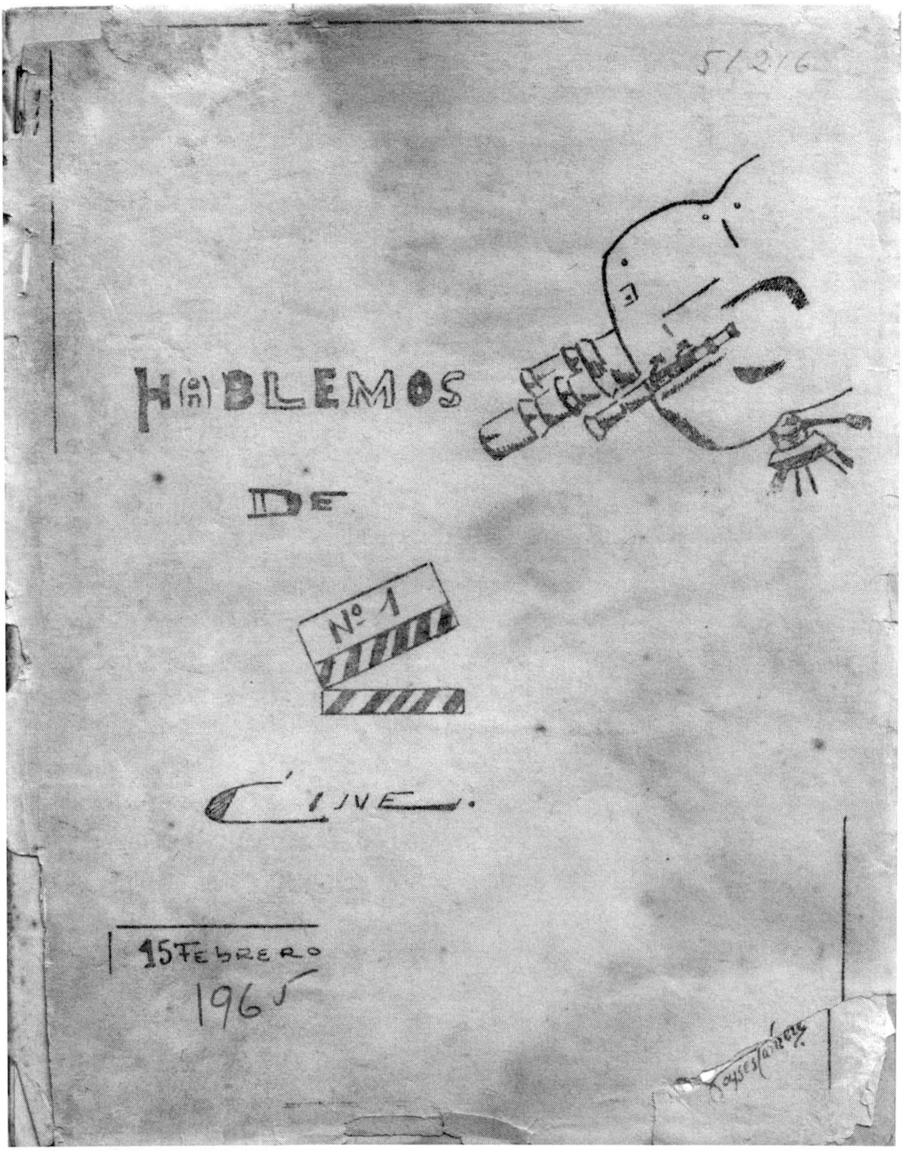

Figure 1: Cover of *Hablemos de cine* 1, originally published as a mimeograph on February 15, 1965. Courtesy of the Filmoteca PUCP *Hablemos de cine* Archive.

well as the shape of cinema itself.[4] Critics and viewers from outside the culture can then gain the opportunity to observe the arbitrary realities defining "national culture" through tracing nationally produced films over time. Traditionally, most histories of national cinema are written and read primarily through the films.

The trajectory of film products that constitute a developing cinema tells a story about the culture whence it comes, but viewers and critics chronicle, nurture and shape that trajectory. Certain films are canonized as emblematic of "national cinema," while others are not considered in the process at all because local critics and/or audiences undervalue the cinematic or thematic qualities such films reflect. In a country where national identity is developing, critics gain their greatest power when they choose to recognize or not to recognize specific national markers; that is, to allow a particular film to be categorized as a "national film." Because the cinematic tradition is not yet strong enough to have these values already determined, the very assessment of these cultural values becomes key to generating and maintaining a sense of national cultural agency. Pierre Bourdieu notes that in the process of validating cultural artifacts, critics also validate themselves:

> *The production of discourse (critical, historical, etc.) about the work of art is one of the conditions of production of the work. Every critical affirmation contains, on the one hand, a recognition of the value of the work which occasions it, which is thus designated as a worthy object of legitimate discourse (a recognition sometimes extorted by the logic of the field, as when, for example, the polemic of the dominant confers participant status of the challengers), and on the other hand an affirmation of its own legitimacy. All critics declare not only their judgment of the work but also their claim to the right to talk about it and judge it. In short, they take part in a struggle for the monopoly of legitimate discourse about the work of art, and consequently in the production of the value of the work of art.*[5]

Given the primary role critics play in evaluating local filmmaking, it also becomes necessary to analyze how these evaluations materialize. Analyzing criticism as primary textual material along with the films illuminates the interplay between these two forces and the influences of one on the other in articulating a more complete vision of national cinema. In many ways, Núria Triana-Toribio's *Spanish National Cinema* uses a similar methodology to provide portrait of contemporary issues within film criticism underlying the development Spanish cinema (a more nuanced, convincing portrait than the somewhat simplified title of the volume implies). Similarly, Anna Everett's *Returning the Gaze: A Genealogy of Black Film Criticism, 1909–1949* focuses more on the writing, but the period of the work corresponds to the dovetailing of the Harlem Renaissance and the accessibility of film equipment that led to the earliest manifestations of African-American cinema.[6] Following these contexts, *Writing National Cinema* sketches the lasting effects of the twenty-year publication run of *Hablemos de cine* alongside the history of local filmmaking and film culture from the 1960s onward to the beginning of the twenty-first century.

A Representative Peruvian Film: *La boca del lobo*

Francisco Lombardi's 1988 film *La boca del lobo* (The Lion's Den; fig. 2), the film that generated one of the largest audience responses to a local film in Peru, serves as a vantage point from which to view the trajectory of Peruvian national cinema and how local film criticism influenced it. The popular response to its release in 1988 speaks to how Peruvian audience tastes as a larger filmgoing society had been shaped to appreciate this kind of film, one that exemplifies a clear, established "Peruvian aesthetic." The film is set six years earlier in the Andean town of Chuspi, where a small army group arrives to defend against the presence of Sendero Luminoso (the Shining Path) terrorists. The naïve *limeño* narrator, Vitín Luna (Toño Vega), and the diverse group that make up the troop are at first unnerved when unseen terrorists come in to disrupt their compound. The guerrillas then kill an ineffective army captain as he tries to accompany a suspect's transport to another vicinity. Rather than be removed from the area, the soldiers soon fall under the command of Lieutenant Roca (Gustavo Bueno), who Luna initially sees as a grounding force in an otherwise confusing environment. The soldiers admire Roca's stern nature and train under his inflexible eye, but also discuss among themselves the rumor of an unfortunate outcome of a game of Russian roulette that prevented Roca from having advanced further in his career. Situations do not improve and they do not find the terrorists. Luna then witnesses his best friend, Gallardo (José Tejada), rape a young shopgirl named Julia (Bertha Pagaza), who had herself desired Luna. When she goes to Roca to denounce her attacker, Luna says nothing in order not to snitch on his friend. Out looking for more trouble, Gallardo and another soldier are attacked when they try to crash a wedding party; claiming they were injured by terrorists, they convince Roca to raid the party and bring everyone in for questioning. During these proceedings, however, Roca accidentally kills one of the townspeople. In order to cover up his error, the next morning Roca and the soldiers bring the townspeople to

Figure 2: Still from *La boca del lobo* (Francisco Lombardi, 1988). Courtesy of the Filmoteca PUCP and Francisco J. Lombardi.

a nearby ravine, where the soldiers shoot them and dispose of the bodies; Luna, however, refuses to discharge his weapon. Following the massacre, Luna returns to the military post where Roca incarcerates him for insubordination. While the other soldiers fret about having knowingly murdered dozens of innocent people, Luna confronts Roca, calling him a coward for murdering the Indians instead of facing consequences. Insulting his superior's manhood, Luna challenges Roca to a game of Russian roulette. Faced with the final bullet, Roca asks Luna to shoot him; instead, Luna shoots the wall, saying "You're dead." Luna then sheds his uniform and leaves the military compound, deserting his post and heading by foot into the mountains.

Up until the bloodbath, inspired by a well-known 1983 massacre from the region around Ayacucho called Soccos, *La boca del lobo* appears to be a socially conscious film where the innocent city-dweller learns about corruption among the powerful by being placed out in a fish-out-of-water situation in the countryside. Similar scenes from other films evoke outrage by placing the viewer on the side of the victims. This aligning is most memorably accomplished in the 1971

Bolivian film *El coraje del pueblo* (The Courage of the People) by Jorge Sanjinés; the film documents a massacre in the mining town of Siglo XX by incorporating semi-documentary footage of actual survivors and employing the same people to assist with development of the script. In *La boca del lobo*, however, the mass execution is not the climax of the film: instead, Luna's conflicted feelings about this event take narrative primacy over the plight of the murdered. Lombardi assures us of this by allowing the soldiers—and the viewers—to sympathize with only one member of the large group of natives who are about to be slaughtered: their guide from an earlier expedition (who actually did not get many lines or much character development prior to his being incarcerated). Throughout the film, Lombardi employs numerous long shots to keeps the native population from the town at a distance, while also largely denying them an actual voice; the exception is Julia, notably the sole woman in the film, whose words must speak for the rest of the subjugated town. Any dramatic tension from the massacre is superseded by the Russian roulette sequence, filmed with sharp angles and close-ups of the participants' strained faces. Contrast this with Sanjinés's film, which opens the movie with a scene of the army machine-gunning a demonstration of native workers marching across an open field: immediately before the massacre, the camera shows many close-ups and medium close-ups within the groups of the striking workers, giving them equal standing with similar, albeit isolated, soldiers on the hill preparing to shoot.

La boca del lobo often earns the sole Peruvian entry in several international retrospectives of Latin American cinema. Alberto Elena and Marina Díaz López's 2004 collection *The Cinema of Latin America* features the film as one of only twenty-four "representative" films from the region from more than a century of filmmaking in Latin America.[7] Mikel Luis concludes his summary of the film for the Spanish collection *Tierra en trance: El cine latinoamericano en 100 películas* by calling the film emblematic of "a trajectory of realistic continuity that seeks to forge the most compact and representative career in all of Peruvian cinema."[8] And in a survey of the best Latin American films, conducted in the 1990s by the film journal *La gran ilusión*, *La boca del lobo* was the highest-placing Peruvian film. The principal idea throughout these reflections is that a particular film can "represent" a national cinematic tradition. To some extent, each critic discusses why *La boca del lobo* is ideally situated within the Peruvian cinematic tradition and articulates specific elements of the mise-en-scène that justify its placement there. Elided in this discussion, however, is the protagonist role that the critics themselves—and specifically, the Peruvian critics associated with *Hablemos de cine*—play in establishing the criteria for national representation. *La boca del lobo* is representative not only because it fits within certain narrative and aesthetic parameters established by other films, but also—and primarily—because it matches those that privileged the value of the auteur and venerated forms reminiscent of American genre films. The assumption of the critic's objectivity masks the cultural and critical biases that are crucial to understanding how criticism influences the shaping of a particular cultural perspective like national cinema.

At the time of its release, the local critical response to *La boca del lobo* was overwhelmingly positive; given that this was his fifth feature film, the film also succeeded in confirming an auteurial trajectory for Lombardi, as exemplified in Isaac León's review for the general newsweekly *Caretas*:

> *While the bonds of domination and aggression remind me of some of his previous work, the prison scene demonstrates some uniquely new qualities in this case since* La boca del lobo *is Lombardi's first feature set in an Andean [mountain] town and the surrounding countryside, the first of his films that really features sun and open space. Despite this, the film reproduces familiar claustrophobic conditions (where the persecuted soldiers are as trapped as the people living in the occupied town), but adds a foreboding sentiment through images of the countryside, thus redefining the limits of how to bring out the sense of claustrophobic spaces.*[9]

León's emphasis on Lombardi's use of the image of the countryside is not accidental. The thrust of the review centers around Lombardi's careful attention to mise-en-scène: literally, how images are arranged on the screen in service of the larger narrative. What might be taken in another film as a pastoral image of freedom (in a Hollywood context, one might think of the opening and closing shots of Robert Wise's 1965 film *The Sound of Music*) instead becomes "foreboding" and "claustrophobic," and León appropriately credits the fresh use of this image to Lombardi. This kind of criticism—examining the mise-en-scène as a way of venerating a director as an auteur—became popular in Europe in the early part of the 1960s as the primary mode of critique employed by the French film journal *Cahiers du cinéma*, which had become influential when writers affiliated with the publication (such as Jean-Luc Godard and François Truffaut) became internationally recognized filmmakers themselves. Note that León uses language that also affirms (or reaffirms) Lombardi as an auteur by referencing "his previous work."

I am privileging the actual wording of the review here because, as Bourdieu notes, the articulation tells us as much about the critics as the film itself. The reference to *Cahiers* and the auteurs it engendered is even more appropriate in this Peruvian example: as it happens, director Lombardi had also been a critic—schooled in criticism, for the most part, by none other than León, the editor-in-chief at *Hablemos de cine* for the entire publication run. Particularly because the film was a box-office success in Peru, this critique is mutually beneficial: the favorable review confirms Lombardi as an auteur while the film's success elevates Lombardi's former status as a critic and, by association, others affiliated with that publication.

Other than this use of mise-en-scène and the thematic use of the contemporary topic of Sendero Luminoso, the vantage point distanced in time and location exposes the lack of novelty in the film. If it is a "representative" text, its quality has therefore been couched in terms of narrative clarity and comprehension, not innovation. For example, the Russian roulette sequence refers explicitly to Michael Cimino's 1978 film *The Deer Hunter*, which reminds viewers that, despite the specific nature of the massacre, the film fits into the tradition of the war film, specifically those expressing the futility of the Vietnam era, whose expressive, expansive shots of the Asian countryside invoke a similarly haunting atmosphere for the American soldiers. Lombardi's film is unique in being the first to dare confront the contemporary threat involving Sendero Luminoso, which by 1988 was waging a strong campaign in Peru, even disrupting and bombing locations within the capital. Nevertheless the film presents this threat to viewers using familiar—one might say "safe," unencumbered—narrative techniques based on American examples of the war film genre. The homage to *The Deer Hunter* actually brings into focus how the Peruvian film mimics a Hollywood war film instead of establishing a unique aesthetic presentation for the local situation. The nationalist terms of that homage are also complicated: the linearity of the film's narrative structure leads us to sympathize with the young military squad instead of the innocent Andean villagers who were massacred immediately before. León does not comment on this, instead praising the more comprehensible narrative structure being served by the mise-en-scène.

I would like to emphasize two converging elements concerning both *La boca del lobo* and León's review. For one, Lombardi's film is not anomalous as a sample Peruvian film from the 1980s: indeed, this genre-oriented, linear narrative placed in a local setting with careful use of mise-en-scène characterized many Peruvian productions of this time, from José Carlos Huyhuaca's *Profesion:*

Detective (1985) to Alberto Durant's *Alias: La Gringa* (1991). The most interesting example of this period is actually one that has been rejected by more recent histories of Peruvian cinema: Luis Llosa's *Hour of the Assassin* (1987). This film explicitly embraces its status as a simple genre picture, with numerous car chases and shootout scenes characteristic of the American action film. Made in English for the direct-to-video market and produced by Roger Corman's Concorde–New Horizons Films, the film was released commercially to theaters in Peru as *Misión en los Andes* (Mission in the Andes), where in recognizing locations audiences could provide an alternate, familiar reading over the otherwise overtly American genre.[10] The large box-office returns achieved by each of these films coordinates with positive reviews from Peruvian critics. As the most consistently successful director and the most decorated at film festivals outside of Peru, Lombardi has become emblematic of Peruvian cinema as a whole—so much so that in the early twenty-first century, young critics now refer to all directors from this period as the "Lombardi generation."

The canonization of Lombardi as a "representative," "iconic" Peruvian filmmaker, however, can also be seen as the natural outcome from nearly twenty years of debate among film critics at *Hablemos de cine*. Lombardi's film in fact embodies the ideal elements critics were looking for in a Peruvian film. Such would be only an interesting side-note if León were writing for a specialized cinephilic audience; we should remember, however, at this point that his review appears for a general readership in a news magazine, evidence that the specialized, analytical language of European film criticism had by the 1980s entered into the Peruvian mainstream.

How did Peruvian cinema get to *La boca del lobo*? Why has this become the "representative" vision of Peruvian cinema instead of a film from the indigenous perspective? This question is particularly cogent within a Peruvian context, considering that after the 1920s, Latin American cultural identity—and particularly the Peruvian—was caught somewhere between *indigenismo*, raised largely by socialist intellectual José Carlos Mariátegui and bringing attention to the enthnocentrism that resulted in the subjugation of native cultures, and the call for "civilization over barbarism" emblematized by Argentine Domingo Faustino Sarmiento.[11] Moreover, Peruvian filmmaking had existed in the Andean region since the early 1960s when members of the Cine-Club de Cuzco released the feature-length *Kukuli* in 1961. However, both cinematic production equipment and spectator culture was centered in the capital of Lima, making it as much a "filmic city" as cultural critic Ángel Rama's "lettered city."[12] Lombardi's privileging of the soldiers' perspective in *La boca del lobo* establishes an outsider's perspective that may be read as *limeño* in the characters' uneasiness and fear of both the "claustrophobic" Andean countryside and the silent, unfamiliar, and visibly "othered" Andean population. The seeming rejection of *indigenismo* by critics and the primary Peruvian filmmakers is not surprising given the relatively young age of the primary cinephilic audience, who preferred to look outside for influences.[13] Peruvian critics and filmmakers largely did not look within their own cultural contexts for inspiration but rather confronted representations from Europe and the United States, concerning themselves with aesthetics as a seemingly "neutral" political concern. Within the context of Latin American cinema in general, however, the stalwart political and aesthetic positions of *Hablemos de cine*—and, by extension, of Peruvian filmmaking in general—are somewhat conservative, which meant that neither attracted the same kind of international attention that was lavished on the cinematic productions and writings from other Latin American countries. Focusing entirely on aesthetic concerns throughout its publication run, the journal avoided the polemic issues that occupied other film journals during the period, such as *Cine Cubano* or even the French *Cahiers du Cinéma*. While this unassuming position made *Hablemos de cine* highly distinctive and assured continued publication and discussions of all kinds of films (long after many other journals closed from lack of interest or were shut down by governmental powers), the Peruvian cinema it helped mold by the end of the 1980s stagnated, resulting in a standard type of genre feature that often, like Llosa's *Misión en los Andes*, flirted with the possibility of not even being considered a "national production." The far-reaching effects of the *hablemistas* continue into the twenty-first century: as late as 2008, the section on Peru in the *International Film Guide* (which calls itself "the most authoritative and trusted source of information on world cinema") was written by Isaac León, even as other, younger critics were available who were more in touch with newer filmmaking trends. These latter-day critics positioned themselves against what they considered the dominant critical mode.[14]

Overview

This book is not so much a strict history of Peruvian national cinema as an examination of how and why that concept was formed and molded by local film critics. As this examination involves tracing the history of Peruvian filmmaking and culture, the book follows a rough chronological trajectory beginning with the period immediately before the founding of *Hablemos de cine* in 1965. Nonetheless, as there is very little written in English on Peruvian cinema, the primary histories in

Spanish may be inaccessible for most readers.[15] To aid in the navigation of what might be an unfamiliar cinematic history, chapter 1 offers a brief history of Peruvian cinema from its inception through the early 2000s.

Each subsequent chapter focuses on a particular issue relating to the influence of film criticism on the developing nature of Peruvian cinema. Chapter 2, "Publication, Authority, Identity: Constructing the Film Journal," begins by tracing the role of cinephilia in film criticism and how this cultish "love of film" in Peru brought together the editors that established the journal. The chapter then explores specifically how film writing—that is, writing about film—nurtured this trajectory of cinephilic identity, how adjustments in the journal's ideology were reflected through both the writing and physical changes in the publication itself and how the ideology reflected in *Hablemos de cine* became the dominant critical perspective in Peru through a series of coincidental political events in the mid-1970s. Chapter 3, "Shaping Peruvian Taste: 'Good' and 'Bad' Peruvian Movies" addresses how the *hablemistas* assessed the "quality" of a film with regard to the national, specifically by concentrating on the myriad "unworthy" or problematic Peruvian films released during the first few years of the journal's run.

Chapter 4, "Latin American Dis/Connections: Peru versus The New Latin American Cinema," locates the Viña del Mar Film Festivals of 1967 and 1969 in Chile as defining moments for the critics—and for Peruvian cinema itself—within the context of the New Latin American Cinema in the late 1960s. Filmmakers from throughout the continent came together at Viña to discover that many concerns they had thought unique to their situations were common throughout the region. As the Peruvian representatives to both festivals, however, the editors of *Hablemos de cine* also realized how their own national cinema was—or, more precisely, was not—developing within the context of what Zuzana Pick has called a continental project.[16] That *Hablemos de cine* happens to have been published during the rise to international prominence of the much-studied New Latin American Cinema movement forces a consideration of (a) how Peru and this journal fit into such a paradigm, and (b) whether Peruvian critics and/or filmmakers chose deliberately not to be pigeonholed into this movement as it gained momentum through the early 1970s.

Chapter 5, "For a Few Minutes: Considering the Peruvian Short Film Industry," explores defining national cinema not through feature films, but through the development of a short-film industry through the mid-1970s. Joint efforts by the government of General Juan Velasco to promote Peruvian identity and by the film community (filmmakers and critics alike) to establish a more viable film industry led to the creation of the Film Law of 1972. Through a tariff levied on all foreign films and an established exhibition circuit established for all locally produced films, the law intended to generate funds for feature filmmaking. While features would be made some five years later, making *short* films that were run in front of all other features in Peru yielded more immediate returns and a profitable short-film industry. *Hablemos de cine* pointedly ignored this format during much of its infancy, but a grudging acceptance led to an eventual realization that the short films were a way to establish *auteurist* trajectories for filmmakers even before they turned to feature filmmaking.

Although four feature films debuted in 1977, which marks a banner year for the rebirth of feature filmmaking in Peru, only Francisco Lombardi emerged into the 1980s anointed as the chosen Peruvian auteur. Chapter 6, "Creating the 'Lombardi Generation': The Rise of an Urban Cinematic Aesthetic," first follows how the critique of Lombardi's filmmaking career in tandem with that of an equally prolific contemporary feature director, Federico García, was viewed in terms of geographic setting, with the former's films associated with metropolitan Lima and the latter with the Andean city of Cuzco. These two primary locations colored how both directors' bodies of work were viewed by *Hablemos de cine* as well as other critics and viewers. This division reflects not only the racial and socioeconomic boundaries that limited both cinemas but also the preferential treatment the Lima-based film journal gave toward situations and ideas with which it was more familiar. The chapter then reflects on how the politics of aesthetics simultaneously grounded the journal's ideology, enabled it to continue publication for twenty years, and help shape the resultant genre-oriented output of the late 1980s and beyond.

This work of the "Lombardi generation" progressed slowly but steadily until 1994 when, during the first administration of President Alberto Fujimori, the Film Law of 1972 was repealed, sharply ending the short-film industry that had proved a substantial training ground for national filmmakers. This action served to inspire the *hablemistas* to regroup with a new publication entitled *La gran ilusión* with financing from the Universidad de Lima, where many of them now serve as faculty members. The changes in content, structure, and even financing of the new publication make an interesting counterpoint for this "second coming" of *Hablemos*, which published eleven issues before morphing in 2004 into yet another title, *Tren de sombras*, this time published by Universidad Católica.

By the beginning of the twenty-first century, the so-called young boys of Peruvian film criticism are now the establishment. But they are also not the only

Peruvians writing film criticism: weaned on *Hablemos*, writers at three additional film publications—*Butaca sanmarquina* (now *Butaca*), *Godard*, and *Abre los ojos*—provide diverse reflections on the contemporary state of Peruvian cinema. Filmmaking has shifted considerably from the "Lombardi generation," with product largely developed by a new generation of filmmakers who did not cut their teeth on the short-film industry of the 1970s and 1980s. Likewise, Peruvian film criticism no longer holds the *hablemista* viewing position as sacred, often confronting these progenitors in much the same way that their elders challenged their own contemporaries forty years earlier. One might also question the relevance of local film writing in print during the Internet-heavy beginning of the twenty-first century. Chapter 7, "The Changing of the Guard: Peruvian Cinema in the Twenty-First Century," looks specifically at the contemporary intersections of Peruvian filmmaking, film culture, and film criticism—and the lingering effects of the *hablemistas* on all three.

CHAPTER 1
A HISTORY OF THE PERUVIAN CINEMATIC TRADITION

> *It is risky to speak of a "History of Peruvian Cinema," mainly because what has been filmed in Peru has been very limited and we can truly affirm that Peruvian filmmaking has not yet gone beyond its "prehistoric" phase. Because of this, think of this "history of Peruvian cinema," as we call it, in the broadest and most general sense.*
>
> —"INTRODUCCIÓN A UNA VISIÓN INFORMATIVO-CRÍTICA," *HABLEMOS DE CINE* (NOVEMBER 1969–FEBRUARY 1970)

Isaac León's introductory statements in his first attempt at delineating a history of Peruvian filmmaking within the pages of *Hablemos de cine* has the characteristic tone of the time of its writing in the late 1960s. Not only in Peru, but in cinematic traditions as varied as those of France, Cuba, and even the United States, the late 1960s marked the rise of "new cinemas," characterized just by using the moniker "new," as disavowing, rejecting, or at best being disdainful of what came before. The reality, of course, is much different: like many countries, Peruvian cinema has a long tradition that goes back to the end of the nineteenth century and the variety of films made within the country since then were shaped by a variety of political, social, and economic influences, both filmic and otherwise.[1]

Early Cinematic Experiences

Motion pictures debuted in Peru, as in the rest of the world, at the end of the nineteenth century with the arrival of Thomas Edison's Vitascope in Lima on

January 2, 1897. The first screening of Edison's short films, attended by President Nicolás de Piérola as well as other invited guests and dignitaries, was held at the Strasboug Salon, an upscale café in cental Lima. Two days later, the apparatus traveled to the upper-class vacation districts of Chorrillos and Barranco, before leaving the country at the end of the month. Exactly a month after Edison's machine had arrived, the same public screened—and preferred—the presentation of the Lumière brothers' Cinematograph and the screening of *The Arrival of a Train* over the more scientific American presentation.

The Strasbourg Salon (described by Ricardo Bedoya as "a recreational area of landholders and electors, of men of the earth and established members of the political class") is notable as exhibition space because it identifies filmgoing as an upper-class activity even at the very arrival of cinema to Peru.[2] As such, local production at the turn of the century logically also catered to the bourgeois cinemagoer, reflecting that perspective of national identity through such images as the Cathedral in Lima (*La semana santa en Lima* [Holy Week in Lima], 1912) or the new road "taming" the wild jungle (*Viaje al interior del Perú* [Journey to the Center of Peru], 1910). Fiction films produced during the silent period were often set in luxurious mansions and estates in Barranco and Miraflores, showcasing a familiar lifestyle for the upper-class viewer. The first major national fiction production, *Negocio al agua* (Business in the Water, 1912), showcased the attempts of two "ragamuffins" vying for the attention of a millionairess who has already been betrothed to an "honorable" (that is, wealthy) man. The film was financed by the same company that owned the major movie palaces in Lima, Cinema Teatro, which produced several local productions during this period, strengthening its connection with the upper-class clientele it coveted.

Despite this catering to the upper classes at the level of content, alternate viewing spaces for lower-class viewers emerged as early as 1908. First-run movies with complete orchestral accompaniment would screen at the European- and Hollywood-style movie palaces built in downtown Lima, also the center of other cultural activities oriented to upper-class tastes such as theaters and concert halls. A "second-tier" business for lower-class families and children known to this day as *cines de barrio* (neighborhood theaters) consisted of smaller movie houses or, more commonly, "movie tents,"[3] accompanied by piano in the working-class and residential neighborhoods of Lima. This two-tier distribution allowed films to be accessible across class divides in Lima, while also effectively maintaining a class division. Not until the coming of the sound era, with its prefabricated soundtracks, would there be a more even exhibition experience among classes.

The 1930s and early 1940s: Amauta Films

The emergence of *cines de barrio* required films that focused on less bourgeois themes and locales. A number of small local production companies generated silent films (including Compañía Internacional Cinematográfica, which was responsible for the Cine Teatro chain of theaters and which produced most of the earliest features geared toward the bourgeoisie, followed by Patria Film and Lux Film later in the 1920s) but the arrival of sound helped found Amauta Films in 1937, which would be the first sustained attempt at creating a production company in Peru. As in most other countries, film was but one of several attractions in a cabaret-type setting that included vaudeville and other comedy acts. In the *cines de barrio*, where actors played out small, locally influenced satires that included "traditional" Peruvian costumes and music, this variety was even more prevalent, because this localized approach was already intrinsic to a certain population's viewing experience. Filming cinematic versions of the same was a natural progression, particularly with the arrival of sound when the local music and accent could be recorded, thereby reaching a bigger audience. Producer Felipe Varela La Rosa flaunted Amauta's nationalistic ideals, publishing the company's overall goals in a local magazine in July 1937, a month before the release of its first film:

1. *To impose our language and our customs on the screen.*
2. *To print them in "books of film"* [libros de celuloide], *which the public prefers.*
3. *To end the prejudice against inferior films in Spanish.*
4. *To reveal our virgin landscape to the world.*
5. *To enable foreigners to admire our music and our environment.*
6. *To elevate the best elements of our local theater and radio.*
7. *To join together elements of good taste and box-office success.*
8. *To exhibit local films because they are of good quality and not because they are Peruvian.*
9. *To conquer the continental market, both economically and in terms of technical ability.*[4]

The intentions of Amauta Films were impressively ambitious, aiming to "conquer" not only the national market but, evidenced from the wording of points 4, 5, 8 and 9, international markets as well.

Palomillas del Rímac (The Rímac Rascals, 1938) is a typical example of an Amauta production.[5] Although some of Amauta's films were set in the northern highlands or the jungle, the film's title references the working-class neighborhood in the capital called Rímac, which is also the name of the only river that runs through Lima; *palomilla*, meanwhile, referred to the Peruvian version of the urban young man on the street corner characterized by his carefree attitude, his penchant for small jobs and his constant chatting-up of young women who passed.[6] In the film, two *palomillas*, Juan and Pedro, are living day-to-day in Rímac. Though Juan loves a neighborhood girl named Julia, he doesn't feel complete because he "never knew his mother"; Pedro is also unhappy because his own mother is extremely ill. Luck comes their way when they win the lottery, allowing them to move to a better neighborhood. They discover, however, that they were much happier where they were before and eventually move back to their old neighborhood. The key to this film's overwhelming success was the re-creation of the *barrios limeños*, complete with the geographical maze of side passages *(callejones)*, the unique personages common to these less elite suburbs of Lima, and the criollo songs heard throughout the narrative.[7]

After four years of financially successful pictures, Amauta Films came to an abrupt halt in 1940. The studio's demise was partially due to the great number of problems surrounding what would be their last film: *Barco sin rumbo* (A Boat Off-Course, 1940), a "comedic film noir" set in the port city of Callao whose plot involved the depiction of a black market. After orchestrating a successful coup in 1933 and invalidating elections in 1936 to remain in power for another three years, President Oscar Benavides maintained a strong rightist government. By the end of the decade, however, two leftist groups — the communist party led by intellectual Marxist Juan Carlos Mariátegui and the leftist APRA led by Oscar Haya de la Torre — both gained enough power to pose a significant threat to Benavides's rule. Seeking to quell any possible criticism of the current regime, the government passed the Law for the Social Defense and Internal Security of the Republic in February 1937, quashing any form of communication, "verbal, written or otherwise," that presented "false information designed to alter the public order or damage the prestige of the country."[8] This law directely affected *Barco sin rumbo*, which, although not explicitly embracing either Aprista or Communist ideas, presented what the censor board called the "false" existence of a black market. Amauta Films spent a great amount of time and money fighting the decision, finally agreeing to certain cuts for a 1940 release. The film nevertheless failed both critically and at the box office. The lawsuit and delayed release subverted the company's business model of spending the profits of each film to increase the production quality of the following film, and the company did not produce any films after 1940, becoming instead a local distributor of primarily Argentine and Mexican films.

The fledgling studio might have been able to afford the materials to make a new film had it not been for a series of events both international and national that conspired against the small company. Most Latin American production companies, lacking both the materials and the expertise to produce celluloid, purchased from firms in the United States such as Kodak. The outbreak of World War II diverted the raw materials used to make celluloid into weapons production, making film stock scarce and causing the United States to limit the amount of celluloid it could send abroad. Of the three Spanish-speaking film industries gaining strength at this time, only Mexico allied itself with the United States against the Axis powers, while the other two (Spain and Argentina) remained neutral. Hollywood thus concentrated its efforts in aiding—both with expertise and raw materials—the quickly developing Mexican industry.[9] While the Golden Age of Mexican Cinema began in the early 1940s, other local cinemas throughout Latin America collapsed soon after 1943, despite the fact that home-grown films might appeal to their own audiences with more familiar themes, dialects, and music. With what amounted to a single production company in jeopardy (as opposed to an entire booming industry in Mexico) Peruvian cinema was of little concern to U.S. interests, political or economic.

Film Culture in Lima in the 1950s and 1960s

In the twenty years following the failure of Amauta Films' *Barco sin rumbo*, virtually no Peruvian films of note were produced. None of the seven feature-length fiction films made between 1940 and 1960 saw favorable critical or box-office results. That said, a number of U.S. productions filmed on location in Peru in the 1950s, including the second units of John Sturges's *The Old Man and the Sea* (Warner Brothers, 1958), then under the direction of Fred Zinnemann, which sent novelist Ernest Hemingway with a crew on a failed attempt to film the catch of the protagonist giant marlin; and *Secret of the Incas* (Paramount, Jerry Hopper, 1953), a Charleton Heston vehicle whose exteriors were shot in Cuzco. The allure of Inca culture, particularly as embodied in the visual representation of the "lost city" of Macchu Picchu, brought several foreign productions to the Andean region. The 1950s also saw some reorganization of the official state censor board, bringing in stricter guidelines concerning its composition as well as the ratings system applied to national films, international films, and the popular new medium of television.

Although cinematic production levels decreased significantly in the 1950s, a film culture fell into place in Peru during the same period, with the cine-club emerging as an alternative form of exhibition throughout Latin America.[10] Polish-born lawyer Andrés Ruszkowski founded the first publicly advertised cine-club in Lima in 1952 while teaching at the premiere private university in Peru, the Pontificia Universidad Católica. Inspired by cine-clubs that he attended while in Europe, Ruszkowki founded both the Cine Forum and the Cine Club de Lima, which screened films "chosen under artistic or cultural criteria and presented with the intention of promoting discussion about the qualities" of the medium itself. The interpretation of these qualities, however, was rather flexible. For example, the first films projected for Cine Forum were *Dieu a Besoin des Hommes* (God Needs Men/Isle of Sinners, France, Delannoy, 1950) and *Rope* (United States, Hitchcock, 1948), while the first film shown at the Cine Club de Lima was *Jeux Interdits* (Forbidden Games, France, Clement, 1951).[11] The club also organized postscreening forums to discuss either the films themselves or the "human values" espoused by the local chapter of the Office Catholique International du Cinéma (commonly known as the OCIC), a group dedicated to both moral vigilance and cinematic education.[12] Previous clubs had existed before this time, but they were usually exclusive events not open to the public; the Cine Club de Lima actively searched for members and almost immediately signed up close to eight hundred subscriptions—a small number in comparison to the several million living in the city, but a large enough population to merit continued interest in cinematic culture.[13] Though attendance at the Cine Club de Lima declined throughout the 1950s and the organization dissolved in 1957, its presence brought together many film aficionados. Indeed, the growing interest in movies in Lima beyond what was shown in the commercial market in the decades to follow has been directly attributed to Ruszkowski.

Affiliated with both the academic and the religious rigors of the Universidad Católica, Ruszkowski stated in an interview: "my personal expectations [in stimulating film activity in Peru] were above all to stimulate a new attitude concerning the cultural and moral phenomenon of film among Peruvian Catholics."[14] This objective, educational both in terms of the medium and the morals the medium could promote, was in fact a directive that was embraced among many in the Peruvian Catholic Church, as evidenced in the 1956 celebration of the twentieth anniversary of the papal edict *Vigilanti Cura*, which stated that the new medium of cinema could be most useful in promoting Catholic values. *Vigilanti Cura*, written by Pope Pius XI in June 1936, began by praising the activities of the Legion of Decency, the entity in Hollywood that brought about the Production Code and eventually the modern U.S. ratings system. While the primary goal of the encyclical was to establish Catholic censor boards around the world similar to the one in the United States, the document also stated that film "should assist in the right education of man and in raising the dignity of morality."[15] It is in this spirit that many Catholics such as Ruszkowski and Desiderio Blanco became, through the efforts of the OCIC, involved in the dissemination of film education around the world. The potential educational virtues of media were also the focus of Pius XII's more detailed 1957 encyclical, *Miranda Prorsus*, which commanded national religious officials to "direct, organize, and assist the many educational projects which have been begun in many countries so that, in this difficult and extensive province of the arts, Christian ideas may be ever more widely spread."[16]

Desiderio Blanco, a priest turned major progenitor of *limeño* film culture, directly sparked this particular type of cinephilia, which would influence criticism for decades to follow. While preparing a screenplay during his seminary years in Valladolid Spain, Blanco started reading theoretical texts, particularly those associated with Soviet montage (Eisenstein, Pudovkin, and the like), which led him to more contemporary theoretical texts. Coming to Peru in 1956, Blanco became involved with the very active Lima chapter of the OCIC by screening selected "human values" films to children at Catholic schools throughout Lima, an activity largely influenced by the *Miranda Prorsus* papal encyclical. Though the program was short-lived, several future significant film critics—including Isaac León Frías, Juan Bullitta, and Carlos Rodríguez Larraín—were first exposed to this serious method of examining films during the large gatherings of school-age students.

Only a few years later, these three young men started attending the Universidad Católica, the only private university in Lima. Although none of them were considering a career in film at the time, all began to attend the various cine-clubs throughout the capital founded in the early 1960s, many of them affiliated with universities, a common practice in many countries. By the mid-1960s, cine-clubs once again thrived in Lima, with many clubs often overlapping both in members and sometimes films. To aid in this endeavor, in 1965, Miguel Reynel founded the Cinemateca Universitaria, a consortium of university resources brought together to collect films to be shown at the many cine-clubs throughout Lima, allowing a permanent collection of films to be maintained in Lima. By 1963, León persuaded

Blanco to give classes on film semiotics at the university, and by 1964 León, Bullitta, and Rodríguez had become friends who frequently debated the aesthetic merits of the films. These three students then persuaded Blanco to help them coordinate a year-long film series about American cinema from the 1930s to the 1950s for the Cine Club de la Católica. Every three weeks throughout the year, the series showcased a different Hollywood genre (such as the western or the gangstar film) featuring three example films. Most of the cine-clubs tended to show "art cinema," [17] a loose term applied to primarily European films of a certain "quality," featuring films from directors such as Ingmar Bergman, Federico Fellini, and many of the French New Wave directors (Truffaut, Godard, and so forth); thus, while the lauding of particular Hollywood auteurs was by this point common among the Parisian cine-clubs (where *Cahiers du cinéma* extolled the virtues of directors like John Ford), the serious consideration of the genre of the American Western marked a significant and uncomfortable shift for Peruvian filmgoers. [18] The significant debate among *limeño* cinephiles brought a considerable amount of attention to this particular club and divided older members of the *cine-club* scene (such as Margarita Guerra and Gerardo Alarco) and the younger university students.

The film journal *Hablemos de cine* was founded in 1965 largely as a response to those who responded negatively to the screenings of classic Hollywood features at the Cine Club de Universidad Católica. Many other young cinephiles were invited to the informal discussion following the films, but by January 1965, the only ones consistently attending were León, Rodríguez, Bullitta, and law student Federico de Cárdenas, along with the principal progenitor of all this activity, Desiderio Blanco.[19] The founding members formed *Hablemos de cine* as something of a justification for their interest in cinema that was not traditionally associated with the *cine-clubs*.

The Cine-Club de Cuzco and *Kukuli*

One of the more notable Peruvian cine-clubs and the first whose members actually produced film was founded far from Lima, in the Andean city of Cuzco. Having become familiar with cine-clubs while an architecture student in Buenos Aires and then while working in Lima during the early 1950s, Manuel Chambi helped form the Cine-Club de Cuzco in late 1955. With only around 150 members, the group was not so large as the Lima-based groups, nor did its programs feature such a large variety, as it was difficult to bring films from the capital. While the group dedicated a significant portion of its activities to viewing and commenting on films, it also shared an interest in making films, an interest that stemmed in part from the increase in foreign productions in and around the Cuzco region throughout the 1950s. For example, Victor and Manuel Chambi, the sons of famed local photographer Martín Chambi, released a number of successful short documentary films in the late 1950s and Eulogio Nishiyama worked on the set of Jerry Hopper's *Secret of the Incas*.

The Cine-Club de Cuzco had important, lasting effects for Peruvian cinema as a whole. Key was the learning trajectory from short documentaries to feature-length fiction films: after the boom of short filmmaking got under way in 1972, this trajectory would prove to be the primary method of training for most filmmakers throughout the country. With titles such as *Corpus de Cuzco* (Corpus Christi in Cuzco, 1955), *Lucero de nieve* (Qoyllur Ritti/Snow Star, 1957) and *Estampas del carnaval de Kanas* (Scenes from the Kanas Carnival, 1963), the shorts generally depicted festival events from around the Cuzco region. The innovative topics and fairly good technical control of images rapidly earned the shorts a number of prestigious international prizes, bringing attention to Peru as a filmmaking entity for the first time. Significantly, many directors—Manuel Chambi, Nishiyama, Luis Figueroa, César Villanueva—shared responsibilities; thus all of these films credited "Cine-Club de Cuzco," rather than a single director.

In 1961, the Cine-Club de Cuzco released the feature-length *Kukuli* (fig. 3) notable for being one of the first films spoken entirely in Quechua, the language common to the mountains of Peru (particularly around Cuzco), the film is a familiar tragic love story set in the mountains of Peru with a translated narration spoken by Peruvian author Sebastián Salazár Bondy. The title refers to a young woman sent by her grandparents to the city of Paucartambo with an offering for the celebration of Mamacha Carmen, a synthesis of native and Catholic deities. Along the way she meets and falls in love with a young man, Alako, but together they meet a wizard who predicts death lies in their future. They arrive in Paucartambo and participate in the opening festivities, but an *ukuku*, a mythical "kidnapping bear" embodied by one of the participants in the celebration, first pushes Alako off from a bell tower and then absconds with Kukuli, eventually killing her with a rock. The local priest informs the celebrants back at the town that they must kill the bear to atone for the collective sins that have caused its appearance. Following the successful hunt of the bear, the spirits of Alako and Kukuli are transformed through death into a pair of llamas, who nuzzle one another as the picture closes. Though somewhat simplistic in its portrayal of the "naïve" Indians, the film demonstrates a relatively sophisticated use of mise-en-scène with its impressive compositions of the Andean countryside and its clear narrative structure.

Considering the distance between Cuzco and the Peruvian cultural center of

Figure 3: Poster for *Kukuli* (Figueroa/Nishiyama/Villanueva, 1961). Courtesy of the Filmoteca PUCP.

Lima, it is truly remarkable that the film achieved success and recognition not only at home but also abroad.[20] Along with several of the cine-club's documentaries, *Kukuli* was viewed at the 1968 Latin American film festival in Mérida, Venezuela, and a festival in Karlovy-Vary, Czechoslovakia, in 1964, inspiring Georges Sadoul in *Les Lettres françaises* to term the collective of filmmakers "the Cuzco school," proclaiming their vision and methods to be inspiring and innovative.[21] *Kukuli* was the first feature-length Peruvian film in more than ten years and became inspirational for filmmakers in the later part of the 1960s. The filmmakers would part ways professionally, in large part becasue of infighting and the failure of the second feature *Jarawi* (1966), but the sobriquet "Cuzco school" would remain.

The Film Law of 1962

The Peruvian government did little to stimulate film production in Peru during the 1940s and 1950s and most legislation from this period generally affected only short documentaries and newsreels. In 1962, however, Law Decree 13936[22] became the first law to directly influence feature film productions. The Film Law of 1962 stated concisely that all nationally produced features would be free from all taxes currently imposed on feature film exhibition. The law did nothing more to encourage distribution, nor did it mandate or regulate exhibition in national theaters.

While a noble first gesture toward the development of national cinema (and providing the basis for the more effective Film Law of 1972), the 1962 Film Law benefited only a small portion of local production companies. Three types of movies resulted from the Film Law of 1962: the films of Armando Robles Godoy and the Cuzco school; locally produced popular comedies; and, most significant, international co-productions. These latter films did little, however, for local film industries as most material and labor was imported from Mexico and Argentina; in addition, most of these films did not enjoy much financial or critical success within Peru. The Cuzco school unfortunately also met with unenthusiastic local reception with their second and final film *Jarawi* (1965). The comedies, mainly vehicles for television personalities, were wildly popular but scorned by critics; nearly all these productions were one-time affairs. Only the work of Armando Robles Godoy gained significant, sustained impact throughout the 1960s: buoyed by a marketing campaign that emphasized the national identity, his first feature, *Ganarás el pan* (You Will Earn the Bread, 1965), earned relatively kind reviews from most critics and a modest financial success. Robles Godoy would become the first major Peruvian auteur, continuing work with *En la selva no hay estrellas*

(There Are No Stars in the Forest, 1967) and *La muralla verde* (The Green Wall, 1970), both of which garnered attention at international film festivals.[23]

Latin American Film Festivals, 1967–1969

In 1967, the fifth Viña del Mar Film Festival[24] in Chile expanded its borders and invited filmmakers from around Latin America to watch one another's films and compare working conditions. Though some of their works had been seen in Europe, Latin American filmmakers had not yet had the opportunity to meet one another, much less see the films that were rarely screened outside their own national borders. Delegates of filmmakers, critics, cine-club directors and/or producers from nine countries—Bolivia and Mexico presented films, while Argentina, Brazil, Chile, Cuba, Peru, Uruguay, and Venezuela sent both delegates and films—met to present the state of the cinematic climate from their own national perspectives. The event began an active discourse among the practitioners of Latin American cinema, who hoped to continue researching ways to ease film distribution between countries.

The film festival had a tremendous effect on Latin American filmmaking as a whole, bringing to light the similarities in working conditions throughout the continent. For the Peruvian delegation—composed of Cinemateca Universitaria Peruana director Miguel Reynel; *Hablemos de cine* staff writers Isaac León Frías and Federico de Cárdenas; and Jorge Volkert's short film *Forjadores de mañana* (Tomorrow's Forgers, 1966)—the festival was a revelation that films produced in Peru were far behind the new features flourishing throughout the continent.

Following 1967, two other major film festivals helped to solidify the image of what would be termed the "New Latin American Cinema." Yet these festivals also exposed the disparate viewpoints of various national delegations. Previously screened to overwhelmingly supportive crowds in Pesaro, Italy, the first part of the polemic documentary *La hora de los hornos* (The Hour of the Furnaces, Fernando Solanas and Octavio Getino, Argentina, 1968) debuted in Latin America at the Mérida film festival in Venezuela in 1968. A scathing indictment of the disparate realities in Argentine society caused by neocolonialist capitalism, the film—along with the manifesto that followed it almost two years later, "Towards a Third Cinema"[25]—called for a different, militant filmmaking style and method of production that worked against the hegemonic aesthetics of European or Hollywood cinema. Rather than constituting a negative component, technical deficiencies were declared necessary to achieve the raw aesthetics that would reflect the Latin American reality. The film's positive reception in Europe continued in

Venezuela where many filmmakers seized Cine Liberación's innovative ideas as welcome signs of a continental filmic ideology.

By 1969, the next major encounter in Viña del Mar, Chile provided a showcase for a number of films from across the continent that reflected, if not explicitly followed, the directives of Cine Liberación. Many seminal works of the New Latin American Cinema were given their first international screenings here. Although the dominant atmosphere at the festival embraced the militant political aesthetics espoused by Cine Liberación—epitomized at the festival with the now complete three-part, four-and-a-half-hour *La hora de los hornos*—a vocal minority also expressed their concern with the idea of a uniform Latin American cinema, particularly one that held such a militant stance. The Peruvian contingency and prominent Chilean filmmaker Raúl Ruiz limited their critiques to the uniform style of militant filmmaking: the former, within the pages of *Hablemos de cine*; the latter with remarks at the festival itself.[26] Hence, although the Viña del Mar festival of 1969 has been seen as concretizing the idea of politically militant filmmaking as the defining force behind Latin American cinema, the festival also marks the separation of the Peruvian cinematic tradition from the rest of the continent.

The Coup of 1968

In October 1968, the moderate-rightist government of Fernando Belaúnde Terry was overthrown by a military coup led by General Juan Velasco Alvarado in response to growing uneasiness from Belaúnde's failure to bring true agrarian reform to the country. In the turbulent history of Peruvian politics since independence, the strong, selfish ruler was a familiar figure. The new leader was therefore unlike anything Peruvians had seen before: neither shrewd nor charismatic, of low-class origin and native appearance, not from the capital but from Piura, one of eleven children who had worked his way up the military ranks and happened to be at the right place at the right time. Velasco's regime outwardly committed itself to sweeping reform, mostly at the expense of the wealthy who had enjoyed advances under Belaúnde. Except for the progressive socialist state of Cuba, the ideals of the Peruvian "Revolution of 1968" were very different from those of other military dictatorships that affected South America during this period, which were primarily rightist and rooted in desire for control. Nonetheless, by the time power was transferred to Francisco Morales Bermúdez in 1975, Velasco's government had shown itself to be somewhat authoritarian, restricting freedom of expression and maintaining strong government control over development. As an example: while filmmakers did not feel direct effect of the government's authoritative nature, the government's nationalization of the press in 1973 significantly changed the nature of popular journalism, having a trickle-down effect on Peruvian art critics.

The Film Law of 1972 (Law Decree 19327) and the Short-Film Explosion

Many within the Peruvian film industry critiqued the ambiguous nature of the Film Law of 1962 (which simply exonerated all national productions from paying any taxes) for not really stimulating local film production. This inactivity would change by the early 1970s, largely due to the influence of director Armando Robles Godoy, who, as much as he was interested in his particular brand of storytelling, also had a great desire to spark more Peruvian productions. In an early interview with *Hablemos de cine*, he mentioned the dearth of film education possibilities within Peru, and that anyone desiring such instruction generally had to travel to a school abroad. Believing a local school outside the university setting would help develop other filmmakers, Robles Godoy founded a small Film Workshop (Taller de Cinematografía) in 1968 that established several major short-film directors over the next few years, including Mario Pozzi and Nora de Izcué, the first female Peruvian director.

Robles Godoy was also one of the original members of the Sociedad Peruana de Cinematografía (Peruvian Society of Cinematography), an organization that originally formed in 1967 to review and push legislation to establish a new, more clearly defined and beneficial cinematic law. The organization published in volume 34 of *Hablemos de cine* (March–April 1967) their declaration of principles along with a list of the board of directors, which consisted of most of the major players in Peruvian film culture at the time, crossing lines of production, criticism, and exhibition: Robles Godoy as president, Cuzco filmmaker Manuel Chambi as vice president, critic Isaac León Frías as secretary, filmmaker Jorge Volkert as treasurer, and filmmaker Luis Figueroa and director of the Cinemateca Peruana Miguel Reynel as additional trustees. Considering that *Hablemos de cine* had trounced Robles Godoy's most recent film *En la selva no hay estrellas* only one issue before, the journal editors had to distinguish their praise for the newly elected president's concerns about national cinema from their disdain for his aesthetic choices in his films:

> *As an organization, we shall greatly support the activities of the Peruvian Cinematic Society. This is perhaps an ideal time to signal that any differences between* Hablemos de cine *and the Peruvian filmmaker Armando Robles*

> *Godoy, president of this institution, are strictly based on* aesthetic-cinematic grounds, *which should be obvious to our readers. Additionally, it seems to us that Armando Robles Godoy is the most suitable person—as it was also thought by the assembly of constituents that elected him, practically by acclaim—to direct this most important institution of our industry.*[27]

The Sociedad de Cinematografía Peruana formed during the rightist government of Fernando Belaúnde Terry and a preliminary law was drafted for Congress within the year, but the hopes of immediate government assistance for the industry would have to wait; Velasco's military coup dissolved Congress in 1968. Over the next three years, the Sociedad grew to more than a hundred members from all facets of cinematic culture within Peru. In 1971, the Sociedad once again started pressuring the government, this time finally getting an audience with Velasco himself, who granted permission with the phrase, "I don't understand a thing about film, but I know that Peru needs to have a national cinema."[28] Velasco's exuberance for national cinema once again seems to go against what most Latin American rulers thought during this period (though similar film laws were being passed in other nearby countries such as Colombia and Venezuela).[29]

The new law, Law Decree 19327 (hereafter referred to as the Film Law of 1972), was much more explicit than the Film Law of 1962, adopting a rigid structure for determining national cinema, as enumerated in article 4-e:

> *A "Peruvian cinematic work" has the following requirements:*
> 1. *It is produced by the National Film Production Enterprise in accordance with the definition of National Business laid out in Law Decree 18236;*
> 2. *The director must be a Peruvian citizen or resident for at least three years;*
> 3. *No less than 80% of the work must be filmed within national territory.*
> 4. *The work must be based on a work by a Peruvian author or the screenplay must be written by a Peruvian;*
> 5. *The technical and artistic personnel must be proportionate for each production as delineated in this Law Decree;*
> 6. *The original version of the film must be in Spanish, Quechua, Aymará [another major indigenous language] or other Peruvian dialects.*[30]

This new law defines a "Peruvian production" mainly to prevent co-productions from setting up a phantom production company to take all the profits out of the country. Other aspects of the national cinematic culture, however, remained unaddressed, resulting in a considerably flawed law. In interviews published in *Hablemos de cine* in 1966, when filmmakers were asked specifically to assess the national situation, for example, easier access to foreign distribution had been a key issue. Yet this access was not even considered in the creation of the law. Government financing for fledgling or unrecognized filmmakers in the form of a cinematic bank, similar to the Mexican model, was also not discussed. The Film Law of 1972 dealt almost exclusively with numbers and funding, primarily benefiting companies that were already created and had some funding available to initially make cinema on their own.

That said, two somewhat obscure articles within the law concerning exhibition became the most significant clauses, leading to the contemporary Peruvian cinematic boom:

> ARTICLE 14 — *A regime of mandatory distribution and exhibition shall be established throughout the whole country to which each approved national production will have recourse, based on the production's quality, by the Cinematic Promotion Commission. Said regime shall be determined in the regulations of this law.*
>
> ARTICLE 15 — *The exhibition of films produced within the country by National Cinematic Production Enterprises that have adhered to the regime of mandatory exhibition will be exonerated:*
> *(a) — in the case of feature-length films, of all taxes and charges;*
> *(b) — in the case of short films, of 25% of taxes and charges; and,*
> *(c) — in the case of newsreels, of 10% of taxes and charges. The exonerations will be of exclusive benefit to said companies.*[31]

To dispense with the legalese of these arguments: article 14 stipulated mandatory exhibition for nationally produced films that were approved by COPROCI; article 15 specified that the already existing admission taxes levied on nationally produced feature films would go entirely to that film's production company, while taxes levied on a film's admission where a short film had been shown would give 25 percent of admission prices to the short's production company. The law did not immediately specify how films were to be assessed by the COPROCI, although this omission would be rectified later in 1972.

Though the percentage of exoneration granted by the Film Law of 1972 would seem to favor the production of features, short-term benefits were found in the short films (*cortometrajes*). A Peruvian feature still had to compete with technically superior films from Hollywood being distributed in Lima; given that local tastes were mostly influenced by the latter type, Peruvian spectators tended to remain wary of the former. A short film viewed before the Hollywood film, however, could take advantage of that film's higher box office and make a considerable profit. Such films were also far cheaper to produce.

As a result of this law, production companies specializing in short films quickly materialized. For filmmakers, here was an amazing opportunity to refine their skills to create product. Most feature-film directors of the late 1970s and beyond experimented with these short films, including Francisco Lombardi, Augusto Tamayo San Ramón, Alberto Durant, Luis Figueroa, Luis Llosa, and Federico García.[32] The process allowed for the filmmakers to experiment and even fail as part of a learning process with little capital at risk. For audiences, however, the influx of short films led to some frustration; the quality of these films was not regulated and most production started solely to generate easy and fast returns, As a result, most films were technically or narratively deficient but nonetheless released for mandatory public exhibition as a "nationally produced product." The law was designed with the intention that the profits from these films would be recycled into the creation of more films, potentially stimulating an industry. Instead, many production companies merely cashed in their profits; the dearth of feature-film production during the late 1970s indicates lack of interest in the long-term promotion of an industry. Filmmakers and aficionados correctly critiqued the law for failing to benefit the industry even as it stimulated it economically.

The ever-increasing number of short films, combined with the finite number of movie theaters, engendered a crisis the system could not accommodate: mandatory exhibition for everything. In July 1978, the market was saturated with the annual maximum of eighty-two short films—and at the time, fifty more were already in some stage of production. This glut caused a significant backlog in exhibiting the shorts, meaning that production companies would have to wait up to eighteen months to see any profit from their investment. The delay coincided with a particularly unstable moment in the Peruvian economy. With the ideals of the revolution fraying considerably and the country heading toward financial crisis, Velasco was quietly ousted in August 1975 by General Francisco Morales Bermúdez, a more right-wing military ruler, in a "bloodless" takeover. With most natural industries (oil, fishing, mining, and so on) depleted or in ruin and the international recession that occurred in the late 1970s having its own effect on Peru, there was little Morales Bermúdez could do to save the national economy other than to institute a severe austerity program. Production companies accustomed to excessive spending could not afford to wait the year and a half to see the returns from their shorts. Combined with plummeting cinema attendance, stemming in part from the growing national economic crisis, the overproduction of shorts in late 1970s forced a number of production companies into bankruptcy.

Muerte al amanecer and the Films of 1977

The entry for Francisco Lombardi in the "Dictionary of Short Films," written by José Carlos Huayhuaca and published in *Hablemos de cine* 71 (April 1980), began by declaring him "the most important filmmaker to have arisen from the Film Law of 1972" (19–20). Alhough Robles Godoy had made more features and Federico García was keeping the same pace of creating films, by 1980 Lombardi was quickly becoming recognized as the premier director in Peruvian cinema. His success also bestowed honor upon *Hablemos de cine*, as Lombardi had first gained attention for his writing with the journal. If *Cahiers du cinéma* contributed to the rise of the French New Wave by presenting François Truffaut, *Hablemos de cine* did the same for Peruvian cinema with Francisco Lombardi.

Lombardi first published in the journal in volume 46 (March–April 1969),[33] though his association with *Hablemos de cine* went back much further. Much younger than the rest of the editorial staff, he was first brought to meetings in 1966 by Juan Bullitta, who had discovered him through a mimeographed journal that he (Lombardi) had started on his own while in high school—similar to the earliest days of *Hablemos de cine*. A 1967 visit to Lima by Fernando Birri, the director of the Santa Fé film school in Argentina, prompted the magazine's editors to encourage Lombardi (who was present at this meeting) to attend Santa Fé to learn the craft. Upon returning in 1969, he joined the staff at *Hablemos de cine*, this time as a participating editor, later becoming a critic for other publications, including *Suceso* and then *Correo*. Historian Ricardo Bedoya credits Lombardi's sharp, insightful critcism (along with that of Desiderio Blanco) for bringing pointed film analysis outside the pages of *Hablemos de cine* to the popular press.[34]

The Film Law of 1972 allowed Lombardi to move away from criticism toward production by aligning with producer José Zavala and forming a lucrative short-film production company called Inca Films. As with many of the directors that would emerge thanks to the law, Lombardi noted in an early interview that the short films were a way of gaining experience specifically to delineate his own style:

> *Robles [Godoy] and Arturo Sinclair have very clear, individual cinematic visions. They work in certain ways that make it possible to predict the nature of their work to come. I am trying to resolve that mystery that is cinema on my own terms and can only do that by actually making films. And I don't expect to arrive at any particular formula, where someone could predict beyond a shadow of a doubt what a Lombardi picture will be like.*[35]

Lombardi's early filmography fluctuated wildly among genres and style and between fiction and documentary, serving as adequate practicum for the feature film. *Muerte al amanecer* (Death at Dawn), Lombardi's first feature film, was released in 1977 and based on the famous 1955 execution of Jorge Villanueva Torres (known as the notorious "Monster of Armendáriz") for raping and murdering a young boy. Although the work was the first major effort of a young, relatively inexperienced filmmaker, *Muerte al amanecer* triumphed both critically and commercially, showcasing a high technical quality unique among the other Peruvian films of the time.

Along with Lombardi, three other directors released their first features in 1977, marking it as the banner year for Peruvian filmmaking: January saw the release of Luis Figueroa's *Los perros hambrientos* (The Hungry Dogs), followed by Jorge Volkert's *La nave de los brujos* (The Witches' Den) in March, Lombardi's *Muerte al amanecer* in May, and Federico García's *Kuntur Wachana* (Where the Condors are Born/Donde nacen los cóndores) in December. Unlike Robles Godoy or Kantor, whose production experience began in the 1960s, all the new directors had had little previous filmmaking practice before making several short films under the Film Law of 1972. The other three films, however, did not share Lombardi's box-office success. Volkert's film was the most flatly rejected of the four films, probably because of its misleading advertising campaign: billed as "a trip around the world of magic and secret rituals," *La nave de los brujos* was actually a feature-length documentary whose technical merits unfortunately mimicked those of the poorly constructed anthropological shorts that prevailed in theaters.[36] One of the three co-directors of *Kukuli*, Figueroa earned the label of "indigenist" by critics for *Los perros hambrientos*'s allegedly perpetuating the "most unfortunate" aspects of the earlier film.[37] The more ambitious and political *Kuntur Wachana* left a strong impression on local critics, particularly those from *Hablemos de cine*, who recognized a direct relationship with Bolivian filmmaker Jorge Sanjinés. While not a box-office hit, García's film did reasonably well within the Peruvian market; more impressively, it became the most-sold Peruvian film to commercial markets overseas. Both of these films were also invited to several international festivals, though not in competition, and García's work miraculously became the film most sold to overseas markets at the time, primarily to the Soviet Union and other Eastern European countries.[38]

The Return to Democracy and Feature Films of the 1980s

The oppressive regime of Francisco Morales Bermúdez yielded to international pressure to bring back democracy and the subsequent ratification of a new constitution in 1979. Democratic elections the following year resulted in the reelection of Fernando Belaúnde Terry as president. Belaúnde's second term would unfortunately be marked by the slow-spiraling economic downturn throughout the early 1980s. The tremendous impact on the national currency, the *sol*, can be measured in any number of ways; as this is a study of *Hablemos de cine*, a brief examination of the continuously inflating price of the journal itself can be used as a measure. Starting with volume 50 in 1970, each copy sold for 20 soles; volume 65 increased to 25 soles; volumes 66 and 67 to 30 soles. Volume 69 (1977–1978) was published in July 1978, a full year and a half after the previous issue, with a price of 100 soles.[39] By volume 72, at the end of 1980, the price jumped to 400 soles; by volume 75 (1982), to 1,000 soles; and 2,000 soles for the next issue in 1983 (volume 76). The final issue, volume 77 in 1984, sold for 4,000 soles.

Despite the economic situation, a relatively fruitful cinematic atmosphere among both spectators and filmmakers prevailed. The abolition of censorship in any form, established in the Peruvian Constitution of 1979 (article 2, clause 4), changed the landscape of Peruvian theatrical exhibition in the early 1980s. Several European films that had been banned for years for a variety of reasons—including Sergei Eisenstein's *Battleship Potemkin* (1925) and the Spanish war documentary *¿Por qué morir en Madrid?* (Why Die in Madrid?, Manzanos Brochero, 1966), two films for which *Hablemos de cine* fought desperately over the years to be shown—finally were screened theatrically. The main change to the cinematic landscape, however, reflected how permissive the new regulations became: banned for years, pornography entered the Peruvian market and the largely male moviegoing public rapidly embraced the genre, causing many movie palaces throughout Lima to switch exclusively to pornography. As late as 1987, a poll conducted by the newspaper *El Comercio* found that a large majority (41 percent) of the moviegoing population attended such theaters.[40]

Peruvian feature films maintained a steady stream of production, averaging two per year between 1977 and 1992. The most notable feature common to all these works is that, with the exception of Robles Godoy, all features were directed by people who had previously participated in the short-film explosion.[41] Several important first works appear in the early 1980s, including *Abisa a los compañeros* (The Abyss of My Comrades, Felipe Degregori, 1980), *Ojos de perro* (Dog Eyes, Alberto Durant, 1982), *El viento de ayahuasca* (The Wind of the Ayahuasca, Nora de Izcué, 1983) and *La familia Orozco* (The Orozco Family, Jorge Reyes, 1983). Of these, "Chicho" Durant has had the most lasting career, having made four films since then, all surrounding some aspect of crime and, in his later work, corruption. *Malabrigo* (1986) follows a woman through northern Peru as she looks for her missing husband; the very successful *Alias: "La Gringa"* (1991) tracks the story of real-life prison escapee Guillermo Portugal while reflecting the harsh realities of the contemporary situation in Lima in the early 1990s. One of the very few Peruvian feature films to center around a black character, *Coraje* (Courage, 1998) is Durant's second biopic, this time of María Elena Moyano, an activist working in the shantytown of Villa El Salvador who was killed by Sendero Luminoso. Durant's *Doble juego* (Con Game, 2004) features multiple storylines concerning small-time corruption throughout Peruvian society and is notable for being the first Peruvian feature to be invited to the Sundance Film Festival in 2004.[42]

Federico García and Francisco Lombardi, whose first films were released in 1977, continued to release films almost annually during a surprisingly productive period throughout the 1980s. García initially emerged as the more prolific director, continuing his interest in Andean affairs with *Laulico* (1980), *El caso Huayanay: Testimonio de parte* (The Huayanay Case: Partial Testimony, 1981), *Melgar, el poeta insurgente* (Melgar, the Insurgent Poet, 1982), and *Tupác Amaru* (1984). The most interesting of these films is perhaps *El caso Huayanay*, whose use of the actual locations and survivors of a particular event once again was compared with the work of Bolivian filmmaker Jorge Sanjinés, particularly his *El coraje del pueblo* (The Courage of the People, Bolivia, 1971). The film examined the case of Matías Escobar, a functionary who committed a number of atrocities against members of the Andean village of Huayanay before being murdered, with the community taking collective responsibility. The film then exposed the failure of the legal system to meet the needs of the community. García's next two films are less experimental, falling into the genre of the biopic. Both of his subjects were popular revolutionary figures: Mariano Melgar was a Peruvian poet who became a revolutionary and was executed by the Spanish, while José Gabriel Condorcanqui took the name Tupác Amaru in one of the major Indian uprisings in the eighteen century. The struggle of the peasant worker against dominant society is García's signature theme through all of these films.

Francisco Lombardi's next two films, *Muerte de un magnate* (Death of a Magnate, 1980) and *Maruja en el infierno* (Maruja in Hell, 1983), solidified his position as Peru's most successful director, both in terms of box-office presence as well as quality of filmmaking. Similar to García's *El caso Huayanay*, *Muerte de un magnate* appears as a critique of the social inequality prevailing in Peru despite the regimes of Velasco and Morales Bermúdez; the film revels in exposing the chaotic debauchery emblematic of the Peruvian upper class. As with his earlier film, Lombardi chose to examine a real event, this time the murder of Peruvian socialite Luis Banchero Rossi. With its grotesque depiction of a white character, the film followed the events leading to the inevitable death of the fishing magnate on New Year's Day, 1972.

Maruja en el infierno marks Lombardi's first adaptation, this time of Enrique Congrains' novel *No una sino muchas muertes* (Not One But Many Deaths). The film struggled to get to the screen, primarily because of the sudden death of long-time Inca Films producer José Zavala. This delay nonetheless allowed the script to be modified to reflect the contemporary economic situation of the country, making the film more immediate. The film centers around a young woman who makes a living by washing bottles alongside a number of crazy, homeless people who are being exploited for their labor; after falling in love with an amateur boxer, she eventually runs away, freeing her fellow captives into the unsure streets of Lima. The film enjoyed considerable financial and critical success, including praise from novelist Mario Vargas Llosa.

In an interview following the release of the film, Lombardi was asked if he was interested in adapting any other Peruvian novels; he replied that he would love to adapt Vargas Llosa's 1963 debut novel *La ciudad y los perros* (published in English as *The Time of the Hero*), the first Latin American book to win the prestigious Biblioteca Breve prize of the Seix Barral publishing house and therefore credited with bringing international attention to the Latin American fiction "boom" of the 1960s. The novel was almost adapted several times during the 1970s, including one effort by Mexican director Luis Alcoriza; however, given that the book explicitly treats the military in a bad light, any attempts under either the Velasco or Morales Bermúdez regimes proved unsuccessful. After viewing *Maruja en el infierno*, Vargas Llosa gave full support to Lombardi and the film was finally screened in June 1985. Though much of the fractured prose that distinguishes the novel was necessarily stripped from the film, *La ciudad y los perros* follows an adolescent boy nicknamed "the Poet" during his final year at a military academy when the death of a friend, "the Slave," is covered up and not investigated. Using the school as a microcosm of Peruvian social structure, the film is Lombardi's first scathing indictment of corruption as it permeates Peruvian society.

Lombardi returned to aspects of the military with *La boca del lobo* (The Lion's Den) in 1988; the film this time, however, takes the perspective of troops deployed to the Andean region held strong by Sendero Luminoso (the Shining Path), the organization that terrorized Peru throughout much of the 1980s. While the military aspects are somewhat derivative of other military films (such as Oliver Stone's *Platoon* [1986] and most notably Michael Cimino's *The Deer Hunter* [1978], which also uses a game of Russian roulette as a climactic plot device), Lombardi's well-constructed, topical drama was the high point of Peruvian filmmaking during this period, lauded by both national and international critics, particularly for being the first film to confront the issue of Sendero Luminoso.

A number of other significant filmmakers entered the Peruvian filmmaking scene with feature films in the latter half of the 1980s. The large majority of these films seem influenced by Lombardi's success through their choice of the crime film as the dominant genre. Augusto Tamayo's first film *La fuga del Chacal* (The Jackal's Escape, 1987) and José Carlos Huayhuaca's *Profesión: Detective* (1986) both follow this trajectory with little innovation, reaping relatively profitable local box-office returns, with the former reaching nearly one million spectators in its run. García's treatment of local Andean populations was also extended; for example, Marianne Eyde's feature debut *Los ronderos* (The Vigilantes, 1987) presents the "good" poor people in Cajamarca going up against the "bad" rich people. García's thematic and stylistic methods were expanded upon most effectively by the collective known as Grupo Chaski, who provided a socially conscious approach to filmmaking with viably commercial narratives. Primarily directed by the triumvirate of Fernando Espinoza, Stefan Kaspar, and Alejandro Legraspi, both *Gregorio* (1985) and *Juliana* (1989) focused on children trying to survive within the ignored underclass of Lima. *Gregorio* (fig. 4) was filmed in a quasi-documentary style evocative of Italian neorealism and, hence, might be seen as a late entry of sorts into the continental movement of New Latin American Cinema. *Juliana*, on the other hand, comes across as less confrontational, with an air of hope—unusual for the year in which it was released. Although both films did well at the box office, Grupo Chaski strayed from their original progressive roots, firing two of the primary directors and entering into a distribution agree-

Figure 4: Members of Grupo Chaski filming *Gregorio* (1985). Courtesy of the Filmoteca PUCP.

ment with Federico García for the disappointing *La Manzanita del Diablo*; largely owing to infighting and financial mismanagement, Grupo Chaski dissolved by the early 1990s.[43]

The other major contribution to Peruvian filmmaking during the late 1980s has been discounted in most national histories as not being Peruvian: the number of low-budget action films produced by Roger Corman's U.S.-based Concorde–New Horizons Productions. Corman entered the Peruvian market through director Luis Llosa, who made several short films during the late 1970s (including a significant contribution to the 1980 omnibus film *Aventuras prohibidas*) and coordinated a number of highly regarded television projects (notably the police series *Gamboa*) before directing the feature *Hour of the Assassin* in 1987. The film starred Erik Estrada, featured locations throughout Peru and was shot entirely in English; nonetheless Llosa retained local distribution and exhibition rights, marketing the film locally as *Misión en los Andes* (Mission in the Andes). The film's success allowed his own production company, Iguana Productions, to turn a major profit, becoming one of the few financially stable Peruvian production companies. Llosa would direct three additional films for Corman in Peru and produce almost a dozen additional low-budget, exploitation thrillers in Peru. Llosa himself secured more commercial productions in Hollywood in the 1990s; his largest production, 1997's *Anaconda* with Jennifer Lopez and Jon Voight, had an estimated $45 million budget and was cofinanced with Iguana Productions.

The End of the Film Law of 1972

The disastrous economic and political policies of the first government of Alan García led to the surprise election of Alberto Fujimori, who bested rightist candidate and author Mario Vargas Llosa in a runoff election. In order to halt what had become a financial free fall, Fujimori's government instituted major economic stimulus packages over the next several years, largely buoyed by international investment in a variety of national interests. In late December 1992, the Fujimori government scaled back the two initiatives from the Film Law of 1972 guaranteeing mandatory exhibition—effectively terminating the law without actually repealing it. Having come together as almost an industry over the last twenty years, Peruvian filmmakers and aficionados protested in the streets for a reinstatement of these two policies, to no avail. Two years after the "repeal," the Fujimori government instated a new law (D.L. 26370) superseding the Film Law of 1972; instead of concentrating on exhibition, however, the new law focused on the production process, channeling resources to a screenplay competition for seed money.[44]

Christian Weiner notes that "the reasoning behind the [new] law is no longer one oriented around the concept of building an 'industry' as much as around supporting a cultural activity."[45] This fundamental difference explains also why the 1994 law did not stimulate nearly so much activity as the one that preceded it. In mandating exhibition and returning a portion of ticket sales to short-film producers, the Film Law of 1972 employed a mechanism of self-generating the funds necessary for production; the screenplay prize, however, required governmental funding up-front with no provision for generating such funding in the future. The idea for the screenplay prize emerged as a result of the contemporary global context of GATT (General Agreement on Trade and Tariff) negotiations in 1993 when France proposed the notion of "cultural exception" applying to audiovisual products—such as film—which needed "protection" as intrinsically national cultural elements.[46] With little idea as to how to maintain funding for this endeavor, however, the prize has not been awarded on a regular basis; even when films are eventually made, the government has more often than not defaulted on the loans to filmmakers, driving these filmmakers to transnational funding sources such as Ibermedia and the Hubert Bals fund.

The immediate weakening and eventual dissolution of the Film Law of 1972 irreparably halted the trajectory of Peruvian filmmaking at the beginning of 1993. The halting of mandatory exhibition stranded the two feature films already in theaters (particularly Eyde's Shining Path–themed *La vida es una sola* (You Only Live

Once) with very little hope of recuperating investments; with no paying venues at all provided for short films, nearly all the production companies that had counted on the funding derived from mandatory exhibition quickly went bankrupt.

The trajectory of Peruvian filmmaking slowed markedly with the dissolution of the Film Law of 1972. The 1990s seemed to offer only a continuation of the cinema of the 1980s with the same directors producing the very few features that were released. During this decade no director that had not worked within the short-film industry would release a film; thus, there was a distinct absence of younger filmmakers. Instead, Francisco Lombardi continued with a series of stylish films, often adapted from literary sources, though also moving away occasionally from dramatic thrillers. His 1990 film, *Caídos del cielo* (Fallen from Heaven), wove three intertwining stories through present-day Lima in a black comedy examining how a middle-class couple must sell their home in order to build a similar structure in the cemetery before they die. *Sin compasión* (No Mercy, 1991) retold Dostoyevsky's *Crime and Punishment* in a modern, localized setting. Although it is now considered one of his minor films, the dark work did travel to a number of international film festivals and is notable for starring local *telenovela* actors in leading roles—including Diego Bertie. *Bajo la piel* (Under the Skin, 1996) cast Bertie in a supporting role for what is arguably Lombardi's most interesting picture: a psychological crime thriller set against an archaeological dig in the northern coast of Peru. *No se lo digas a nadie* (Don't Tell Anyone, 1998) is based on Jaime Bayly's sordid exposé of gay men among the upper class; starring actors-of-the-moment Christian Meier and Santiago Magill, the scandalous movie met with tepid reviews but outrageously successful box-office returns, successfully beating the Hollywood feature *Godzilla* when it opened in July on Independence Day weekend. Salvador del Solar and Angie Cepeda starred in the adaptation of Mario Vargas Llosa's *Pantaleón y las visitadoras* (Captain Pantoja and the Special Service, 2000), yet another satire of the Peruvian military, this time following an army captain who is ordered to create a floating fleet of prostitutes on the Amazon in order to placate soldiers who otherwise suffer from low morale.

Lombardi's most recent films maintain an interest in his constant themes of corruption at the highest levels. Starring Giovanni Ciccia and Spanish actors Fele Martínez and Lucía Jiménez, *Tinta roja* (Red Ink, 2000, adapted from Chilean author Alberto Fuguet's novel) tackles yellow journalism, as a young journalist becomes embroiled in the preying techniques he is initially horrified at. *Mariposa negra* (Black Butterfly, 2006, based on Alonso Cueto's story) similarly targets yellow journalism, but here specifically for being in the hands of Vladmiro Montesinos, Fujimori's real-life righthand man; set just before the fall of the Fujimori government, the film focuses on a young woman who resolves to murder Montesinos after her husband is murdered and slandered for attempting to expose his activities. Significantly for this most masculinist director, this film focuses on a woman's viewpoint instead of a man's.

A New Perspective: Peruvian Filmmaking in the Twenty-first Century

Lombardi's most ambitious project of the twenty-first century remains *Ojos que no ven* (What the Eye Doesn't See), a complex, nearly three-hour epic of interlocking stories, all treating the subject of corruption throughout contemporary Peruvian society—so contemporary, as a matter of fact, that the "Vladishow" (the televised trial of Montesinos) is playing in the background of nearly every scene of the film. Lombardi was one of the first Peruvian directors to embrace coproductions with Spanish companies (starting with *La boca del lobo* in 1989) and to subsequently develop a considerable following among Spanish audiences. It is thus significant that this film found little support outside Peru, instead gathering money from a wide variety of private sources in the country. Finding little traction among Peruvian critics, the film failed with local audiences as well, perhaps because of media fatigue with the "Vladishow," perhaps because of the extremely long running time of this very serious film. Even so, the film was selected as that year's 2003 representative for the Academy Awards.

In virtually any other year, a Lombardi film would seem to be the natural choice as the most representative and/or best Peruvian film produced in a particular calendar year—often because it was the only one. As the Film Law of 1994 did not provide any further stipulations concerning exhibition, nor was funding available for all filmmakers, feature film production remained steadily underdeveloped throughout the 1990s and early 2000s. Usually only a handful of feature films were commercially released to theaters; moreover, the films that were completed during this period were directed either by already established directors or new ones who had gained experience primarily through short films. If the level of detail concerning Lombardi's films above seems overstated, it is also true that there are few other films made during this period that are markedly different. Perhaps predictably, the largest divergence comes from Lombardi's companion auteur, Federico García—but his films from the mid-1980s onward failed to find commercial audiences in the country, despite attempts at both broad comedy (*La Manzanita del Diablo* [The Devil's Block], 1992), science fiction (*El forastero* [The Outsider], 2002) and, more predictably, the political biopic (*El Amauta*,

2004, in limited release on video). Besides García, only Augusto Tamayo has steered in a completely different direction in the 2000s, concentrating solely on period pieces set during the colonial period in *El bien esquivo* (The Elusive Good, 2001) and *Una sombra al frente* (Crossing a Shadow, 2007).

It is worth noting the year—2003—that *Ojos que no ven* was nominated for the Oscar. Because of the sudden and somewhat unexpected rise in Peruvian production, ten feature films were released during 2003, seemingly heralding a new era in national filmmaking much as 1977 had before. This particular year's productions are notable primarily for their diversity; in addition, an overwhelming number had been made by new directors with little or no experience from the short-film production period.[47] Sarah Barrow has noted that this surge did not continue into the immediate future in terms of numbers of productions, in part because of the Peruvian government's defaulting on both the national screenplay contest winners and on participation in Ibermedia.[48] By 2007, the Peruvian cinematic feature film landscape featured both older, established filmmakers from the short-film period—Tamayo's *Una sombra al frente*, for example—as well as younger filmmakers benefiting from international programs. As an example of the latter, Claudia Llosa's *Madeinusa* (2006) was completed with assistance from the Sundance Screenwriters Lab in the United States after she received university degrees in both New York and Spain. In 2009, Llosa's second feature *La teta asustada* (Milk of Sorrow) won the prestigious Golden Bear Award as the top film of the Berlin Film Festival.

CHAPTER 2
PUBLICATION, AUTHORITY, IDENTITY
Constructing the Film Journal

> *All serious film journals are necessarily minority publications, even those that assume a decidedly political militancy, pretending to escape the elitist reductions to which cultural publications almost always subscribe.*
>
> —OPENING EDITORIAL OF *HABLEMOS DE CINE* (NOVEMBER 1969–FEBRUARY 1970)

Before the first issue was published, Isaac León Frías, Federico de Cárdenas, Carlos Rodríguez Larraín, and Juan Bullitta put to paper the initial plans for *Hablemos de cine*. According to a typed, unpublished document dated January 2, 1965, the publication would comprise a one- to two-page editorial, written by the editor-in-chief but discussed with the rest of the staff; two to six pages of "reflections" on film, to be written by the "adviser"; one to two pages of news to be culled from other magazines such as the Spanish *Film Ideal*; four to eight optional pages to be filled with articles, interviews, and other material; two pages of advertising; and four to ten pages of the reviews of current films shown in Lima. The two more important sections were to be the reflection, which was used to discuss more theoretical issues, and the reviews, to be divided among the staff with "the most interesting film having two reviews, one by the person who most enjoyed it and another by the one who least enjoyed it."[1]

Surprisingly, this format can be seen through almost all of the seventy-seven issues of the journal. Though the theory-oriented "reflection" fell away when Desiderio Blanco left the country briefly, and advertising did not often materialize beyond small notices for the printing company and local bookstores that carried the journal, the "news" section survived throughout the run under the title "Cine de aquí y de allá" (Movies from here and there), as did the reviews under the heading "Aquí opinamos" (Here we opine). The journal expanded in size as well, maintaining an average of 68 pages and growing to 108 pages for what would be its penultimate issue in 1983.

Much as some of the structural features were fine-tuned throughout its publication run, *Hablemos de cine*'s identity as a publication also became modified over its twenty years. How does a journal in fact construct an identity? What sort of film culture must exist to generate interest in writing about film in the first place? What sort of borrowing must take place to establish authority early in the publication run? These are not small questions: if we claim that *Hablemos de cine* has a significant influence on how Peruvian cinema was articulated and developed, then how the journal itself constructed and maintained its authority as the primary voice of Peruvian film criticism in a general sense ties in directly with its views on the specific issue of national cinema.

In establishing its original identity, the journal responded to two precedents: first, reviews in local general publications to which the journal reacted against; second, the European film journals to which they had the most access and which they largely imitated. In many ways, the reaction against the first entity was maintained through the close, almost intimate connection established through cinephilic activity at screenings in Lima, which played a direct role in the criticism that followed. While there was still an emphasis on national cinema this early in the publication run (as I shall detail in the next chapter), the legitimization of the film journal through European parameters and the subsequent acquisition of European personnel parallel ideas concerning art criticism and reception within contemporary Latin America. This dependence on European models changed once the journal developed an autonomous identity in 1967.

Local Cinephilia, the Cine-Club, and Film Writing

The close, almost intimate connection established through cinephilic activity at screenings in Lima plays a direct role in the criticism that followed. The premise of the film journal depends on the slippery concept of *cinephilia*, or the "love of film."[2] Those involved with films—those who watch them, those who make them—tend to align themselves within a unique cultural field where what is shown on the screen (and what is said about what is shown on the screen) becomes more than a form of entertainment. As a medium in and of itself, film tends to be passive: the spectator willingly watches the images and sounds on the screen before him without any participation in manipulating such images. The spectator cannot enter into direct dialogue with either the filmmaker or the film itself. Cinema is thus at the core a solitary act, characterized purely by the reception of individual viewers to a stimulus. Once the lights come up, however, the theater reveals many seats with other spectators, who have all had the same experience — or have they? A film might enthrall one viewer, bore another, and offend a third. The difference lies in the subjective nature of each viewer: no two viewers have come into the theater with the same experiences, so each viewing experience is unique. Because the actual movie-watching experience is communal — a theater with many spectators — interactions can take place using the film just viewed as a point of departure for discussion. Films thus inspire a search for discourse among the viewers, serving the films up as textual objects to be discussed, citing anything from the political influence of a film's theme to questions of aesthetics to the gaudy hairstyle of a particular actor. Whereas watching a film is a solitary experience, the resulting discourse establishes a community.

In a film-journal article, the personal emotional investment of the author in the reception of the film is evident, an individual pleasure (or displeasure, which is the same thing) that he/she wishes to share with others, presumably to bring them to his/her view. Metz identifies this feeling as a "love" where the critic aims "to save as many films as possible; not *qua* copies, *qua* celluloid, but the social memory of those films and hence a by no means unfavorable image of them."[3] The importance of an individual film as object is thus subverted by the impression of the experience generated by that film; the film journal records the impression of the film rather than the film itself.

Cinephilia, this desire for discourse concerning cinema, should be distinguished from *scopophilia*, particularly how the latter term has been used in the work of Laura Mulvey.[4] In her essay "Visual Pleasure and Narrative Cinema," Mulvey uses a Freudian analysis to read the relationship between the observer and the cinematic apparatus, finding the pleasure derived from film as an unadulterated objectivizing gaze from a masculinized subject toward a feminized screen. For her, "analyzing pleasure, beauty, destroys it. That is the intention of this article."[5] If scopophilia as defined by Mulvey is a negative process, cinephilia does not see the film apparatus as being so sinister — or, if it does, finds a positive outlet for it. Beyond the obvious "love of film" implied by its name, cinephilia has been more loosely defined, particularly by Paul Willemen, by anecdotal confluence: he reads cinephilia in the gathering of French critics in the 1950s and 1960s as "represented by the fact that they all saw one another in the front rows of the cinema, grooving on their relationship to cinema which they then went away and rationalized into different types of positions."[6] The actual cinematic experience generates position-taking in relation to the shared event, be it positive or negative: cinephilia is the "groove" established by those who experienced the event. Unlike the private, voyeuristic nature of Mulvey's scopophilia, where the film "unwinds magically, indifferent to the audience,"[7] cinephilia as sketched by Willemen is necessarily social, stimulating interaction between similar enthusiasts who have experienced the same "vibe" from having been spectators at the film. The private, voyeuristic relationship with the screen, coded as dangerous and menacing by Mulvey, becomes a public, social interaction that transcends the scopophilia that might have inspired it. In essence, cinephilia creates a community through the medium of the screen by providing a context for contact with another filmgoer: "What you are reconsuming is the moment of revelation experienced in an encounter between you and cinema, which may be different from the person sitting next to you, in which case you have to dig him or her in the ribs with your elbow to alert them to the fact that you've just had a cinephilic moment. This is a mode of ordinary consumption containing a critical discourse which is quite valid on its own terms and which is actually being relayed in more rationalised film discourses."[8]

Mulvey proposes that the cinematic apparatus maintains a pseudosolitary relationship with the screen that cannot be broken during the actual viewing of a filmic event. Cinephilia bypasses the screening event—and even the film itself—to achieve a positive (read: not voyeuristic) postviewing relationship with the film through interaction with other filmgoers. If, as Roland Barthes says, the photographic image confirms the dead, human interaction concerning the photograph brings it back to some semblance of life.[9] The scopophilic moment is too private, too perverse: announcing the pleasure behind the moment allows the pleasure to be diffused, effectively normalizing the perversity.[10] Whereas other forms of entertainment periodicals serve a promotional purpose, the film journal becomes a meditation on an experience of viewing a particular film as much as (if not more so than) a discourse on the actual film viewed. It is also a vehicle with which to share the positive meditations on the cinematic experience with others. Rather than promote the critic as being above the ordinary filmgoer, cinephilia establishes the connection between these two spectators, mitigating the distance between them.

These functions of normalizing and forming community around the cinematic experience can, and have historically been applied to both the film journal and organizations that formed with the express intent of venerating the cinema.[11] Termed *cine-clubs* (see chapter 1) after their institution in Paris in the 1920s, these societies developed their repertoires around particular types of movies, themes, places of origin, or—particularly after the rise of the *politique des auteurs* (auteur theory)—directors. David Bordwell has argued that the earliest cine-clubs formed to canonize certain silent films as examples of "quality" cinematic representations of an idealized narrative structure.[12] Often accompanied by spirited discussions, forums and/or other events that served to informally educate audiences about auteurs, national cinemas, or even genre classifications, the continuation of these societies remained key to further dissemination of cinephilia. Their presence gained additional purpose as governing powers attempted to censor certain films for public consumption. The cine-club's status as a small, private, alternative space for films outside the realm of mainstream distribution often allowed screenings of films that might otherwise not be viewed. Sometimes this was in the name of "art," "aesthetics," or "cultures," though by the 1950s, many cine-clubs would organize and feature movies with political or social orientations.

Many film journals—*Hablemos de cine* included—were active, collaborative endeavors that built upon the encounters at the cine-clubs. These self-selected, highly motivated viewing groups that discussed films following their screenings served as testing grounds for cinematic writers eager to test their mettle, often forming their positions through interaction with the cine-clubs. The cine-club patrons also served as an ideal writing audience: if nothing else, they would share the viewing experiences of the journal's editors. The association between a film publication's genesis and a particular cine-club has historical precedent and international breadth. In France, the formation of various cine-clubs in the 1920s led to the creation of a cinephilic culture that in turn produced the first version of *Revue du cinéma* in 1928.[13] During World War II, *L'Ecran Français* was originally a mouthpiece for an organization of clandestine filmmakers as part of the Resistance in 1943.[14] Antoine de Baecque's exhaustive history of *Cahiers du cinéma* lists several cine-clubs as significant to the journal's formation in 1951, including "Cine-club du Quartier-Latin," the "Cercle Cinémane," "Objectif 49" (frequented by André Bazin and Alexandre Astruc), and especially Henri Langlois's Cinémathèque and the subsequent screenings in the form of the "Cercle de Cinéma."[15] Cine-clubs also contributed to the rise of the Spanish journals *Film Ideal* and *Nuestro Cine* in 1956 and 1961, respectively.[16]

The amorphous group of people who frequented the cine-clubs came together to view and discuss films, and the journals that follow seem almost inevitably to espouse the position of a very small group, or perhaps even of one person. For the French, for example, the young Jean George Auriol who founded *Revue du cinéma* in 1928 was seen as the driving force behind both versions of that journal, as well as the later *Cahiers du cinéma*. With his emphasis on the objective nature of the cinematic image as crucial, André Bazin was associated both with *L'Ecran Français* as well as the early *Cahiers*. In Cuba, the founding of *Cine cubano* is less seen as the brainchild of one person than of the ICAIC, a cultural division affiliated with and commissioned by the Castro government. Even periodicals that were not interested in "art cinema" per se have sometimes been ascribed to a single person: for example, the Chilean *Ecran* was founded in 1930 by Roberto Aldunate, who simply felt that Santiago should have a film magazine similar to those found in Paris. By 1940, *Ecran* would be associated with María Novaro, whose journalistic recounting replaced the previous editorship that had lacked a central vision.[17]

Australian critic Noel King's comments in a conversation with Paul Willemen aptly address the community-building roles and connections of cinematic written discourse:

> *Maybe the cinephilic act of "reading" a film involves aligning the film's image-discourse with other more or less fanzine writings that attach to, or can be attached to, the film. You don't have to read* Sight and Sound *and* Film Comment *on Eastwood's* Unforgiven *but a cinephile probably would. And perhaps it is that sort of combinatory act that goes some way to defining the reproduction of the cinephile. One account of the history of cinephilia might say that, in the 50s or whenever, cinephilia produces the institution of the magazine/fanzine which in turn helps recruit future cinephiles.*

Willemen counters this neatly: "Cinephilia has more to do with writing in magazines than with reading them,"[18] a comment that I shall return to shortly. Earlier in the essay, however, he states the usefulness of reading certain magazines as "short-hand" for solidarity with certain ideologies:

> *I think film magazines created their following in areas of obscurely perceived overlaps which were translated into the way we say: "I like that magazine*

> *and I hate that magazine." Very loosely articulated, short-hand designations were in play which were actually covering the complex processes in which a multitude of possible pleasures were imbricated, of obscurely perceived coincidences of relationships which you felt this magazine shared and that magazine inflected in a way you were out of sympathy with.*[19]

King and Willemen cannot identify precisely *why* readers would feel a certain way about a film (or, significantly, any other topic of discussion), merely that they generally agree with the editorial practices of this particular mouthpiece, even if it is only expressing an opinion and trying to convince others to share his opinion of a film.

Though cinephilia does not necessarily manifest itself exclusively in film journals, all film journals (even the writings despising the films being discussed) are necessarily cinephilic. King's comment that these journals seemed to "recruit future cinephiles" should therefore not be taken lightly. Once alignments are made within groups of readers, those writing for the journal obtain power that can influence the viewing experiences of similarly oriented cinephilic readers. A critic can only gain respect when readers agree with his opinions, but their agreement in turn gives him greater power over their ideas. This theoretical power translates directly into economic and social power, as a critic's opinions and relationships with his/her readers can encourage or dissuade viewers concerning a certain film. Both the film (in the form of box-office receipts) and the journal (in the form of subscriptions and sales) can thus be directly affected by cinephilic criticism. If, after all, a person likes a particular magazine Q, which did not care for motion picture X, the reader might not go to see the film or might have to rethink his alignment with either the movie ("Why did I like X, when the critics at Q did not?") and/or periodical ("If I liked X, what does that say about my entirely subjective affiliation with Q's ideology?").

In the case of the Peruvian critics at *Hablemos de cine*, there is an even larger connection between cine-club activity and cinematic writing: the former directly funded the latter. Over its run of seventy-seven issues, the journal never gained significant revenue from advertising sources. It thus would have had to derive its entire funding from subscriptions (of which there were few) or sales, neither of which could be considered fiscally stable. With only five hundred copies printed during the mimeographed stage (the first twenty issues) and two thousand copies during the rest of the run, the journal could not stay afloat financially on the revenue from sales; the Cine-Club de la Católica, however, did enough business to keep the journal afloat. The editors of the journal also programmed the cine-club, thus also bringing their influence into cinematic exhibition. By aligning with the cine-club, the journal retained its editorial independence for as long as the cine-club remained financially viable. The lengthening delays between issues over the last few years of publication correspond to the drastic reduction of cine-club attendance in the 1980s.

This delineation also highlights the problematic characteristics of elitist cultural politics within Peru, particularly when considering modern art forms such as the cinema. For example, *Hablemos de cine* accurately mirrored the patriarchal nature of Peruvian cinephilic culture. Though undoubtedly women attended cine-club functions, not a single woman graced the masthead of *Hablemos de cine* during its entire run. Only one article by a woman was ever even published: an introduction to the work of French director Eric Rohmer by Sonia Goldenberg in issue 71 (April 1980), which may have been reprinted from another publication. When asked in 1998 why no women became staff members of the journal, Isaac León Frías could not identify a precise reason, stating that it was not intentional but that women tended not to come alone to film events and therefore did not develop the same cinephilia as men did. This gender divide would extend from cinephilia and criticism to production as well: only one female Peruvian director, Nora de Izcué, emerged during the twenty years of publication at *Hablemos de cine*. That gender issues never surfaced as a topic of an full-length article at the journal—especially considering the attention paid to other dichotomies such as national versus foreign, rural versus urban—reflects the patriarchal nature of cinematic culture in Peru and, to a large extent, Peruvian culture in general.[20]

Early Spanish (and French) Influence on Hablemos de cine

At the founding of the journal in the beginning of 1965, serious study of film was still almost exclusively European: the major film festivals were still held there (Cannes, Berlin, Venice, Moscow, and so forth), and the major critical publications were European. The model for a film periodical in the 1960s was the French *Cahiers du cinéma*, not only because of its revolutionary methods of seriously considering films, but because several of its writers were also significant filmmakers of the French New Wave; hence their contributions to cinematic culture were both theoretical and practical. The *cahieristas* were young, brash, and innovative young men, more contemporary and in agreement with the *hablemistas* than with the older critics working throughout Latin America.

The mark of the French journal is, of course, very apparent on the early issues of *Hablemos de cine*. Surprisingly, however, at the very beginning, the French journal was not the primary influence on the Peruvians. The most significant European influence came instead from a pair of Spanish film journals, *Film Ideal* and *Nuestro Cine*. As articulated by Iván Tubau in *Crítica cinematográfica española*, these two periodicals differed significantly at their beginnings in the early 1960s. The former followed *Cahiers* and with it, Bazinian notions of mise-en-scène and the younger critics' almost obsessive worship of the *politiques des auteurs* as defining the shape of film. *Film Ideal* embraced Hollywood filmmakers as much as the French did. *Nuestro Cine*, however, followed more closely the Italian journal *Cinema Nuovo* and the ideals of founder Guido Aristarco, who championed elements of an orthodox form of Marxism in the works of artistic European directors such as Visconti and Antonioni, flatly rejecting the classic Hollywood cinema that *Cahiers* embraced.

Because *Hablemos de cine* mentor Desiderio Blanco was himself influenced by the writings of *Cahiers*, his pupils gravitated toward *Film Ideal* (though a shift within the Spanish cinephilic community in the mid-1960s made this genealogy more complex). The document listing the initial plan for the Peruvian periodical in fact specifically mentions the Spanish journal as being the primary source of information for the "News" section.[21] In 1967, however, an interruption in the publication of *Film Ideal* caused the majority of its staff to join and eventually take over *Nuestro Cine*.[22] By the time Jesús Martínez León, originally a staff writer at *Film Ideal*, was listed on the masthead as a contributor to the Peruvian journal, he was writing for *Nuestro Cine*. All the later Spanish collaborators would come from this magazine, which modeled itself entirely after *Cahiers*.[23]

The influence of *Film Ideal* (and indirectly of *Cahiers du cinéma*) on *Hablemos de cine* was primarily evident in the fierce defense of mise-en-scène as the only legitimate way to view and critique film, though how that term was ultimately envisioned is somewhat hazy. Traditionally defined as the way in which an image is composed on the two-dimensional screen, mise-en-scène was also a primary force behind *Cahiers*' development of the *politique des auteurs*, privileging the director as the primary agent in creating a film as a work of art. Particularly in the early years, *Hablemos de cine* professed a strict adherence to judging mise-en-scène to the detriment of any other contributing factor to film style. The first issue, for example, featured two scathing reviews of Basil Dearden's *Woman of Straw* (1964), a Sean Connery–Gina Lollabrigida thriller vehicle. In his summary, Federico de Cárdenas is the only member who rates the film a 1, while the rest give it a 0.[24]

Given that the rest of the review is so damning, it is questionable why he would ever give it a 1:

> *The mise-en-scène of the Majorca exteriors is excellent, and the naturally achieved atmosphere at [Ralph] Richardson's Victorian mansion is also quite good. But...the director's lack of imagination is evident in the conventional camera movements and the poorly executed, standard effects used to create suspense (focusing on Richardson's open eyes at least six times while trying to create "suspense")....Perhaps [the film's failure] isn't entirely Dearden's fault, but he is just as guilty of filming and commercializing a script whose only value is in bringing together three actors (especially Connery) who are sure to bring in big box office. Again, the exteriors and the sets save this film from a "0."*[25]

This last line shows the tunnel vision of the four members: they attribute some value to a film they clearly deplore solely on its the use of mise-en-scène. However, no one at *Hablemos de cine* ever articulated what this term actually meant for a reader who might not have been familiar with it. The editorial of the premiere issue professed,

> *Our basic point of departure is our love for cinema whereby, in assessing the films, we shall avoid the dichotomy between content and form, since we believe that a film is fundamentally the act of expressing the vision of an auteur's world through the use of mise-en-scène. When said mise-en-scène most assumes the vision of an auteur's world, the film will be of higher quality. In this way, there is no reason to separate between content and form when analyzing a film, as the film is the realization in images of a way of viewing the world and mise-en-scène establishes the auteur in contact with the world. Film analysis can only be done through mise-en-scène. This is what we shall do at* Hablemos de cine.[26]

This editorial tells the reader nothing about how mise-en-scène works, nor how it should be evaluated. Admittedly, the concept is not the most concrete, but even in two articles written as "Reflections" by Desiderio Blanco, it is more talked around than defined. Citing the first volume of Bazin's *What Is Cinema?* Blanco lists three "fundamental principles of mise-en-scène" in volume 10

(July 1, 1965): that it is demonstrated phenomenologically, that the filmic image only reveals its being as it is projected, and that aesthetic value is a function of such an appearance. Whereas Bazin elaborated on his view of film criticism as a combination of examining aspects such as montage and depth of focus, the *hablemistas* never really define for their readers their specific strategies for viewing cinema.

The preceding passages also stress another problematic Cahierist notion: the privileging of the auteur. Subsumed by the *politiques des auteurs*, the French critics established clear, if underdeveloped, hierarchies based largely on personal preference and adherence to the visual poetry of "pure cinema." This perspective, while popular abroad and especially in the United States, provoked a warning from Bazin in *Cahiers du Cinéma*: "[The] strictest adherents of the *politiques de auteurs* get the best of it in the end for, rightly or wrongly, they always see in their favourite directors the manifestation of the same specific qualities. . . . I beg to differ with those of my colleagues who are the most firmly convinced that the *politiques des auteurs* is well founded, but this in no way compromises the general policy of the magazine."[27] For the Peruvian critics, this emphasis on the auteur meant that, in the context of Peruvian cinema, critics were looking desperately for someone to fulfill their ideals. An "auteur," for these critics, would legitimize their national project. This issue will become crucial as they begin to laud Francisco Lombardi in the late 1970s.

Establishing *Hablemos de cine*'s original theoretical position and identity as derived from other (particularly European) periodicals is unavoidable, albeit—given the international influence of *Cahiers du cinéma*—predictable. By beginning this way, however, the journal quickly gained an authoritative (if borrowed) voice through which to talk about cinema, without a trial period of determining *how* to write about the medium. The ideas stimulated by the French magazine provided a foundation that the Peruvian journal would modify through the course of its publication.

Given that in 1965, film writing from elsewhere in Latin America (much like fiction) did not travel to Peru, *Hablemos de cine* had access to few other alternatives besides these Spanish and French journals. This basis in a European model can also be seen as a simple way to be accepted as a valid critical voice within the local *limeño* cultural society. The fact that this brand of criticism was derived from European sources would make it *already* acceptable to other cultural critics in Lima. This concept of "validation through visibility," where a mode of expression is accepted primarily *because* it has already been accepted abroad,[28] would provide immediate validation within the larger local cultural community the journal was simultaneously writing for and trying to enter.

In truth, *Film Ideal* should not be seen as a "father figure" influence on the formation of *Hablemos de cine*, but rather as a sibling publication, as both publications experienced similar growing pains. Granted, both journals were run by very young critics who were excited by the ideas originally postulated by *Cahiers du cinéma*, but even though both Spain and Peru had developed lively cinephilic societies, many films were not exhibited in those areas with enough frequency or regularity for critics to develop their own theories or ideas about filmmakers or even genres. In Spain, this scarcity was caused by the authoritarian nature of Francisco Franco's military regime, which lasted from 1939 to 1975. Although in the 1960s filmmakers were allowed more freedom under the appointment of José María García Escudero as general director of cinema in Spain, and films appeared at film festivals that espoused artistic ideals instead of necessarily fascist ones, the threat of film's influence to work against fascist ideals in Franco's regime caused many American and Italian neorealist films to be either censored or banned outright.[29] In 1965, Peru was not yet under such a repressive rule, nor was the censor quite so active; there, the dearth of films reflected the physical distance of Lima from other centers of film production abroad. Nonetheless, critic Iván Tubau's description of the Spanish situation in the early 1960s sounds very much like what was also happening in Peru:

> *In effect, the young Spaniards were "cinephiles without films = cultured without culture." [Spanish critic José Luis] Guarner confessed that at the cine-club Monterols, they postulated entire cinematic theories based on three films by Rosselini and two by Renoir. There was a hunger for film and very few films to feed off of. We at* Nuestro Cine *often wrote about films that were not screened in Spain. The rigid Spanish censorship prevented the majority of the films seen throughout Europe from being seen here.... This is particularly grave when we consider that the sixties was the era of the British Free Cinema, the French New Wave, the Cinéma-Vérité, the Brazilian Cinema Nôvo, the American Underground—all these movements were read about instead of seen.*[30]

Tubau finds this obsessive demand for material a step beyond cinephilia into what he calls *cinephagia*, or "the devouring of films." In this respect, much more so than *Cahiers du cinéma*, *Film Ideal* and *Nuestro Cine* were excellent models for

Hablemos de cine, which, because of its location in Peru, would also be forced to write about films never screened locally in order to supplant its readers' demands for material. As *Hablemos de cine* established itself internationally, it solved this problem by enlisting foreign correspondents.

Becoming an International Publication

The connection with the Spanish journals *Film Ideal* and *Nuestro Cine* became explicit in *Hablemos de cine* 23 (March 1966) with the introduction of Spaniard Jesús Martínez León as one of two new collaborators to the journal. Martínez did not contribute a text written specifically for *Hablemos de cine* in this issue, but rather an article and filmography of Hollywood director Henry Hathaway that had been originally printed in *Film Ideal*. This was not the first time that an article had been reprinted: a short excerpt from *Film Ideal* on Otto Preminger had been published in issue 19 (December 15, 1965), and Peter Bogdanovich's interview of Alfred Hitchcock had been reprinted from the British Cahierist journal *Movie* in volume 22 (February 1966). Unlike the previous appearances, however, Martínez's name appears on the masthead as a collaborator to the journal. His presence marked the beginning of a significant change in the journal's scope, expanding the reach of the journal far beyond the Peruvian borders into Europe.

Quickly joining Martínez on the masthead were Chilean Mariano Silva in volume 24 (April 1966) and fellow *Film Ideal* (and later *Nuestro Cine*) correspondents Augusto M. Torres in volume 26–27 (June–July 1966) and Vicente Molina Foix in volume 33 (January–February 1967). The impact on the journal's contents was seen almost immediately. *Hablemos de cine* 25 (May 1966) contained a retrospective of contemporary Spanish cinema by Martínez as well as a firsthand view of the 1966 Mar de la Plata festival in Argentina by Silva, the first international festival covered within the journal's pages. Volume 26–27 regaled *Hablemos de cine* readers with portraits of even bigger festivals: Martínez detailed the eleventh edition of the Semana Internacional de Cine Religioso y de Valores Humanos (International Week of Religious and Human Rights Cinema) at Valladolid, Spain, while Torres provided an exclusive look at the premier European festival at Cannes. Volume 30–31 (September–October 1966) supplemented a retrospective of Czech cinema in Lima with an interview with directors Milos Forman and Ivan Passer by Martínez and Torres, now both at *Nuestro Cine*. For nearly three years, the foreign correspondents covered a variety of film festivals throughout Europe and Latin America, and subsequent issues of *Hablemos de cine* featured their significant contributions.

There are clear reasons for these international additions to the *Hablemos de cine* masthead. As young men independently financing a publication that was isolated completely from the film-producing centers of the world, the editors found it impossible to travel to other parts of the world to cover film happenings that other serious journals could. Despite the emergence in the early 1960s of significant film movements (such as the Brazilian Cinema Nôvo) and film festivals (such as the growing Mar de la Plata festival in Argentina or the pre-1967 Viña del Mar festivals in Chile) in Latin America, the Peruvian editors did not consider these as important as the European activities and made little effort to include them in their coverage. As cinephilic culture expanded in Peru, interest in foreign festivals documented by *Film Ideal* and *Nuestro Cine* (both commercially available in Lima) developed among the cine-club circles to which the journal was catering. Martínez's inclusion on the masthead began a significant internationalization of both the scope and the staff of *Hablemos de cine* that would establish it as one of the major film publications in Latin America. Though some other regional film periodicals had affiliations with Hollywood,[31] the Peruvian journal chose to focus on the European art-house festival material that appealed to their peers in cine-clubs. The decision to affiliate with the Spanish publications meant connecting with the publication that most directly inspired *Hablemos de cine* to begin with (not to mention the fact that the Peruvians did not need to translate any of their articles). With correspondents at many different locations, a wide number of film experiences were added to which Peruvian cinephiles would not otherwise have been exposed. These events also led to interviews with international directors who did not travel to Lima. An exclusive interview with Roger Corman conducted in part by Augusto M. Torres and published in volume 37 (September–October 1967) was a major coup for the Peruvians, who in 1965 had written many enthusiastic reviews of the American independent director's work.[32]

Hablemos de cine's cultural cachet rose significantly with the addition of the foreign correspondents: what could only have been seen as a local, specialized periodical now received international attention and scrutiny. Through their Spanish correspondent Martínez León, the Peruvian journal acquired its most significant international correspondent in volume 39 (January–February 1968) with French critic (and later director) Bertrand Tavernier.[33] His contributions can only be found in four issues, but he is listed on the masthead as a significant correspondent for nine issues, probably because his status as a French critic brought the highest credibility to the Peruvian journal by making that tangential connection to the country that produced *Cahiers du Cinéma*.

New Identities, New Looks

All the foreign correspondents disappeared from the masthead and from the journal with the publication of volume 50–51 (November 1969–February 1970). An exchange of free advertising for plane tickets with Air France enabled Federico de Cárdenas and Isaac León Frías to travel to Europe to cover several festivals themselves, thereby eliminating the immediate need for the European correspondents.[34] Volume 50–51, however, marked a shift in direction for the journal on a number of levels: this is the same issue where they report on how events at the Viña del Mar film festival of 1969 made them feel distanced from the current militant, political, and aesthetic trends evidenced in other Latin American national cinemas.[35]

This new vision manifested itself physically in a marked format change. For any periodical, a format switch through physical changes in layout can indicate a major ideological shift. It is rare for a periodical to undergo such a radical format shift without considerable forethought. Once a journal has achieved some reputation, changing its format will mean readers will have to adjust their personal methods of accessing and reading the material. Even if only the cover is altered, readers will not easily recognize the periodical with which they are familiar—though this may in turn attract other potential readers who had not noticed the periodical previously. The motives for reformatting a periodical's layout cannot be generalized, as they are often unique to the individual magazines being altered.

A study of layout variations and the stated motives behind such changes of the French film journal *Cahiers du cinéma* (figs. 5 and 6) will show how a periodical with similar goals and ideals to *Hablemos de cine* had very different reasons for change. Despite its having been published since April 1951, *Cahiers du cinéma* did not modify its format until September–October 1972 with issue 241. This change would be radically significant, not for what was added but for what was missing: for the first time, the "magazine" ran a cover without a picture. By the late 1960s, the journal's contents concerned the development of a militantly Marxist politics as much as theory, criticism, or star/auteur power. Early in 1972, political drawings replaced cover photographs as a harbinger of the format change. The physical appearance of volume 241 thus graphically represented the journal's austere ideological change: printed on heavy paper, the cover featured a banner masthead featuring the title of the journal and a listing of the table of contents in large print with nothing else. Clear and without frills, the plain, deliberately unspectacular cover set the serious tone of the contents inside and marked a transformation from what the editors considered a popular "magazine" to a

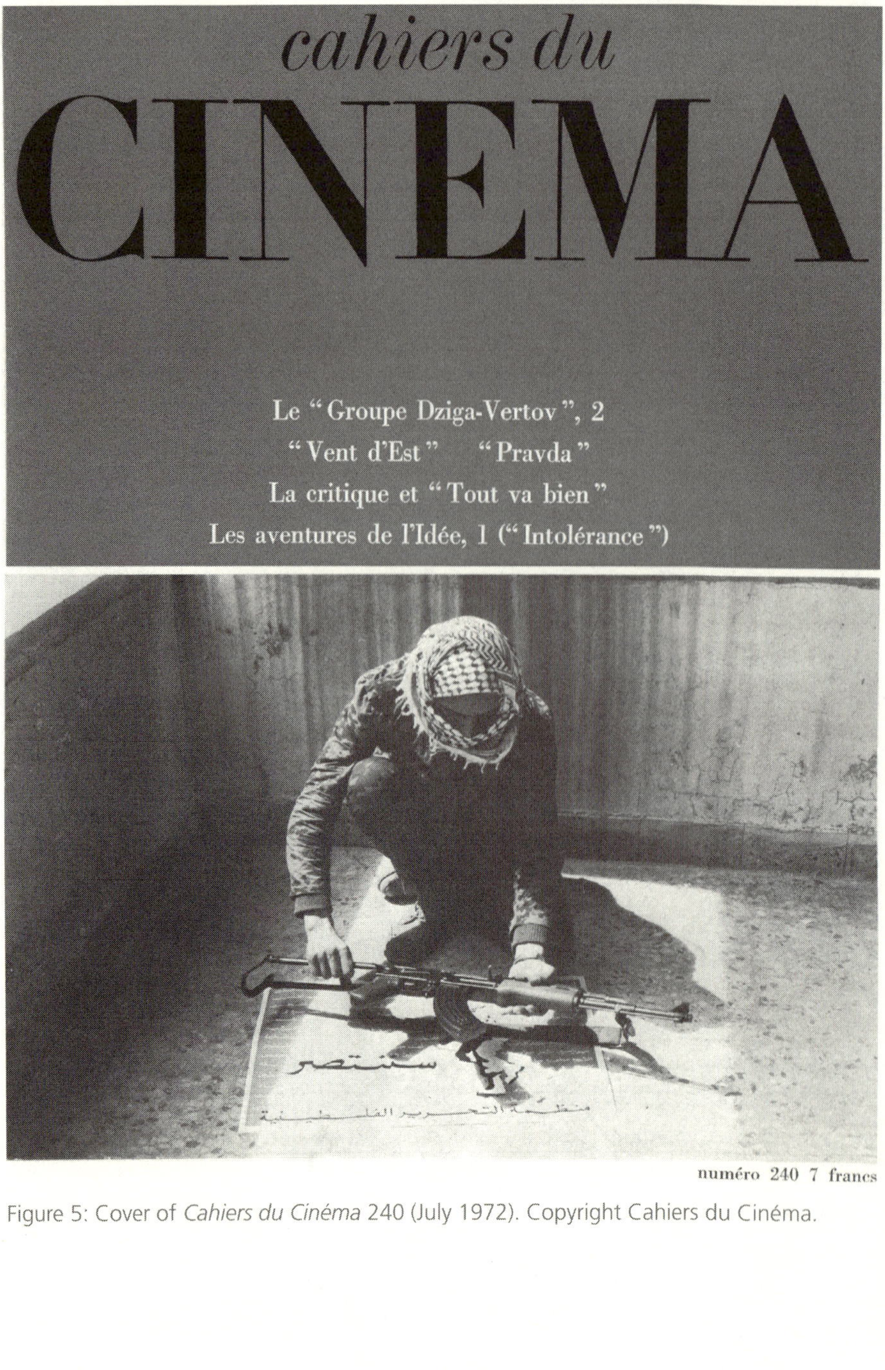

Figure 5: Cover of *Cahiers du Cinéma* 240 (July 1972). Copyright Cahiers du Cinéma.

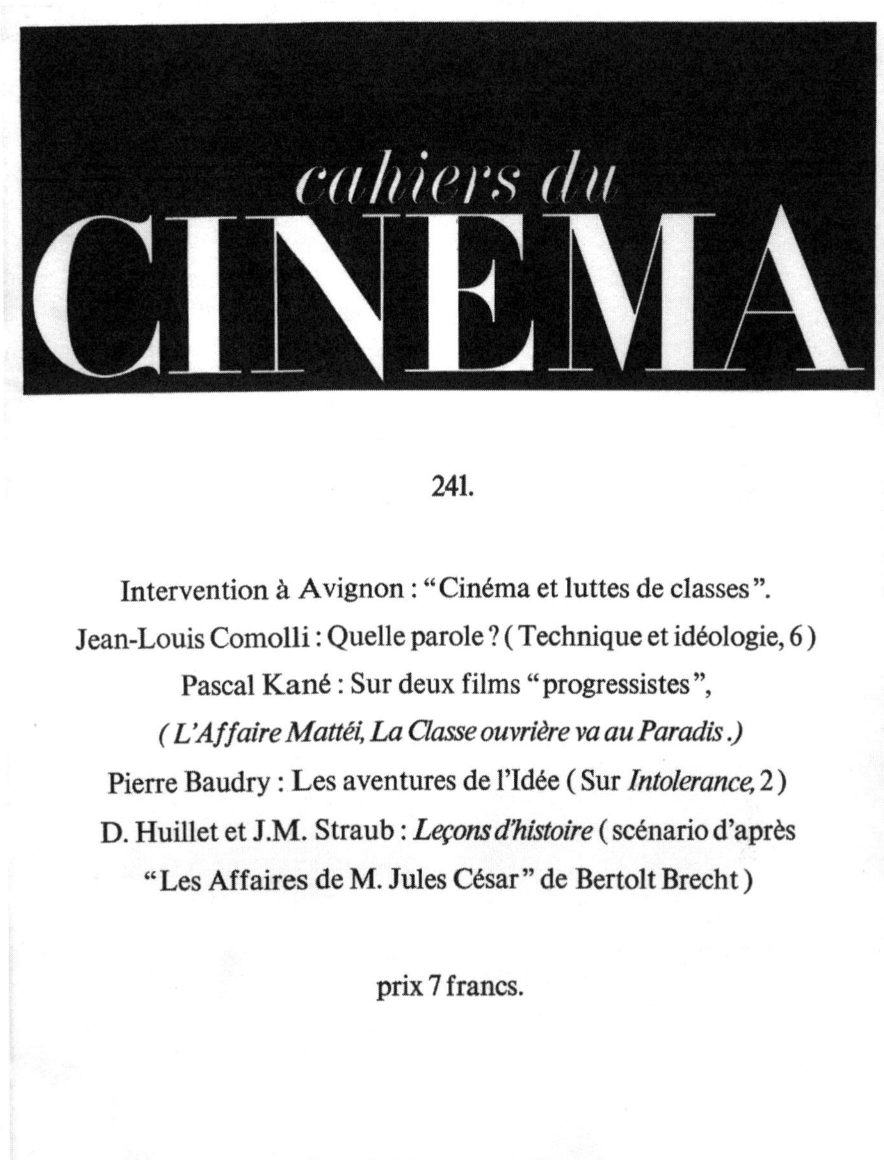

cahiers du
CINEMA

241.

Intervention à Avignon : "Cinéma et luttes de classes".

Jean-Louis Comolli : Quelle parole ? (Technique et idéologie, 6)

Pascal Kané : Sur deux films "progressistes",

(*L'Affaire Mattéi, La Classe ouvrière va au Paradis*.)

Pierre Baudry : Les aventures de l'Idée (Sur *Intolerance*, 2)

D. Huillet et J.M. Straub : *Leçons d'histoire* (scénario d'après "Les Affaires de M. Jules César" de Bertolt Brecht)

prix 7 francs.

Figure 6: Cover of *Cahiers du Cinéma* 241 (September 1972). Copyright Cahiers du Cinéma.

more serious "journal," challenging the passive, accepting readers of the former to become the actively committed reader of the latter.[36] Significantly, it is during this period that *Cahiers*, with its many articles about class struggles and political manifestations through cinema, became highly interested in the New Latin American Cinema, which had been ignored up until this point. *Cahiers* would shift emphasis again in 1978 when it renewed its interest in American "spectacle" films such as *Jaws* and *Star Wars*. This emphasis was made visible in their replacing the stark versions of the decade's earlier covers with ones oriented around photo stills. In November 1989 (425) in the "spirit of the fall of the Berlin wall," *Cahiers du cinéma* transitioned to a sleek, glossy, modern "magazine" style, with articles displayed in a three-column layout, a modern font, and liberal use of boldface type for easy readability.

Hablemos de cine changed its layout twice during its twenty-year run. The first occurred a few months after its founding in February 1965 (fig. 7). Originally a cheaply produced mimeographed publication, the journal took a major step forward by turning into a printed publication with volume 21 (January 1966). Many cinematic publications throughout Latin America (and worldwide during the mid-1960s) started out in mimeographed form; most never published more than a few issues before folding. Note that, as an independent publication, *Hablemos de cine* did not depend on advertising to support the publication; instead, during this period, sales at cine-club screenings and profits from running the Cine-Club de la Católica kept the journal afloat. Though the number of pages decreased between volume 20 and 21, the printed format actually allowed more room for articles as the typeface was smaller than the large typewritten lettering used during the mimeographed period.

The transition marked a major commitment on the part of the editors to a more expensive—and therefore riskier—format; it also confirmed, however, that there were sufficient numbers of readers to cover such an enterprise. The format change corresponds to a quadrupling of the printing run from five hundred to two thousand copies.[37] Ideologically, to be printed meant to become a true periodical, one whose appearance reflected that the content within should be taken as seriously as that of other magazines. In addition to a more professional appearance, *Hablemos de cine* could now accompany the text with photographic stills that were not only more aesthetically pleasing for readers, but also the ideal accompaniment for a critical text about a visual medium. The two-dimensional images on the screen, after all, are what separate film from the novel or the theater, arguably the two artforms most closely related to narrative cinema. Though the

Figure 7: Cover of *Hablemos de cine* 21 (January 1966). Courtesy of the Filmoteca PUCP *Hablemos de cine* Archive.

photographs could not possibly move on the pages of a magazine, stills allow the reader a frozen moment to appreciate the filmic medium.[38]

The change in identity was cause for great excitement at the periodical. As *Hablemos de cine* exulted in its editorial "Birth of a Journal": "Maestro [D. W.] Griffith would excuse the paraphrasing. Surely, if he could see this volume 21 of *Hablemos de cine*, he would be as happy as we are" (3). The same sentiment was echoed in the first cover photograph: a publicity photo from Richard Lester's Beatles film *Help!* (1964), featuring the musical "fab four" smiling and walking toward the camera. The connection with the four founding members of the journal was not lost on its readers.

Though there was some flexibility in terms of how big individual sections of each issue would be, the journal consistently gave pride of place to certain sections, such as the reviews and the news areas. Rather than constricting the amount of information disseminated, this hierarchy allowed other material to be spread out over several issues, assuring that a future issue could still be published using older material if there was relatively scant information at that time. The practice was particularly evident once *Hablemos de cine* staff members started attending international festivals themselves. The amount of information amassed during each festival could not be published in a single issue without removing several regular features or producing a prohibitively large issue. Interviews of major Latin American film personalities (critics, filmmakers, producers, and festival organizers) were therefore often deferred to a later issue. Thus the information published in a particular issue might have been collected months earlier, at a festival that had already been commented upon. That interviews collected at one festival were divided over several issues can be ascertained by comparing who attended a particular event with the resulting interviews published over the next few issues. Following the 1968 Mérida (Venezuela) festival, relative newcomer Antonio González Norris, the only staff representative in attendance, produced the write-up of the festival in volume 43–44 (September–December 1968), an interview with Mexican director Arturo Ripstein and Italian critic Guido Aristarco in volume 45 (January–February 1969), and a particularly intimate interview with Argentine director Fernando Solanas in volume 46 (March–April 1969). Similarly, as the only member to attend an otherwise lackluster festival in Rio de Janeiro in 1969, Federico de Cárdenas obtained a massive amount of information about Cinema Nôvo, published between volumes 47 and 49 (May–October 1969).[39] Interviews were also stockpiled whenever prominent Latin American cineastes came to Lima, such as Mexican director Luis Alcoriza (vol. 37 [September–

October 1967], 17–23) or Venezuelan festival organizer Carlos Rebolledo (vol. 42 [July–August 1968], 13–18), who visited before the important festival in Mérida that would take place later that year.

The second format shift in 1970 (vol. 50–51) was written about with more decorum in the journal's opening editorial, though it expresses complete awareness about the implications of change: "We have adopted a new format, not without some resistance. A periodical is to a large extent characterized by its outside presentation and it is somewhat painful to go through a metamorphosis.... Beginning with this issue, you will notice a more agile and modern layout, without the 'smashing' of texts in our previous format. But the [larger] size will permit a more original, 'relaxed' layout of headlines, texts, and pictures" (7). This newer layout allowed more freedom in terms of using columns and pictures for a more dynamic look. The editorial fails to mention, however, the subtler ideological shift that occurred within the journal's content. As previously mentioned, for the first thirty-three issues, until the journal covered the Viña del Mar film festival, it operated under the Bazinian criticism first exposed to them through *Nuestro Cine* (and by association through *Cahiers du cinéma*), emphasizing almost exclusively the importance of mise-en-scène. The Viña del Mar festival in 1967 shifted their focus away from finding such qualities in Euro-American films to more immediate issues of production in Latin America. Volume 50–51 (fig. 8), however, coincided with the summary of events at the Viña del Mar festival of 1969, which caused the critical view of Latin American films by the Peruvian journal to become slightly more reactionary, away from the militant aesthetics that had dominated participants' concerns at the festival. Although the standpoint of *Hablemos de cine* mimicked the sentiments of some of the Chilean filmmakers who spoke out against some of the proceedings at the festival, the position expressed within volume 50–51 concerning Latin American cinema was quite different from its earlier, all-embracing position toward New Latin American cinema—and therefore from other Latin American positions in general.[40] Hence, the format change could also be seen as an emblem of the journal's independence concerning regional issues, announcing the development of a unique identity.

During the 1970s, *Hablemos de cine* would go through one other major identity shift, though this one did not manifest itself by any outward physical change. After two issues produced in an attempt to be a quarterly, the journal slowed to an annual publication with volume 65, published in 1973. Though physically the journal remained the same, two major changes were happening in the cinematic culture of Lima. The first, of course, was the Film Law of 1972, which was passed

Figure 8: Cover of *Hablemos de cine* 50–51 (November 1969–February 1970). Courtesy of the Filmoteca PUCP *Hablemos de cine* Archive.

late in the year and was first briefly reported on in volume 65. The journal regarded the law with disdain, an attitude exemplified in Isaac León's article "Peruvian Cinema: Nothing Here Has Changed," which only mentions in a postscript at the end that several short films were going into production as the issue went to press (6). The journal would eventually change its mind about the law—but it was going through a number of changes itself at the time. The masthead for volume 64, published in June 1972, featured nine members on the editorial board; of these nine, only three—Blanco, de Cárdenas and newcomer Ricardo González Vigil—carried over to volume 65 (1973). A number of longtime contributors, including Pablo Guevara, Mariano Molina, and founders Juan Bullitta and Carlos Rodríguez Larraín, were replaced by four new, young contributors, two of whom would have a considerable impact on the journal: Colombian author and film critic Andrés Caicedo, who would found his own film journal in Cali, *Ojo al cine*, based on the *Hablemos* model; and Ricardo Bedoya, who would much later become the country's only major film historian. Bedoya, Caicedo, and the other two new editors (who only worked on volumes 65 and 66) were the beginning of a new wave of film critics who themselves had been influenced by the *hablemistas*, having received their formal introductions to film and film culture when the journal was already in place. Although the turnover rate for these newer editors was somewhat high—fifteen new contributors joined the staff over the next twelve years, most staying for an average of four issues—the publication itself came alive with a new interest in film genres, auteurs, and even some theory. While seasoned veterans like de Cárdenas and León traveled and acquired information on Latin American films, the newer members brought revitalized energy to the reviews of the films shown on the local screens. A section called "Studies" began with volume 65 with an article by Ricardo González Vigil on French director François Truffaut and a joint article on American director Peter Bogdanovich by González Vigil and Caicedo. Former academic adviser Desiderio Blanco (who by this point had left Universidad Católica) often collaborated with the younger members on many of the articles in this section, which attempted grander cinematic reflections with fresh perspectives on concepts of "genre" and "auteurs."

Without a noticeable physical change, volume 65 marked the beginning of what would be the final, gradual transformation of *Hablemos de cine*. There would be increased interest in the possibilities of a Peruvian film industry brought on by the results of the Film Law of 1972. The journal focused more on national product as both short and feature-length films found their way to Peruvian screens. This understanding of a national identity affected the coverage of

Latin American cinema: as attention moved away from the militant politics of the New Latin American Cinema in the early to mid-1970s, *Hablemos de cine* began to look at other cinemas in the region by comparing them with what was happening at home. By the beginning of the 1980s, the journal had a much clearer picture both of its personal aesthetic and of what Peruvian cinema in general should look like.

CHAPTER 3
SHAPING PERUVIAN TASTE

"Good" and "Bad" Peruvian Movies

> *We stand by Peruvian cinema. . . . Our position is a logical result of our commitment to and solidarity with the our dear nascent cinema. We are sure that you, Friendly Reader, will rightly surmise that if we are hard on a particular Peruvian film today, it is only because* those who love you the most will make you cry.
>
> —OPENING EDITORIAL, *HABLEMOS DE CINE* (MARCH 18, 1965)

From the very first issue in February 1965, the fostering of active local film production was a major goal of *Hablemos de cine*. As stated in its opening editorial: "The purpose that we have proposed is to make films in Peru, to which end we wish to stimulate an eagerness in the development of the art of our time."[1] A noble idea, but "our cinema"—Peruvian cinema—was one that was also necessarily underdefined. Only three feature films made in Peru had been released in the ten years preceding the founding of the journal: *La muerte llega al segundo show* (Death Comes to the Second Show, Roselló y Beltrán, 1958), a failed thriller; *Kukuli* (Nishiyama/Figueroa/Villanueva, 1961), produced and released by the Cine Club de Cuzco; and *Operación Ñongos* (Operation: Kiddies, released in Mexico as *Un gallo con espolones* [A Tough Guy with Spurs], Gómez Urquiza, 1964). With no industry and not enough immediate examples to construct a trend, *Hablemos de cine* could only imagine Peruvian filmmaking at its founding as an abstract concept.

On March 4, 1965, however, Lima saw the release of Manuel Antín's *Intimidad de los parques* (Intimacy of Parks), an art film advertised as a Peruvian production. Reviewed in *Hablemos de cine*'s next issue, volume 3 (March 18, 1965), the film also provided the subject for that issue's editorial, "National Cinema is Born." The editorial, however, indicated a somewhat qualified interest in Peruvian cinema: "From this third issue, we therefore salute Peruvian cinema and *sincerely hope that our cinema can be worthy of the word 'Peruvian.'* In such a way, we can discount the huge space that separates us from, for example, Argentine cinema."[2] Though Argentine cinema was redeveloping a small industry by this point in the 1960s,[3] the tone of this passage indicated that *Hablemos de cine* did not consider Argentine cinema as superior. Hence, the derogatory reference to Argentina should be seen as a deliberate and nationalistic response; more important, however, is the additional comment that it be "*worthy of the word 'Peruvian.'*" For many, a national production only indicated perhaps the presence of Machu Picchu in the background of certain sequences; the journal, however, was more interested in *quality* as a determining factor in defining Peruvian filmmaking.

But what constituted "quality" filmmaking in Peru? *Hablemos de cine* constantly used the phrase "quality cinema" (*cine de calidad*) without ever explicitly stating what such a subjective phrase meant, neither as it applied to national filmmaking nor as it pertained to other productions from Europe or the United States. Certainly, "quality" did not necessarily mean the same thing to the critics at *Hablemos de cine* as it did to the *Junta de Supervigilancia de Películas* (the Film Supervision Board, or state censor) who, upon its creation in 1947, was commissioned to give ratings to films to ensure and uphold the moral values of potential audiences. In what appeared to be a Nietzschean paradox, *Hablemos de cine* instead had to consider what were the aesthetic considerations of "good" cinema.

At the beginning of the publication run, the editors simply desired a film to make "good use" of mise-en-scène. As their critical experience expanded, this relatively vague definition would be refined. National cinema was particularly scrutinized by the journal, most of the time resulting in damning evaluations of Peruvian product. In fact, the journal did not publish a positive review for a single Peruvian production until Pablo Guevara's short film *Semilla* (Seed) in volume 45 (March–April 1969)—and not again until eight years later, when the first feature films resulted from the Film Law of 1972. Instead, the writers at *Hablemos de cine* considered and refined qualities of their own local cinema through the various negative reviews. Put simply, if the *hablemistas* could not identify a film that reflected their ideals, they could instead clarify why each successive release did not meet their standards of representative national cinema, which had more to do with aesthetic analysis of mise-en-scène than about the images of the Peruvian countryside.

Six different locally produced feature films—the first feature by Peruvian auteur Armando Robles Godoy, an "insipid" art film that seemed more Argentine than Peruvian, the second (and final) film by the Cuzco School, two popular comedies based on popular television personalities, and a Japanese production filmed on location in and around Cuzco—contributed to *Hablemos de cine*'s contextualization of the shape of Peruvian national cinema.[4] Robles Godoy offers a particular example of how, of all things, becoming an auteur can be a bad thing—at least through the eyes of the editors at *Hablemos de cine*.

Establishing Taste

It is commonly thought that critics apply their own sense of "taste" to determine the worth of a particular film, but in their pedagogical role, critics can also help to shape taste in a larger sense. In his long work *Distinction*, Pierre Bourdieu defines taste as something learned yet internalized and therefore indescribable: "Taste is an acquired disposition to 'differentiate' and 'appreciate,' as Kant says—in other words, to establish and mark differences by a process of distinction which is not (or not necessarily) a distinct knowledge... since it ensures recognition (in the ordinary sense) without implying knowledge of the distinctive features which define it."[5] Put very simply, "taste" allows a person to say, "This is good, although I cannot exactly articulate why." Ideas of culture, already previously determined by others, are absorbed and accepted into a popular, unquestioned sense.

Ideally, critics must not rely on "taste," but instead qualify their decisions: this is good, *and here is why*. Critics may in fact follow commonly held constructions and their "tastes" should match those of their readerships in order to maintain that population. Critical justification thus becomes essential when what the critic considers to be "good" (or "bad") goes against conventional contemporary notions of taste. On one hand, a contrary position may alienate the critic from his readership; on the other hand, a strong argument for taking a stance against popular opinion would bring attention to the critic.

Such a position would distinguish the critic, positively or negatively, from those following status-quo interpretations of taste; instead, the critics then become arbiters of taste. The implied interactions between critic and reader-viewer bring an added perspective to how film is being viewed in a particular culture. As noted in the previous chapter, part of the film critic's work involves "the establishment of a pantheon of artists" created by "reassessing [canonized] Hollywood cinema."[6] The French critics at *Cahiers du cinéma* performed a similar service in examining their own cinema by rejecting high-art historical pieces ("la cinéma de qualité") for more contemporary pictures that broke with traditional narrative and stylistic construction. A clear consensus on what was included as part of "national cinema" was unclear—in this case simply because there were not enough examples to construct any sense of "national cinema." Nonetheless, Peruvian critics applied their skills—sharpened from reviewing more commonly viewed (American and European) films—to this new context. In many ways, a film is just a film, regardless of national origin, but the editors at *Hablemos de cine* believed they had a duty to educate the viewing public in order to craft high-quality, aesthetically oriented Peruvian films.

Reviews from the inaugural issue reveal what the journal considered "better" filmmaking at the start: by necessity, European and American films, not Peruvian ones. Only two films earned an average score of 4 or higher in this first issue: Ingmar Bergman's *Wild Strawberries* (with an average of 4) and Gordon Douglas's *Rio Conchos* (with an average of 4.25). Giving the former title a relatively high grade was fairly understandable: by the late 1950s, Bergman was considered the quintessential "art film" director by most critics throughout the world; even reviewers at nonspecialized publications recognized his talent and stature. The slightly higher veneration of *Rio Conchos*, however, can be considered a bold move as elevating Douglas to the level of Bergman would raise a few eyebrows among other cine-club attendees in Lima in the 1960s.[7] Though considered a good western, *Rio Conchos* was dismissed in the United States and elsewhere as standard genre fare; Howard Thompson's review in the *New York Times* praises the film and "Douglas' crisp direction," but the thrust of the article remains within generic terms: "The blunt, wry dialogue, the gritty fiction and the harsh adventures along the way are consistently credible and persuasive."[8] The ratings summary in *Hablemos de cine* lists two other Douglas westerns—*Murallas de sangre* (Walls of Blood) and *15 balas* (the latter is presumably *Fort Dobbs* [1958])—that also earned relatively high ratings from the editors, averaging 3.5 and 3 respectively. Even more curious, no commentaries appear for any of the three Douglas films in the first issue.

The journal offers an explanation in volume 2 (March 1, 1965) with an analysis of Gordon Douglas, the first single-director *acercamiento*,[9] or "analytic approach," of many during the initial phase of the journal's publication run. These analyses provided commentaries on individual films to clarify the artist's auteur status. An unsigned introductory piece justifies the need for this *acercamiento*; it was

> *to make clear our reviewing criteria which some readers may interpret the wrong way. As you know, our review summary for volume 1 featured three films directed by Douglas, which all received relatively high average scores. Some readers have been upset because we put* Rio Conchos *on the same level with* Wild Strawberries *or, even more, that two of our editors [Bullitta, Rodríguez Larraín] thought that the former was better. In the following pages, we shall try to address this seeming discrepancy at some length.*[10]

Elevating Gordon Douglas to auteur status similar to that of Ingmar Bergman would align *Hablemos de cine* with European publications such as *Cahiers du cinéma*, whose young editors wished to reclaim Hollywood cinema—particularly genre films—as comparable if not superior to European art cinema. In addition to fomenting interest in the auteur, the French critics found that their notions of mise-en-scène and its use by specific directors were easily demonstrated in many Hollywood genres such as the western and the gangster film. By taking an unusual stance on a less commonly venerated director, *Hablemos de cine* afforded itself an opportunity to educate its audience about qualities and concepts of mise-en-scène as it defended the claim that Douglas was "an artist, a true filmmaker whose films consistently demonstrate good taste, individual style, and dominion over the cinematographic arts to achieve his desired results."[11] The commentary provided for each of the four examined films reveled in long, detailed descriptions of specific elements of each film's mise-en-scène, as evidenced from a passage in Isaac León's remarks on *Walls of Blood*:

> *Sure, there is also a certain brief yet useful influence by John Ford in [Douglas's] film; the fight sequence where Kalker and Byrnes take on the cavalry is very Fordian. But in every image in* Walls of Blood, *you sense a certain characteristic that is very much his own: the tangible presence of things, of objects, of beings. It's the vivid presence of the landscape, of the deep red earth that serves to mark each battle, of the water that spatters on the soldiers' coats, of the bodies wounded by bullets, of the casings falling away from the rifles. Juan Bullitta rightfully claimed that in Douglas's films, "the water is water and the earth is earth." Indeed, that material presence ap-*

> *pears to be simply* discovered *by Douglas, integrated into his mise-en-scène without need of obvious photographic grandstanding or picturesque effects that some films make a big deal about. Douglas's film does the opposite: the living objects are restored in three dimensions, in all their phenomenological intensity. This is what causes the fulfilling vitality that breathes through his films, that human totality that appears in the films made by those who really know how to communicate their world in cinematographic images, without false rhetoric or pretentious posturing.*[12]

The passage tells the reader nothing about the film's story or theme; it instead assumes that the reader is already familiar with the film. Given that these films were probably shown in repertory, León's comments may even be directed to a particular screening's audience. In any case, the brief references detailed in almost loving fashion are meant to highlight the impact of mise-en-scène to identify to the reader-viewer that these remembered passages are enough to justify Douglas's standing as an auteur in the best meaning of the word. From this, we can also assume that imagery that embraces "false rhetoric or pretentious messages" would be a sign of poor filmmaking.

Unfortunately, it would be difficult to compare this kind of criticism to what was normally printed in the Peruvian popular press at this time. Other critics seem to have ignored this particular film, perhaps believing cine-club screenings of what was still considered to be a genre film to be outside their purview. To show how innovative this criticizm was, we turn to a more popular contemporary film.

Hablemos de Minnelli

Though the five early editors of *Hablemos de cine* sometimes agreed in their assessment of poor-quality films, they rarely agreed on what they considered excellent films, ones that earned a 5 on their rating scale. This divergence must have contributed to interesting private or cine-club discussions among the members that spilled onto the pages of the fledgling journal when films earned multiple reviews from editors with disparate opinions. For example, in the second issue (March 1, 1965), the 1964 Roger Corman film *The Secret Invasion* was reviewed by Isaac León and Carlos Rodríguez Larraín, who rated the film a 4 and a 2 respectively. In the sixth issue (May 1, 1965), however, all five editors—Isaac León Frías, Federico de Cárdenas, Juan Bullitta, Carlos Rodríguez Larraín, and Desiderio Blanco—gave the rerelease of Vincente Minnelli's *Some Came Running* a 5. The editors marked the occasion ("the first time in the [short] history of the journal that a film has unanimously been regarded as 'excellent'") by deciding to "move up the *acercamiento* of Vincente Minnelli...considered by the staff to be one of the most important, developed and laudatory directors in the world."[13] The tone may be excessive, but it points to a new direction in Peruvian criticism.

First, the film. *Some Came Running*,[14] overshadowed now in both general and critical examinations of Minnelli for being released the same year as his hit musical *Gigi*, follows a complex plot typical of the American melodrama of the 1950s. Based on the James Jones sequel to the World War II epic novel *From Here to Eternity*, the film stars Frank Sinatra as Dave Hirsh, a veteran who returns to his midwestern hometown after having written a novel. On the bus ride, he meets a carefree, loose young woman named Ginny (Shirley MacLaine), who instantly falls for him. In town, Dave meets up again with his brother Frank (Arthur Kennedy), who had put him in an orphanage when their parents died. Frank is now a shopowner and respectable citizen. Married with a teenaged daughter, Frank is having a clandestine affair with his secretary, an event eventually discovered when his daughter goes to the same Lover's Lane with her boyfriend. Meanwhile, Dave meets Gwen (Martha Hyer), a pretty but frigid English professor who loves his writing but cannot commit to his free-spirited life. Dave and Ginny also start cavorting with a newfound, lowlife friend, a drunk and gambler named Bama Dillert (Dean Martin). The characters' stories interweave until Dave, having been rejected by Gwen, marries the starry-eyed Ginny. While leaving the courthouse, the couple is pursued through a local fair by one of Ginny's ex-lovers, who tries to shoot Dave but kills her instead. As a symbol of her passing, Bama takes off his hat at her funeral, something he had up until now refused to do under any circumstances.

Though it made a respectable $4 million at the U.S. domestic box office, *Some Came Running* is now a little-remembered film, primarily noted for the breakthrough performance of Shirley MacLaine, who was nominated for her first Academy Award for this role. The film also marks her offscreen induction into the "Rat Pack," the informal group of performers founded by Humphrey Bogart; after Bogart's death, Sinatra and Martin were signature members. At the time of the film's original release in 1958, reviews in the United States varied widely, but primarily concentrated on the star issues surrounding the cast. Industry-oriented publications such as *Variety* and *Harrison's Reports* indicated that the film was likely to do well with audiences, praising the casting selections as well as their performances. In particular, *Variety* chose to highlight MacLaine, who with this role "moves into the front row of film actresses. She isn't conventionally pretty.

Her hair looks like it was combed with an eggbeater. But it doesn't make any difference, because she elicits such empathy and humor that when she offers herself to Sinatra, she seems eminently worth taking."[15] At the other extreme, many of the reviewers from popular general magazines, such as *Newsweek*, *Saturday Review*, and *Time*, savaged the film. Said *Time*, "[As] bromide follows bromide, the spectator slowly comes to a drugged realization that the script is not making fun of anybody's beliefs, but simply stating its own. After that, there is simply nothing to hang around for except occasional flickers of brilliant overacting by Shirley MacLaine, the chance to watch Frank Sinatra play Frank Sinatra and the spectacle of Director Vincente Minnelli's talents dissolving in the general mess of the story, like sunlight in a slag heap."[16] This emphasis on stardom over other issues also parallels reviews from general (not film-specialized) periodicals in Lima, such as the one written by Percy Gibson, the main film reviewer for the Lima daily newspaper *El Comercio*:

> *The re-release of the film for which Shirley MacLaine won the Oscar [*sic*]*[17] *some six years ago allows the opportunity to appreciate the immense, authentic talent by which the actress deservedly won that highest American honor. However, it also allows us to see how filmmakers have since insisted on stereotyping her and exploiting her by casting her in several similar roles, some nearly identical to the original. We need only remember the recently released* Irma la Douce, The Yellow Rolls-Royce, *and* Operación: Haren *[possibly* My Geisha? *1962] to list a few poor imitations. The blame should not rest on her, but rather on those who persist within this lucrative game.... Except perhaps for Dean Martin's role—the gambler/hustler played so many times by the former singer-comedian that only demonstrates the actor's natural sense of ease and sympathy—the remaining characters are psychologically impressive and well developed. Sinatra's characterization of the temperamental, bohemian writer is truthful and certainly acted well and, even better, it's one of his most complex roles to date. Also impressive and portrayed well is the role of the hypocritical town leader played by Arthur Kennedy, the other side of Sinatra's coin. And the intellectual, repressed English professor played by Martha Hyer acts as an interesting foil to Shirley MacLaine's character.*[18]

Typical of his style of writing, Gibson's review says little about the film itself, preferring to comment on star interests that extend far beyond the text (MacLaine's and Martin's stereotyping, Sinatra's exceptional performance here in context, and so on). Gibson says nothing about the director—or anything about the film's visual qualities—save for a single line at the very end of the review: "Vincente Minnelli's directing talent is also evident, particularly in sequences such as the one at the fair, where strident use of color dramatically brings the story to a close."

Contrast this with the review of the film published in *Cahiers du cinéma* 97 in July 1959, written by Philippe Demonsablon. The article is negative toward the film: "How do Americans live, how do they portray themselves, what do they do, and what do they dream? *Some Came Running* turns these questions around rather than answer them: but they are only sketched vaguely with generalities."[19] In contrast to the previous reviews, discussion of the cast and their acting is relegated to a single line near the end of the article: "We remain with Frank Sinatra, Shirley MacLaine, Dean Martin, and Carmen Philips, whom I am wary of omitting in their full and beautiful absurdity; and this fantasy opposing the lives of one group of people too caged in by order and reason, and another group too constricted by a false balance, which itself is the only evidence of truth [in this film]."[20] Notably, Demonsablon refuses to be concerned with factors regarding stardom and their contributions to the film. The measured structuralist and post-structuralist analyses in *Cahiers* set the film journal apart from reviewers from general publications.

Hablemos de cine's approach runs closer to this Cahierist approach by eschewing the more popular, star-centered elements. While the latter type of review catered to a wider readership, a more detailed formalist approach that focused on the auteur served a different, analysis-oriented population. Carlos Rodríguez Larraín opens his review by taking popular critics to task for dismissing the work of the director: "Few directors are so undervalued as Minnelli by the 'serious' critics—mostly from the newspapers—who completely dismiss him. And yet there are so few directors who display such genius. He is a pure *artist* in the complete sense of the word."[21] That is not to say that the editors were loath to drop names, only that those names belonged to critically established directors over actor-oriented gossip. Rodríguez continues by noting "Minnelli expresses to us, in a certain way, ideas similar to Bergman or Fellini, with the exception that they completely serve the development of the characters and situations, emerging from them without overrunning them."[22]

The editors realized that, for an audience unfamiliar with certain basic critical film knowledge, *Hablemos de cine* also needed to assume a pedagogical role: to educate readers in formal cinematic terminology and analysis. This issue marked the beginning of a series of short articles concerning cinematic study written by editor Desiderio Blanco, the Universidad Católica professor who originally brought the four other editors together for discussions as students. Hence, Blanco's remarks concerning Shirley MacLaine concern neither stardom nor social issues, but rather the acting itself within the context of the auteur:

> *Shirley MacLaine is a marvelous actress in Minnelli's hands. Compare the depth of this acting job with that of the idiotic, banal, and apparently brilliant acting of the same MacLaine in [J.] Lee Thompson's* What a Way to Go! *[1964] The same thing happens with all the female characters in that film. A single gesture by MacLaine in* Some Came Running, *such as the one where she puts on perfume in the school stairway, which ends with a complacent look at her own perfume, gives us a better indication of her true characterization—not false and obviously acted, but rather a performance that is lived authentically.*[23]

Through this brief passage, Blanco delineates what makes this performance significant as compared with other MacLaine roles, asserting Minnelli's agency in manipulating blocking on screen over MacLaine's stardom.

By not even referring to MacLaine's star status here, Blanco reaffirms the journal's zealous commitment to critique through mise-en-scène. It seems their overwhelmingly positive reaction to *Some Came Running* stems from the film's transparent use and manipulation of these different visual cinematic elements. Rodríguez Larraín calls attention to the final sequence at the fair where "his stylization becomes delirious. A true 'ballet' of images accomplished through masterful movement of actors, color, camera movements and orchestrated blocking combine into a virtual symphony. The montage alone earns it [the highest rating]."[24] Blanco goes even further in demonstrating the importance of mise-en-scène by explaining how décor helps to define characterization: "The many settings help define each character's behavior. Minnelli's use of mise-en-scène takes full advantage by using props to either distance or draw in the viewer. None of the characters are separated from their environment. Rather, with very subtle use of blocking, Minnelli drives his characters to lonely situations where they can be free to let themselves go with everything they have."[25]

Particularly from a general or international perspective, the point here is certainly not that *Hablemos de cine* is publishing anything significantly new or different with respect to film studies or even the interpretation of this particular film. In Lima in 1965, this type of review only shows how pervasive the French-inspired cult of mise-en-scène among international film criticism had become. It is with this perspective that the *hablemistas* turned to look at their own nationally produced films very early in the publication run.

Myopic Auteurism: *Ganarás el pan*

Neither the editors nor the readers of *Hablemos de cine* were strangers to European art cinema of the early 1960s, particularly as their cinematic diet largely consisted of screenings at the cine-clubs, which showed the likes of Antonioni, Eisenstein, and the French New Wave. However, it must be remembered that the editors at *Hablemos de cine* first made a name for themselves by rejecting such programming at the Cine Club de Universidad Católica in favor of American genre films. Ingmar Bergman's films were greatly appreciated, but so was the latest low-budget thriller from Roger Corman. Overpretentious cinema that proclaimed its artiness for art's sake, where style superseded all narrative convention, was deemed reprehensible by the journal in their early period; this precept held even more firmly when it concerned Peruvian filmmaking that embodied a bad copy of what was already undesirable.

Shortly after the founding of the journal, the editors at *Hablemos de cine* found their first local example of this negative kind of auteur. First known as a film critic for *La Prensa*, Armando Robles Godoy claimed to have taught himself the filmmaking craft, had already made three minor short films and was in the process of shooting his first feature-length film, *Ganarás el pan* (You Will Earn the Bread) when *Hablemos de cine* published an interview with him in volume 4 (April 1, 1965). The idea for the film came from Yugoslav-born producer Vlado Radovich, who had been acting, directing, and producing a number of newsreels and short documentaries for Estudios Roselló, a major local newsreel production company.[26] The film was originally conceived as a documentary about work; under Radovich, however, a narrative frame was added about a Peruvian man who inherited a fortune while he lived in Europe, but would only get the money if he and his French girlfriend returned to Peru and learned about the country's working conditions. At the end of the film, the son nevertheless does not internalize much of his experience, collecting the money with little reflection. Initally titled *The Parasites*, Robles Godoy suggested the name change because the characters would have to discover how others "earn their bread" before they could earn theirs; later, he would declare that the only good thing about the film was the title.

The prerelease interview in *Hablemos de cine* was only one entry among a considerable amount of local press coverage afforded to the film—justifiable as it was the first feature to be made in Lima in nearly ten years. The tone of the article was friendly and the questions were standard for a movie magazine (asking about the film currently being made, the influences on this film and the director overall, and the like). When asked for his opinion on general impressions of national cinema, Robles Godoy responded indifferently to the topic:

> —*Are there films of any particular nationality that you prefer?*
> —No. *I realize that nationality may incorporate determined historical attributes into a film, but nothing else. At present, there is no national cinema more important than another. Actually, nationality is not an attribute so much as a characteristic. A film is neither better nor worse just because it comes from one country or another.*[27]

Though he recognized the interest in the topic of a Peruvian cinema, Robles Godoy had little hope in any sort of local movement or genuine local activity: "There is great anticipation among people concerning national cinema. They don't know what kind of cinema they want, but they want one to exist."[28] This position, in fact, mirrored *Hablemos de cine*'s own. Nevertheless, Robles Godoy recognized that his own film depended on the reception of a national audience who wanted to see images of Peru. The interview therefore also specified a number of comments that served to distance his own film from the failure of the just-released *Intimidad de los parques*: "There is a lack of confidence in Peruvian filmmaking and [the local failure of] *Intimidad de los parques* only made things worse, particularly as it was such a 'serious film.' That is why it is important that *Ganarás el pan* succeed. Then [potential producers] will invest again."[29]

Ganarás el pan became the first Peruvian box-office success story in more than twenty years, with a full release in some of the top-tier theaters in Lima. Buoyed by an advertising campaign that stressed the Peruvian roots of the film, the film was swamped by large audiences wanting to see the "national film." Critics made allowances for a Peruvian production with limited resources and cited its unique blend of documentary and narrative techniques. Even the slightly negative review from *Oiga* magazine noted that the film "is a special 'case,' a noteworthy and laborious essay from Peruvians who are attempting to produce films with their own national characteristics."[30]

Nonetheless, the collection of reviews in volume 11 (July 15, 1965) made clear how much the four editors at *Hablemos de cine* loathed the film. As a sign of the importance of considering *Ganarás el pan*, all four editors published reviews, the only occurrence of this in the seventy-seven-issue run. Each review built on the one before, starting with the one penned by the verbose Juan Bullitta, which continuously cited the publication's interview with Robles Godoy seven issues earlier:

> *Robles Godoy . . . insisted on pointing out the film's unique take on the documentary form: "This is a documentary in dialogue with a linking character that is in reality an intermediary, living on the screen what the director wants to show to the public."*[31] *Robles Godoy's words makes this idea sound interesting, though one of the more complicated ways to structure a documentary. . . . The results are not so interesting. As a documentary,* Ganarás el pan *has acceptable and even some good characteristics but as* cinema, *it is a complete failure (hence the 0), precisely because there is no discovery of the nature of work in Peru by the linking character. During the entire film, you very clearly see that there is no true integration between the narrative (the story of the rich young man) and the documentary on Peruvian working conditions. It seems to me that even the subjective elements of the film—that is, the whole story of the young man—gets in the way, limits, sinks the documentary.*[32]

Bullitta's five-page analysis accused the film of being "literary cinema," the most unforgivable sin for these editors who single-mindedly thought mise-en-scène was the only valid way to evaluate a film. The remaining three reviews, each with a spin unique to its author, echo and reference Bullitta's sentiments: Carlos Rodríguez Larraín opined that "personally I think there is no worse defect than imitation—let us not descend into the horrible example of Argentine cinema, which in addition to being bad is completely sterile," calling for Peruvians to "search for our own forms of expression."[33] Ever the critic committed to the technical aspects of filmmaking, Isaac León Frías focused on the purely cinematic problems concerning framing and "the search for aesthetically pleasing takes (those of Machu Picchu, etc.) which, when placed alongside the simplicity of other shots, creates a tremendous imbalance that, along with the lack of pacing and the cold presentation, dominates the entire film."[34] In their numerical assessments, Bullitta, Rodríguez, and León all gave *Ganarás el pan* a 0.

Federico de Cárdenas, however, bestowed a 1 upon the film by comparing it to the previous Argentine co-production that had been released and marketed as Peruvian: "I am talking about and judging national cinema and I am forced to compare this film to *Intimidad de los parques* . . . and so I continue to maintain the 1."[35] While dismissing Robles Godoy as an overly auteur filmmaker, de Cárdenas still praised him solely because he was Peruvian; here, national pride trumped cinematic quality. After completely damning the film with a negative evaluation, each analysis ended with a favorable note stimulated by this tone of nationalism. Despite the scathing, detailed nature of his review, Bullitta concluded by encouraging all readers to go see the film anyway:

> *In any case, it is plain to see that if the film had not been of any interest to me I would have dismissed it with a four-line review. I went to see the film on opening day . . . with that special enthusiasm of being Peruvian, with my additional affection for film and my own aspiration to be a director. I wouldn't change my evaluation of "0" for anything. Despite that, I love the film and hope that anyone who believes himself to be a true Peruvian cinephile will go to see it. . . . At least this film has the right to present itself as truly national, something that not all the films shown in Peru can do.*[36]

The phrasing and placement of the "accolades" accorded to *Ganarás el pan* by *Hablemos de cine* were shoehorned into otherwise extremely negative reviews. The editors clearly felt it important, particularly at this early stage of the journal's publication, to show solidarity with a nationally produced feature film. Such accord was not only crucial for the overall ideology of the publication, having committed itself to critical examination of Peruvian cinema, but also to maintaining a favorable readership. Assuming that the readership was interested in national productions—and the box-office success of the film indicates that it was—the journal had to concede some support for the film to agree with, and thereby maintain, their fledgling readership. Although the four editors were still determined enough to detail their individual opinions without apology, the conciliatory attitude acknowledges the necessity of catering to the specialized audience among the moviegoing public in Lima.

The "Peruvian" aspect of Robles Godoy's cinema was more pointedly addressed in a later interview following the release of his second feature *En la selva no hay estrellas* (In the jungle, there are no stars, 1967). The editors accused the filmmaker for being "too obvious" in his aesthetic decisions, provoking a fiery response: "Dammit, the worst thing a critic can tell me is how did you use a opposing traveling shot without anyone noticing it? No, sir! I want it to be noticed and noticed well!"[37] Robles Godoy more effectively defended the quality of his film by forcing the journalists to consider the popular response in terms of box office:

> A.R.: *You say that the general public is losing interest [in the film]. In that case, why do they continue to go see it? The public has taken to it and it's not just because of the advertising. . . . En la selva . . . has entered its fourth week—which is something no other Peruvian film has done—and audiences keep coming because of word of mouth.*
> J[ORGE] CH[IARELLA]: *It seems to me that the fact that some critics have called this film "the best Peruvian film ever" is an important factor. Second, word of mouth has been favorable primarily because the film is Peruvian and they find certain values in it; there's also the curiosity factor . . .*
> I.L.: *I think the public isn't passionate about the film, but then again, it hasn't been rejected.*[38]

Hablemos de cine's response to *En la selva no hay estrellas* demonstrated how out of step the journal was with the general Peruvian public of 1966. While they admit that the public response to claims of "the best Peruvian film ever" was effective, and other critics and the box office confirmed this claim, the journal still derided the film (and its filmmaker) for its auteurist tendencies in the most negative sense, reaffirming its unique (or perhaps isolated) critique of national cinema. It can be argued that the Peruvian public had already decided that the film was sufficiently nationalist to at least go to see it—but because it was derivative and not reflecting an appropriate national reality, the journal maintained that Peruvian cinema did not have to be this way, that it could be better.[39]

Hablemos de cine's opinion of Robles Godoy's filmmaking style did not change over time, but the editors' own status within Peruvian film culture did, particularly as they began writing at less specialized periodicals during the Velasco government in the early 1970s. Hence, whereas they were out of sync with other critics in the mid-1960s, by the time of the release of Robles Godoy's *Espejismo* (Mirage) in 1973, they wielded much more influence than they had at a young, fledgling specialized publication. Interest in other up-and-coming directors and productions and the journal's diminished periodicity starting in 1973 allowed the journal to pay less attention to Robles Godoy's films.

Nevertheless, Armando Robles Godoy had a large impact on the history of filmmaking in Peru. With two additional feature films produced before the Film

Law of 1972, *La muralla verde* (The Green Wall, 1970) and *Espejismo*, Robles Godoy was the only Peruvian director making feature films before 1977. Considering his early comments on national cinema, it is somewhat ironic that he was one of the earliest forces to stimulate actual production, founding the first cinematic educational program in Peru in the 1960s as well as being the driving force behind the creation of the Film Law of 1972. Because of these activities, Robles Godoy maintained an amicable relationship with several of the editors of *Hablemos de cine*, who were also actively concerned with national cinematic production, particularly León and de Cárdenas.

It is also significant that, despite Robles Godoy's influence on creating filmmaking opportunities in Peru, future directors chose not to follow his style of filmmaking.[40] The scant influence of Robles Godoy on later Peruvian filmmaking cannot be attributed to *Hablemos de cine* entirely. In the 1970s, cinematic aesthetic styles internationally moved away from the "artist auteur" cinema that had characterized other early major Latin American filmmakers such as Brazilian Hugo Khouri, Argentine Leopoldo Torre Nilsson, and Mexican Emilio Fernández. The next internationally recognized Peruvian auteur, Francisco Lombardi, starting in 1977 with a prize won at the Havana Film Festival for *Muerte al amanecer* (Death at Dawn), would not have the same art-film characteristics in his films as Robles Godoy.

Unfortunate Coproductions: *Intimidad de los parques*

As noted at the beginning of this chapter, *Ganarás el pan* was not the first "Peruvian" film examined by *Hablemos de cine*. Manuel Antín's *Intimidad de los parques*, was released less than a month after the inaugural issue of the journal to a universally scathing critical reception. One of the leading popular film reviewers of the day, Alfonso Delboy of *La Prensa*, stated: "it is difficult, if not impossible, for the spectator to understand what is going on."[41] *Hablemos de cine* went even further, finding the film not only difficult, but derivative of European cinema: "It would have been preferable, more comfortable, and less painful to let ourselves forget about such a tragic 70 minutes of celluloid. . . . [The film] aspired to be a version of [Alain Resnais's *Last Year at*] *Marienbad*. It is shameful that such an unoriginal experiment in plagiarism was made in our country."[42]

Much of these same accusations could be levied at Robles Godoy (and, indeed, that is why this chapter runs out of chronological sequence to explore the Peruvian auteur first) but the issues behind Antín's film are complicated by its status as an international coproduction—and, more precisely, a foreign film loosely disguised as a national film. Director Antín, most of the crew and even the textual source for the script (two stories by Julio Cortázar, "Continuidad de los parques" [The Continuity of Parks] and "El Ídolo de las Cícladas" [The Idol of the Cyclades]) were all Argentine. Having little to do with Peru in and of itself, the production chose to shoot there to take advantage of the weak Film Law of 1962. This first attempt at a cinematic law was designed to stimulate interest in national filmmaking by freeing any Peruvian production from having to pay heavy taxes on exhibition within the country; unfortunately, some foreign filmmakers set up puppet companies in Peru to reap the benefits of what amounted to an expanded exhibition market.

Therefore, as the very first exercise in critiquing a national film, *Hablemos de cine*'s review expressed very little in terms of why the film was aesthetically bad, but offered many choleric perspectives as to why the film was an affront to Peruvian nationalism. Unlike the treatment that would be given to Robles Godoy, whose work the editors simply didn't like, this review took a strong stance of national pride. Hurt and enraged, the editors reveled in exposing the non-Peruvian characteristics of the film, often using heavy sarcasm:

> *Mr. Antín, apparently a director of some prestige in his own country, has made a film that, other than the actor Ricardo Blume and the backgrounds, has not a single Peruvian quality. . . . Mr. Antín took advantage of the opportunity to come to a country just beginning its national film production and experimented randomly, with little regard to the quality of the results, surely believing that here we know nothing about how to watch a film and that any absurdity would appease us. Mr. Antín was very wrong: in Peru, thank God, there are many people who know how to watch a film and, because of that, will ensure that this film is an economic failure. Unfortunately, this only works against the Peruvians who have invested their money with patriotic intent, while Antín lives happily in Argentina with a conscience that is "free from shame."*[43]

Accusing Antín of being a "tourist posing as a director,"[44] the editors signed all four of their names to the review. This unusual display of solidarity—all four signatures, as opposed to the all-encompassing term "The Staff"—would not appear again in the entire run of the journal. Demonstrating their collective ire at how the film was presented in Peru, this reaction also recognized the importance of this first defense of "the Peruvian" to be presented as a clear, united front.

More problematic for the editors than local reaction to the film was the possibility that other respected foreign film critics unfamiliar with the Peruvian reality would have nothing else with which to compare the film. Both the review and the editorial in volume 3 respond with grave concern to a rumor that the film was to be submitted for competition at the most prestigious film festival in the world:

> *The only thing left for us to add [to our critique of* Intimidad de los parques*] is our conviction that this film should not represent Peru at Cannes. Our reasons are included in our review of the film; we only mention this here [in the editorial] because we believe it is essential for the well-being of our cinema that a wrong impression of Peruvian cinema is not communicated abroad—and particularly at such an important festival.*[45]

Considering the strikingly negative evaluation and reception both in Peru (and, coincidentally, in Argentina), it is unlikely that the film was ever seriously considered for Cannes. Nevertheless, the journal's overanxious concern that non-Peruvians would assume this to be representative of Peruvian cinema reflected the specialized journal's obsession with quality local cinema. Because European spectators and critics would not know—or care to learn more—about such a (cinematically) insignificant country's national cinema and might only have had the opportunity to see this one film from the country before making a sweeping decision about the state of that industry, *Hablemos de cine* took it upon itself as the local publication to ensure that its cinema was both aesthetically and technically acceptable as well as representative of an appropriate national reality.

By the 1990s, most Latin American films (including nearly all of those made in Peru) were co-productions: a necessity to gather sufficient funds during times of economic instability throughout the region. Fortunately, the stigma of the earlier films did not carry over to the later films. Later regulations would clarify how "national films" were to be defined (by percentages of crew, setting, cast, and so on). Auteurist co-productions (like *Intimidad de los parques*), taking advantage of the local Film Law of 1962, constituted the largest number of films made throughout the decade: of the twenty-one national productions produced and exhibited in Peru between 1962 and 1970, thirteen of them were co-productions, most of them with Mexico and Argentina and a large number of them exploitation films similar to those produced in Ecuador around this same time.[46] Of these co-productions, however, *Intimidad de los parques* was the only one examined at length by *Hablemos de cine*. Two other Mexican examples, Guillermo Fernández

Jurado's *Taita Cristo* (Daddy Christ, 1967) and Alfredo Crevenna's *El tesoro de Atahualpa* (Atahualpa's Treasure, 1968), were summarily dismissed as insignificant, "worthless co-productions" in short reviews.[47] These films were never even mentioned in passing in editorials, interviews with fellow Peruvian filmmakers, or even in blurbs about current film screenings within Lima. The distaste left by *Intimidad de los parques* thus impacted the perception of these co-productions to the extent that the journal went out of their way to ignore them completely as they appeared on Peruvian screens throughout the 1960s.

Patronizing Indigenism: *Jarawi*

The editorial opening the issue that contained the review of *Intimidad de los parques* began: "It is evident that Peruvian cinema is being born these days; a new impulse of cinematic creation appears to have arrived in this country since the experience of *Kukuli*."[48] The invocation of *Kukuli* is significant in its use as a sign of the expected rebirth of filmmaking in Peru in the 1960s.[49] As in Lima, the Andean city of Cuzco formed its own cine-club in 1955, founded by a number of aspiring filmmakers who quickly gained considerable experience directing a number of short documentaries as well as assisting various foreign feature productions that came to use Machu Picchu as a background setting in the late 1950s and early 1960s. None of the filmmakers had a formal filmmaking education, but the documentaries that resulted were considered elegant in their simplicity; indeed, they were later compared with the work of documentarian Robert Flaherty. The Cine-Club de Cuzco brought international attention to Peru with their prize-winning shorts and the successful 1961 release of *Kukuli*, the first Peruvian feature made entirely outside Lima. Co-directed by three of the club members, Luis Figueroa, Eulogio Nishiyama, and César Villanueva,[50] the film was an eighty-minute fable set in the outskirts of Cuzco and is notable for being one of the first films spoken entirely in Quechua, the language common to the mountains of Peru, particularly in the Cuzco region.[51]

Kukuli's significance lies not only in that it was one of the only fiction features made in Peru at the time, a shining example during the dearth of nationally produced films in the 1950s and early 1960s, but also that it was *not* made in Lima. Between documentary experiences and location shoots for several foreign productions, fledgling filmmakers in Cuzco were the only ones gaining practical experience in Peru during what is otherwise considered a fallow period in Peruvian cinema, the years between World War II and the mid-1960s. Nevertheless, cinematic raw materials and equipment for editing, developing, and sound were already difficult to obtain in Lima, the primary commercial entrance point for the country, so the completion of a feature-length film in Cuzco was an astounding achievement.[52] Most important, *Kukuli* exposed viewers to a fictional narrative with Andean faces—a vital aspect of Peruvian identity missing from virtually all previous Peruvian films.

The film was criticized for some noticeable technical defects, including some amateur editing and filming techniques and problems with color processing; more important, however, was the film's focus on the idea of the "innocent native." Cinematographer Eulogio Nishiyama admits that the visuals were in part inspired by Peruvian painter José Sabogal, a founder of the "indigenismo" movement earlier in the twentieth century, whose work emphasizes the landscape and simple compositions of native faces. Appropriately, therefore, the film earned the label "indigenist" from some critics, though this is now seen as a negative implication that the film too easily resorted to an unreal, reductive representation of Andean life. Some international criticism gave grounds for these fears: Spanish critic Juan Francisco Lasa wrote in *La Vanguardia de Barcelona* in 1962 that *Kukuli* "reflected all the Incan grandiosity simultaneously with the primitivism of the native soul."[53] At the time of its release, however, local critics attributed this reductionism to the Cuzco school's documentary experiences now being applied to fiction filmmaking. As such, the film's deficiencies were regarded as an appropriate aesthetic choice reflecting a rough, beautiful, simple life in the Andes.

Local critics also expected many of these deficiencies to have been corrected with the Cuzco school's second feature film, *Jarawi* (The Ballad, 1966), an adaptation by Eulogio Nishiyama and César Villanueva of José María Arguedas's story "Diamantes y pedernales" (Diamonds and flint). The film follows a young politician who, though he first loves an Indian singer, one day falls for a young woman visiting from Lima. Out of jealousy, the indigenous woman asks an Andean harpist for help in getting her lover back. The harpist instead dies and the peasant population rises up against the politician. While *Hablemos de cine* had not been in publication at *Kukuli*'s release, Juan Bullitta's review of *Jarawi* drew largely on a comparison between the two films. Though quantitatively the editors split on the low end of the scale (the film garnered ratings between zero and two), this film was viewed as a considerable failure, primarily due to its poor technical quality:

> *Cinematically,* Jarawi *shares many qualities with* Kukuli, *although the latter film has a simpler narrative structure and less ambitious intentions. The inevitable comparisons between the two films does not give much credit to*

> *the directors who, instead of cleaning up their style and correcting errors (including some very large ones, such as arbitrary and confusing editing), have only aggravated these errors. If anything, their new film adds bigger and undisguised problems.*[54]

These "additions" included "poor color processing (with differences in tonality in every sequence), deplorable synchronization of sound, poor actors who don't for a single moment convince the viewer of their characters, etc." Bullitta compared *Jarawi* to a South African film released in Lima around the same time, Jamie Uys's *Dingaka,* as both films mix historical elements with folklore and come from countries without strongly defined national film industries. As such, Bullitta speculated on how the Peruvian film would fare if screened internationally: "The exoticism of the customs featured in the film might prove attractive overseas (particularly in Europe), but I think that no critic could overlook the flaws of this Peruvian film. In contrast, *Dingaka*, although it's not something to talk about from an aesthetic point of view, is at least free from major technical errors."[55]

Bullitta also chastised the film for its reliance on stereotyped and simplified characterizations that were confusingly depicted. Bullitta is more concerned with the lack of technical improvement with this film; the problem of the "folkloric depictions" of Indians, however, is something that the journal would later criticize heavily in later films. While the editors acknowledged that Andean characterizations were something new and unique in Peruvian films, such simplified depictions, recorded without analysis or commentary, were derogatorily labeled "indigenist" and a disservice to the *serrano* population.[56] A comparison of what were seen as positive and negative depictions of this population would be offered later in 1977. One of *Kukuli*'s directors, Luis Figueroa, adapted Ciro Alegría's novel *Los perros hambrientos* (The Hungry Dogs, 1977) to similarly negative reviews, especially when compared with the director's earlier work. In his overview of the year's releases, Isaac León noted that while the narrative seemed to show the conflict between the landed and the landless classes around Cuzco, the visual structure itself was too reminiscent of a documentary for a feature. Figueroa's film was again labeled "indigenist" and was seen as a problematic return to the aesthetics and era of filmmaking associated with *Kukuli.* In contrast, Federico García's *Kuntur Wachana* (Where the Condors Are Born), released in the same year, presented a more multifaceted depiction of Andean life while telling virtually the same story, even though García employed a more active documentary practice and methodology in shooting the film.[57]

Bullitta wrote in 1966, "It is possible that *Jarawi* will succeed at the box office, but it is also easy to see that the everyday spectator will not be completely satisfied by the film."[58] As it turned out, even this qualified estimate was overoptimistic: confusing and mystifying for viewers as well, *Jarawi* flopped in Peruvian theaters, not even coming close to recouping its investment. Its failure subsequently forced the members of Cine-Club de Cuzco to work independently on short projects, mainly documentaries. Figueroa would continue to make features in his own, but the group never made another feature film again.

Popular Comedies: *El embajador y yo* and *Nemesio*

Television arrived in Peru in the 1950s with its first nationally produced show airing in 1958.[59] By the end of the 1960s, the medium was extremely popular and had generated its own set of local stars. It was only a matter of time before several television personalities attempted to transfer their successes to the big screen. We shall discuss four of them here: two *telenovelas* (soap operas) and two comedies, concentrating primarily on the comedies. More often than not, the general moviegoing public received these films enthusiastically—and they made an obscene profit, enjoying the same benefits from the Film Law of 1962 that the coproductions did. But once again *Hablemos de cine* weighed heavily against these films, deeming them beneath the category of cinema. In truth, *none* of the four so-called television films (not films made for television, but films featuring television stars) made before 1972 were even reviewed by the journal, despite their immense popularity. By 1968, the journal had developed a clear aesthetic elitism that did not attempt to speak for the popular viewer. Although the television films screened widely across the city's cultural and socioeconomic divisions (opening at theaters across the city in completely different districts), the division between the cultural elite and the popular filmgoing public was still very wide.

This distance is strikingly apparent in *Hablemos de cine*'s omission of commentary on the two films based on extremely popular *telenovelas*: Enzo Bellomo's *Simplemente María* (Simply Maria, 1970) and Tito Davison's *Natacha* (1971). Originating on Peru's Panamericana Televisión (channel 5), which also produced the cinematic versions, the two melodramas had almost identical plots: a young woman comes to the city, becomes a domestic servant, and is seduced by the son of the household; she eventually escapes this situation and is redeemed in the eyes of the community and her true love. The earlier film was set in Buenos Aires; the latter in Lima. *Simplemente María* became something of an international cultural phenomenon in 1969 as a televised serial, eventually airing internationally in more than twenty countries.[60] Nevertheless, *Hablemos de cine* completely ignored both films. At least in the case of *Simplemente María*, the journal might not have considered the film to be sufficiently "Peruvian": although it did feature the Peruvian lead actress Saby Kamalich, it had been filmed entirely in Buenos Aires. It is also possible that the journal, typically demonstrating the intellectual's disdain for popular melodrama,[61] did not believe the film's narratives held any agency in the development of national identity. Most likely, however, the film versions were seen as merely copies of the *telenovelas* from which they derived and therefore fell under the scope of television as opposed to true cinema.

The two comedies, on the other hand, had the potential to impact more directly on Peruvian identity, which the *hablemistas* considered a significant threat to developing a responsible national film identity. The first, *El embajador y yo* (The ambassador and I, Oscar Kantor), was a vehicle for television game-show host Kiko Ledgard, who also produced and cowrote the film. Not aiming to be an artistic triumph, the film focused instead on Ledgard's already established comic personality in a simple action-adventure narrative.

El embajador y yo was released in May 1968 and was an immediate financial success. The plot is familiar in the action-comedy genre: a television personality gets confused with a visiting ambassador who is being pursued by a number of bad guys who wish to obtain secrets involving a drug trade; in the process, our hero foils the plans, shakes off the crooks, and gets the girl, all the while performing various action sequences throughout Lima. The film's goal focused on the comic personality of Ledgard, already proven on the small screen. Advertising for the film also emphasized the setting in the capital, touting it as "the only film that has not taken advantage of Machu Picchu." Major settings included the newly opened Jorge Chávez International Airport, the posh suburb of Miraflores, the coastal playground of Ancón—all icons of cosmopolitan, upper-class Lima.

Given *Hablemos de cine*'s previous embracing of genre films, it may seem unusual that a popular comedy would be so flatly rejected, but the film was released during a crucial juncture at the journal's trajectory with the result that the film has not figured significantly as part of the canonized history of Peruvian cinema. *El embajador y yo* happened to be the first Peruvian feature film released following the journal's return from the 1967 Viña del Mar film festival, an experience where contact with filmmakers from throughout Latin America exposed to the editors how embarrassingly far behind their own national cinema lay.[62] Rather than explore the quotidian Peruvian reality, the film showcased the districts and the social atmosphere of the elite. The film was directed either narcissistically at the upper class (of which the editors of *Hablemos de cine* were themselves members) or at the nonelite to show how the elite lived. Either way, such a depiction was largely seen as irresponsible and was received negatively by many popular critics.[63]

For *Hablemos de cine*, however, *El embajador y yo* was also the antithesis of the "new cinema" they had chosen to embrace following Viña '67. Thus their editorial, more than commenting on the film itself, served to discourage any idea that the film signified a trend in national activity:

> El embajador y yo *remains an isolated work. Its relative commercial success means little in view of the current situation concerning the future of our infant (or almost nonexistent) cinema. . . . First, the film caters openly to the grand populace...much as the television programs of Tulio Loza or Ledgard himself. . . . It is not that we demand an intellectual argument that we don't believe in. We affirm that even the most banal or routine genre still results in acceptable or even quality works. What is unacceptable is the assumption that Peruvian spectators are "sub-mental." National films should not be made like an inexpensive drug that anyone could take, similar to many television programs.*[64]

Though they stated they did not believe in an "intellectual" cinema, their disdain of the "grand populace" clearly proved otherwise.

El embajador y yo was also released five months before a radical change occurred within the Peruvian government. Though the journal never mentioned it at the time, Peruvian critic-historian Ricardo Bedoya has noted that the film's flaunting of the city's new architecture effectively displayed the accomplishments of the first government of Fernando Belaúnde Terry.[65] In October 1968, the military coup of Juan Velasco Alvarado radically changed the political and social landscape of the country. The Velasco government explicitly favored the celebration of a national identity that embraced the indigenous from all parts of the country.

The release of *Nemesio* in 1969 provoked a similar response to the one generated by *El embajador y yo*, but this time the editorial reflected an internalization of the ideals of the Velasco revolution of the year before, emphasizing considerations of national cinematic identity.[66] Again directed by Oscar Kantor, the film this time appropriately starred Tulio Loza, the other television personality mentioned in the editorial on *El embajador y yo* eight issues earlier. The comedy for which Loza was known depended entirely on the implicit racism prevalent throughout *limeño* society. The title of the film is derived from Loza's familiar characterization of a *recién bajado*, an Indian who had just "come down" from the mountains to the capital and who must use his provincial mettle to make it in the city. In the film, Nemesio must find the right paperwork to settle a land-ownership dispute going on back home in the province of Abancay that threatens to kick his grandmother out of her house. Not only does the problem get solved, Nemesio also gets the girl, a *limeña* flight attendant. The film suggests the triumph of the *recien bajado* over the city with a final sequence that includes Nemesio standing in front of a waving Peruvian flag, seemingly in line with what the new Velasco government would have approved.[67] An exceptionally popular character on television, *Nemesio* broke box-office records for a Peruvian film, doing 250,000 soles' worth of business on its first day.

With a particularly racist comment, one review bitterly attributed the success to the "*serranitos* [little ones from the mountains] eager to see themselves in the mirror of Tulio-Nemesio."[68] The response of *Hablemos de cine*, well versed in the ideals that both the new military government and the New Latin American Cinema were trying to represent, denounced the film in a different manner:

> *We feel it is our obligation to fiercely repudiate this favorable campaign for a film that, in its complete aesthetic ineffectiveness, twists and deforms the struggle of the Indian and of the Peruvian* mestizo. *The characterization by Tulio Loza (who is hardly funny and can't act) does not represent the Peruvian* cholo . . . *nor does the film contribute to the process of revalidating the* mestizo. . . . *If Peruvian cinema is going to hold up* Nemesio *as a model, it is better to hope that cinema is not made in Peru.*[69]

Invoking the language and ideology behind more progressive cinema, *Hablemos de cine* also remained contemporary to current political and cultural trends within the Peruvian government. Ironically, with such comments, the journal began to align itself away from the cultural elite that generally characterized most film criticism in Peru up until the 1960s (the same dismissive criticism that refers to Indians living in Lima as *serranitos*, "little mountain people").

Hablemos de cine's response to these two popular comedies advanced their ideas of national cinema in two major ways. First, they reaffirmed the journal's general stance that "quality cinema" was not one derived from television; many years later, similar distaste would be expressed by Peruvian critics en masse for the film version based on the 2000 *telenovela* adaptation of the Mario Vargas Llosa novel *Pantaleón y las visitadoras* (Captain Pantoja and the Special Service), even though it was directed by Peruvian auteur Francisco Lombardi. More interesting, however, while indigenism was not desirable, neither was comedy derived from the hardships and travails of working-class Peruvians. The journal believed that a certain reality must be portrayed, not a stereotype. The result of influences from both its exposure to the New Latin American cinema and the ideals of the Velasco regime, *Hablemos de cine*'s reaction to these comedies demonstrated a significant step away from their original perspective favoring style (mise-en-scène) over content.

Possibly Peruvian: Andesu no hanayame

While *Hablemos de cine* rejected every national feature production released in the 1960s as not being of sufficient "quality" to earn the label "Peruvian cinema," one film was so designated by the journal precisely because it *did* meet such qualifications, though other factors complicated its being canonized within the category of "national cinema." Japanese director Susumu Hani's *Andesu no hanayome* (Bride of the Andes, 1966) caused a serious debate on the topic of how national cinema should be defined.[70] Filmed on location in Peru in 1965, the picture follows a young Japanese couple honeymooning in the highlands of Peru, Bolivia, and northern Argentina. Hani's arrival in Lima had been greeted with enthusiasm by the *Hablemos de cine* staff who, at the last minute, procured only their second filmmaker interview ever (after Robles Godoy) for volume 10 (July 1, 1965). News had just arrived in Lima through the Spanish journal *Film Ideal* that Hani's most recent film *Kanojo to kare* (She and He, 1965) had just been awarded the Golden Bear at the Berlin Film Festival. The editors acknowledged their relative ignorance about Japanese cinema, asking Hani's opinion about the current state of his own national cinema as well as his place in it. Hani replied, "Kurosawa's and Mizoguchi's pictures, for example, generally situate their arguments in the past. I prefer to make films that deal with current issues."[71] The director turned the questioning around in the middle of the interview to ask the editors about their own national cinema:

> HANI: *Why do you think films are not made in Peru?*
>
> LEÓN: *First of all, a lack of funding makes it so that there are no capable technicians to direct.*
>
> BULLITTA: *The proportion of cinematic production is very poor. We still don't have here a* cinemathèque, *or a film library, nor support for cultural organisms or film schools as an artistic phenomenon.*

HANI: *Do you want to direct films someday?*
UNANIMOUS RESPONSE: *We* all *do.*[72]

The editors also saw the director off at the airport in Lima following the shoot and Federico de Cárdenas reported the scene at the airport as shockingly uneventful considering the status of Hani as an international director: "No reporters were present, but humble people from the community in Cuzco were there to say goodbye. And among them, Susumu Hani was happy. Much like the anonymous protagonists of his film."[73]

By the time *Andesu no hanayame* was released in Lima in 1967 (under the Spanish title *Amor en los Andes* [Love in the Andes]), the film had already been screened at the 1966 Venice film festival.[74] At this point, the journal was well into considering how to define Peruvian film: a film was "Peruvian" if it reflected Peruvian ideals and themes and used national actors and/or landscapes. On these grounds, the editors argued that *Andesu no hanayame* should be considered national and thereby included as part of the fledgling (and admittedly weak at the time) canon of Peruvian cinema: "The film is made by a foreigner, but in focusing on a Peruvian reality there is a significant tie to what until now we have been able to call Peruvian cinema." The relative simplicity of Hani's film inspired Juan Bullitta to compare the film with Robles Godoy's *En la selva no hay estrellas*, his most recent release:

> *But I want to stress that the tone of indifference with which our cinematic milieu has received [Hani's] film is one of the most tragic examples of corruption because if Hani's film is seen as foreign, what can we say about Robles Godoy, whose aesthetics is much more foreign than Hani's?* En la selva no hay estrellas *not only does not reveal a Peruvian reality, or help us understand the Peruvian person, it does not even attempt to do so, at least on the filmic level.*[75]

No one picked up Bullitta's comparison, and the issue remained unresolved: if Hani was ideologically and aesthetically closer to detailing the realities of Peruvian life than Robles Godoy—who publicly admitted that his impression of filmmaking was more influenced by Europe than anything else—then why was the latter's film worthy of status within national cinema and not the former's? Part of the issue concerned financing: Hani clearly indicated in his first interview that this film was not a co-production but entirely funded through Japan. Like *Intimidad de los parques* above, most co-productions took full advantage of the Film Law of 1962 by setting up a cloaked Peruvian company to open up the local market and conveniently bypass national import tariffs. *Andes no hanayame* therefore stands out as an unusual "local" production for this period. Because no Peruvian money was used to make the film, no history of Peruvian cinema has considered it as part of its national cinema. Even the debate at *Hablemos de cine* ended with Léon's claim that "It has been said that this is the best picture filmed in Peru, not that it is the best Peruvian film."[76] The editors were clearly torn, however, having admired Hani's work and expressing at least some desire to claim the film as part of national cinema. Nevertheless, the journal also realized that the Japanese film was even more of an isolated cinematic event in Peru than the stalled efforts of the Cuzco school. Hani's cinematic glance did not bind him to a Peruvian community of "comradeship," to the building of a national cinematic identity. Other directors from abroad who did make "Peruvian films"—for example, Oscar Kantor and Manuel Antín from Argentina—were soundly criticized for inaccurately portraying Peruvian life because of their nationality. Hani was a more difficult prospect, having *accurately* depicting life in the mountains, arguably even more so than the Cuzco school did. *Andes no hanayame* was curiously not referred to as a milestone in filmmaking in Peru in any later issues, nor does it even appear today in Ricardo Bedoya's otherwise comprehensive film encyclopedia—a significant omission, given that the encyclopedia includes many other "questionably national" co-productions, such as the Roger Corman co-productions of the 1980s and early 1990s. The debate that lingered within the journal's pages at the time of its release nevertheless reflects the insecure, changing notions that the editors had concerning national cinema—and whether "quality" did in fact trump "nationality."

To be sure, *Hablemos de cine* found fault with nearly every Peruvian production it examined in its first ten years of existence. It seemed the few exceptions were short films such as *Estampas del Carnaval de Kanas* (Scenes from the Kanas Carnival, Cuzco school, 1965) and *Semilla* (Seed, Pablo Guevara, 1969), which at the time were still seen as peripheral to the national cinema project—though this view would change when a short film industry developed following the Film Law of 1972.[77] Nevertheless, the journal's negative reactions to these features publicly announced their convictions of what Peruvian cinema *should* look like. Films should avoid the auteurist pretension that characterized the work of Armando Robles Godoy, the feigned nationalist characteristics of co-productions such as *Intimidad de los parques*, the native "indigenism" of *Jarawi*, and the general poor quality and lack of interest in cinema qua cinema found in popular comedies such as *Nemesio* and *El embajador y yo*. If anything, Peruvian films should instead emulate the careful, measured examination seen in *Andesu no hanayame*. With each negative review, the journal refined and reestablished its criteria for national productions, preparing for the feature filmmaking that would emerge in Peru in the latter half of the 1970s.

CHAPTER 4
LATIN AMERICAN DIS/CONNECTIONS

Peru versus the New Latin American Cinema

> *The sketched reflections that follow should be taken as provisional and partial. They do not indicate concluding judgments, but rather brief evaluations of trends in Latin American cinema that might be called "advanced" or "vanguard," in their aesthetic or political sense. As such, we take into consideration our admittedly fragmented knowledge of this continent's cinema and risk making some generalizations that tomorrow—or even today—might appear arbitrary or careless. But the opportunity of having seen a more or less representative portion of our continent's cinema and the knowledge of some preceding works stimulates us to write these lines, the statement of which we consider inevitable for a Latin American film journal.*
>
> —ISAAC LEÓN, FOLLOWING THE 1969 VIÑA DEL MAR FILM FESTIVAL, IN *HABLEMOS DE CINE* (NOVEMBER 1969–FEBRUARY 1970)

Filmmaking in the late 1960s and the early 1970s from several regions throughout the world often reflected and embraced a politically motivated activism. Referred to by many Eurocentric critics as "new cinema," these films reacted to productions, strategies, themes, and aesthetic considerations that were regarded by some as "dominant" or hegemonic within most Hollywood and European commercial films. This activism was especially prominent in Latin America, where the troubling political and social realities at local levels were exposed in films such as *Deus e diablo na terra do sol* (Black God and White Devil, Rocha, Brazil, 1964), *La hora de los hornos* (The Hour of the Furnaces, Solanas and Getino, Argentina, 1968) and *Yawar Mallku* (Blood of the Condor, Sanjinés, Bolivia, 1968). A film publication from the region would logically offer a good perspective on these films as they were being produced.

Hablemos de cine only discussed one Latin American filmmaker during its first thirty-three issues: Peruvian Armando Robles Godoy, who released his first film, *Ganarás el pan* (You Will Earn the Bread), in 1965. During the beginning of its publication run, the journal placed its emphasis on Hollywood and European productions shown at cine-clubs across Lima. The absence of any information on Latin American films within its pages is indicative of how films did not travel across borders within Latin America rather than the historical absence or paucity of these films elsewhere. The only films from the region that appeared on Peruvian screens were primarily Mexican and Argentine popular comedies or melodramas—which the journal universally discounted as "Latin American subcinema."[1]

All this changed in 1967, when several of the journal's editors traveled to the film festival held in Viña del Mar, Chile. Within the historical context of the region's cinema, that year's festival is now seen as a key moment: filmmakers and critics from around the continent shared their experiences and their work, exposing common cinematic traits throughout the region that would eventually define what was to be known as the "New Latin American Cinema."[2] The Peruvian response to this encounter, however, was unique and had serious repercussions for the journal in particular and its connections with concepts of national cinema both at home and abroad.

Solidarity: Viña del Mar, 1967

The invitation from Viña del Mar festival organizer Aldo Francia allowed two of the founding editors of *Hablemos de cine*, Isaac León Frías and Federico de Cárdenas, to join their Chilean correspondent, Mariano Silva, in Viña del Mar in early March 1967. This marked the first film festival abroad that the journal would cover using Peruvian reporters. Up until this point, the journal had relied almost entirely on Spanish colleagues from *Film Ideal* such as Jesús Martínez León, Augusto M. Torres, and Vicente Molina Foix for reports on the major European festivals at Cannes and Venice, as well as local festivals at San Sebastián and Valladolid. Silva had also chronicled his experiences at Mar de la Plata, Argentina, a year earlier, and Peruvian cine-club organizer Andrés Ruszkowski detailed his experiences at the Rio de Janeiro festival early in 1965.[3] Neither León nor de Cárdenas, however, had had the opportunity themselves to report on a festival that went beyond Peruvian short films.[4]

Considering there were no articles in previous issues of the journal announcing either the upcoming festival itself or the editors' plans to attend, it is unclear whether *Hablemos de cine* knew the impact the festival would have. The festival had certainly not been seen as significant before 1967.[5] Started by the Cine-club de Viña del Mar in 1963, the first three events were mostly showcases for the small Chilean film scene. All three of the festivals were nevertheless billed as international events and awarded prizes to several non-Chilean films. The fourth festival in 1966, however, focused exclusively on Chilean filmmaking in an unsuccessful attempt to prove both the interest and the need for a film law to stimulate a national industry. The announcement that organizers for the fifth festival were broadening the scope to include Latin America in 1967, however, might have interested *Hablemos de cine*.

The other objective—and a major draw for the international participants—was the opportunity to show films made throughout the continent in a single location. In 1967, the stranglehold of the North American "majors" over distribution and exhibition throughout the region was a reality shared by all of the filmmakers.[6] Only in the small cine-clubs was it possible to watch non-Hollywood cinema, but even these outlets did not necessarily have access to other Latin American films. The Spanish correspondents for *Hablemos de cine* had reported on some Latin American films viewed in Europe at festivals such as Cannes, France, or Pesaro, Italy, the latter venue being an early supporter of new cinema. The festival at Viña del Mar, however, provided a space for the screening of several short- and medium-length films for the first time in Latin America of *only* Latin American productions. The festival allowed a considerable range of styles from emerging directors to be viewed by their international peers for the first time. As a specific example, much had been written at the time in international film periodicals about the bursting onto the scene of the Brazilian *Cinema Nôvo*, yet none of these films had crossed Peruvian borders. With no organized network among filmmakers or independent exhibitors within the continent, there was little communication among countries to know that films were even being made, much less how they could be distributed.

Hablemos de cine's coverage of the Viña del Mar film festival of 1967 is the primary focus of volume 34 (March–April 1967), starting with the front cover (fig. 9) featuring a still from the festival-winning film, *Manuela* (Cuba, Humberto Solás, 1966). The breakdown of the individual film's ratings by reviewer provided at the end of the main article indicate that at least three other film journals sent representatives who attended the festival: *Cine cubano* and two Chilean publica-

Figure 9: Cover of *Hablemos de cine* 34 (March–April 1967). Courtesy of the Filmoteca PUCP *Hablemos de cine* Archive.

tions, *Ercilla* and *CEP*. Yet *Hablemos de cine* provided the most in-depth coverage and analysis of the event. As if to acknowledge this exceptional coverage festival organizer Aldo Francia selected *Hablemos de cine*'s printed account of the 1967 festival as the primary summary in his history of the festival published in 1990. This selection was a breakthrough for the journal in expanding its scope beyond national borders. However, even as *Hablemos de cine* became a more "regional" publication with its coverage of the festival, it did so by exposing many aspects of the film experience within Peru.

The festival featured films from nine countries. The great majority arrived from Argentina, Brazil, and Chile, with three films coming from Cuba, two each from Uruguay and Venezuela, and a single representative film from Bolivia, Mexico, and Peru. The introduction to the journal's report on the festival by de Cárdenas and León included a paragraph comparing the different national cinemas and their respective states of progress. Note particularly the placement of the Peruvian cinema within this spectrum of cinematic achievement:

> *It has been our great fortune to see how the films' technical and narrative qualities differ from country to country. On the one hand, a vigorous cinema, technically and artistically vibrant, like the Brazilian; another important cinema, the Cuban; an industry that is currently undergoing a moment of crisis but remains active, the Argentine; finally, the most solid film industry in Spanish America, although perhaps, due to its commercialization, without the same expressive level as those from Brazil or Cuba: the Mexican. On the other hand, the remaining countries. Some like Chile, Venezuela, Uruguay, and Bolivia with a short history (or, better said, a prehistory) but likely to advance soon. Others, like ours, in an infant state. There was no news of the rest of the countries, particularly from Central America.*[7]

Along this continuum of cinematic development, the Peruvian cinematic example is placed dead last, seen as being in an "infant state," not far enough along to represent even a "prehistory." This pronouncement was not entirely true: the Peruvian cinematic tradition from the silent period through the early sound period had produced a number of films, ending with the short-lived success of Amauta Films in the late 1930s.[8] For the young men writing for *Hablemos de cine*, however, these films were far removed from current filmmaking practices. With scant few productions in recent history—and all of them isolated endeavors—any significant example of significant Peruvian filmmaking had been forgotten by 1967;

thus the journal could not attest to a "national cinematic history."[9] Then again, this attitude was endemic among other Latin American cineastes who chose to indicate a break with their cinematic histories (which they found derivative of Hollywood and European ideals) by referring to their own films as "new cinema." The "New Latin American Cinema" that emerged would seem to have developed without any prehistory at all; even Zuzana Pick's excellent, detailed examination of the "movement" begins in the mid-1960s, avoiding any discussion of film traditions prior to this time.[10]

Hablemos published reviews of all the films shown in competition at Viña del Mar, conspicuously organizing the reviews by country. Laudatory remarks were bestowed upon the Cuban films as well as upon most of the Brazilian and Argentine shorts. Most interesting, however, were the remarks made about some of the "lesser" cinemas. De Cárdenas's notes on the Chilean entries, for example, indicated that although the "level of production as a whole is still below the minimum technical and professional proficiency that the Argentine and Brazilian industries already possess . . . [the industry] continues on a clear path that, we don't doubt, will soon be fruitful."[11] With historical hindsight, the Chilean short films shown at the Viña del Mar Festival in 1967 serve as some of the first cinematic examples made by Chilean filmmakers who soon were to play major roles in the national cultural climate with the rise of Salvador Allende and the Unidad Popular government. Reviewed in this article were short films by Rafael Sánchez, Miguel Littín, Patricio Guzmán, Pedro Chaskel, Helvio Soto, Jorge Di Lauro, and Nieves Yankovic. (Two additional filmmakers were omitted, Fernando Balmaceda and Augustín Squella.) Under the Allende government, Soto became head of the government-run television station, and Littín was named director of Chile Films. Many of these directors would receive international attention when exiled in 1973 with the fall of the Allende government.[12] From the contemporary Peruvian critical perspective, however, this display demonstrated the active, preliminary stirrings of an industry, but nothing particularly notable.

The Chilean films were directly compared with the sole Peruvian entry in the festival competition, Jorge Volkert's *Forjadores de mañana* (Tomorrow's Forgers). The editors of *Hablemos de cine* were already familiar with this film as two years earlier it had won second prize in the short-film contest sponsored by the journal.[13] At that time the journal had offered a relatively positive review:

> *We liked the film, and the jury was right to award it second place. This documentary's use of montage can be contrasted with [Manuel] Chambi's*

> [Estampas del Carnaval de Kanas, *the competition winner].*[14] *They are two different types of films each of which should be judged on its own merits, that is, in accordance with what appears on the screen. Volkert uses skillful editing to create an excellent cinematographic rhythm, firm and sustained. The same goes for the film's soundtrack, based on toccatas, fugues, and partitas by Johann Sebastian Bach, which is perfectly coherent and accompanies the images logically. On the other hand, some of the questionably skewed frame compositions might have been avoided. The weakest point of the film is the grandiloquent, falsely poetic narration, which serves only to highlight how such strong imagery does not need such support. [Nevertheless,]* Forjadores de mañana *does what the director has set out to do and, as such, deserves to be exhibited commercially in our theaters.*[15]

An amicable interview with Volkert was also published in the same issue. The goodwill demonstrated in both the review and the interview might stem from the fact that, as the introduction stated, Volkert was "more than a stranger, but rather a friend of *Hablemos de cine*," again reinforcing the close connection between critics and filmmakers in the early stages of developing a cinematic climate in Peru.[16] The staff also admitted that there were very few "good" films shown at the festival, so that it was relatively easy for both the judges and the editorial staff to agree on the winners.

Viewed again at Viña del Mar and now compared with the other films from across the continent, *Forjadores de mañana* was a major embarrassment. Given high praise in the first commentary in 1965, the film now received a numerical assessment of 1 (out of 5) from both León and de Cárdenas, a 2 from Cinemateca Universitaria Peruana director Reynel, and a 0 from Chilean *Hablemos* correspondent Silva as well as the rest of the international critics attending the event.[17] The reevaluation of *Forjadores de mañana* subscribed to the journal's commitment to review films within their contemporary contexts as opposed to merely reprinting the reviews previously published (though it chose to refer the reader to the earlier review for specific information about the film). The discussion of the film is at the end of the article and its last two sentences are particularly damning:

> *Finally Peru, with Jorge Volkert's* Forjadores de mañana. *This film was reviewed in issue 12 of* Hablemos de cine. *It was out of place in the festival and very badly received. It concerns a film commissioned by the Universidad de*

> *Ingienería with a stupidly patriotic script. We don't doubt that if it had been screened without its soundtrack, at least it would have passed unnoticed. It is neither better nor worse than the Chilean films, for example. But this serves as a call for Peruvian cinema to forget such ingenuousness if we are to somehow move forward.*[18]

Nothing had changed about Volkert's film in the two years since its viewing at the 16mm Festival in Lima, yet viewing it within the context of many other more ambitious and explicitly oppositional politically cinematic projects radically altered the perception of the film. Extremely poor production values, narrative structure, and cinematographic techniques, combined with an over nationalist theme, resulted in an unfavorable representation of national cinema. Other publications blamed the festival selection committee for admitting this film in the first place,[19] but the Peruvians took this reception to the film as a slight to national cinematic pride.

Perhaps as important as the films that were screened was a landmark meeting held between the various cineastes to present the state of the Latin American cinematic climate from their own national perspectives. Each of the seven delegations[20] was composed of a diverse mixture of filmmakers, critics, cine-club directors, and producers. As active participants in this meeting, de Cárdenas and León outlined the highlights of the encounter, which dealt "primarily with the problems of production and, above all, distribution of independent Latin American cinema," as well as the goals articulated for a "Center for New Latin American Cinema":

> *[The Center] will bring together the movements of new independent filmmaking from every country in Latin America. . . . It will [also] take on the task of cataloging a complete list of New Latin American films as well as initiating studies of markets to organize adequate distribution of films. In addition, [the Center] will promote the constant interchange of productions and filmmaker experiences. Finally, it will develop ways to allow for the recognition of Latin American cinema, as much in countries of this continent as well as in Europe.*[21]

The 1967 Viña del Mar festival has been acknowledged throughout the literature on the New Latin American Cinema as having played a tremendous part in uniting the filmmakers by revealing their shared causes and interests. Before relationships between filmmakers and distributors could be established, however, the actual films (particularly features) had yet to be made.

Hablemos de cine and the New Latin American Cinema

The experience at Viña del Mar profoundly altered the perspective of *Hablemos de cine*. Though the publication of the article on Viña '67 put them at the forefront of the new movement as active participants, it also exposed how little they knew about the rest of the region, as well as how embarrassingly little Peru appeared able to contribute at the time in the way of filmmaking. Peruvian film historian Ricardo Bedoya provides an appropriate metaphor for this radical shift of the journal's focus: "*Hablemos* seemed to lose its virginity and the spiritualism of its early Bazinian affirmations to make way for the polemics and discussions of Cinema Nôvo, the militant Argentine cinema, and the appreciation of the fervor stimulated by the Cuban documentaries."[22] The journal recognized that the cinematic revolution that was taking place throughout the continent would quickly leave Peru behind if something were not done locally to actively stimulate an industry.

Inspired by the accomplishments of the festival, *Hablemos de cine* opened the following issue (vol. 35, May–June 1967) with a striking editorial, "Concerning Latin American Cinema," where the editors noted that, if only "at the journalistic level" (*al nivel periodístico*), the lines of communication between the Americas had been opened and that "we desire to continue, in the best possible way, to shed light on filmmaking in Latin America." Nevertheless, the editors in Lima continued to be frustrated by their inability to collect information on productions from abroad. In order to accomplish this, *Hablemos de cine* called for a stronger and better-articulated link between new filmmaking and criticism:

> *We were so . . . ignorant about what was happening in Brazil or Argentina that there was no other alternative than to wait for the right moment to learn about it. That moment has arrived. Even so, any effort to keep the information current is insufficient without the possibility of having more direct contact with New Latin American films. A journal cannot stimulate sufficient interest when curiosity is frustrated, when expectations are not satisfied. But we will insist on writing about these films because we are convinced that Latin American film critics should commit themselves to the films made—and those that will be made—in their own countries. We have been*

able to verify that this does not occur everywhere. Argentine criticism is isolated, for example, with a tense compromise with the new cinema done in that country. Something similar occurs in Brazil, where several critics feel separated from the Cinema Nôvo movement. From now on, we will discuss the New Cinema, now that a stance of solidarity with a stagnant cinema cannot be justified.[23]

This perspective, however, did not negate the writers' status as "critics" by proposing unequivocal support for any and all Peruvian films produced. The best thing they could do *as critics* would be to maintain high standards in evaluating their own cinema, not to espouse a "blind or unconditional justification of everything that is produced." Rather, *Hablemos de cine* wished to "share as much in the accomplishments of the industry as it did the errors."[24] The journal wanted to note the change from its previous indifference toward national or regional product, going so far as to reprimand other Peruvian periodicals for not having attended Viña del Mar: "We truly lament . . . that at a festival as important as Viña del Mar, far fewer Latin American critics attended than at the press junket that Twentieth Century–Fox held in Lima just a few weeks ago. It is still not too late to correct such errors."[25] This reference to other critics demonstrates the maverick historical and ideological positioning of the staff of *Hablemos de cine* within local Peruvian criticism. Previously seen by others within the cultural elite as the "chicos" [boys] who tended to "waste their time with film," the editors now stood apart from other critics by boldly embracing a new regional cinema that questioned the hegemonically dominant aesthetic and narrative techniques of Hollywood cinema, daring to move away from solely examining European and American films.

Hablemos de cine's presence at Viña del Mar in 1967 yielded valuable direct contacts between the Peruvians and other international filmmakers. A great number of interviews were acquired quickly over the course of the festival, to be disseminated throughout the course of several issues. The articles following the festivals in Viña del Mar in 1967, Mérida in 1968, and Rio de Janeiro in 1969 allowed the journal to publish some of the first contemporary accounts on the continent of the New Latin American Cinema, offering a unique perspective on many of the Latin American directors who gained international acclaim during this period. Articles by the Spanish correspondents, who contributed interviews with prominent members of the Latin American literary "boom" and their interest in the movies, supplemented these pieces.[26] Antonio González Norris's interview with Argentine director Fernando Solanas at Mérida—published the same month in Peru as a similar interview with Michel Delahaye, Pierre Kast, and Jean Narboni in *Cahiers du cinéma* in France—offers a good example of the kind of interviews the journal was now able to procure. Over the next few years as the first part of *La hora de los hornos* gained notoriety throughout Europe and among readers of the leftist film journals of the United States (fig. 10), Solanas was repeatedly interviewed and asked to discuss the politics behind Cine Liberación and the making of this aesthetically daring film. González stated nearly as much at the beginning of his article: "Praised by many and criticized by others, the extensive reports and commentaries on the film from critical journals from many different geographical areas remain prominent."[27] Despite the grand acclaim Solanas had already received at the Pesaro Film Festival in 1968, Latin American audiences had yet to experience the raw power of the film.[28] Considering the paucity of "New Latin American" films that made it into theaters in Lima, readers probably associated any film coming from Argentina with Manuel Antín's 1965 co-production *Intimidad de los parques* (Intimacy of the Parks), which was cited as being too "literary" and a "bad copy" of the worst of auteurist European cinema. González therefore noted the difference between Solanas's film and the Argentine cinema most Peruvians were familiar with: "For the Peruvian cinephile, it is probably difficult to imagine what [the film] is like and, given the current circumstances, it is improbable that it will come [to Peru]."[29] Though the first part of *La hora de los hornos* was screened early in the festival, the tone of the interview seems to indicate that González had not viewed it before interviewing Solanas. Intentional or not, his questions mimicked the Peruvian—or other Latin American—reader who certainly could not have viewed the film. The first four questions concerned general conceptual issues of the film and its structure: for example, "From what I know, *La hora de los hornos* comes from a new or different conception of what cinema means, of its usefulness and necessity. How much of this is true?" Solanas offered lengthy responses to each question that mirrored other early writings, including his famous polemical essay "Toward a Third Cinema."[30]

Within many of his responses, however, some details concerning the actual production of the film also emerged:

> *The most interesting—and the most difficult—thing for us to do was to break with the structural, stylistic and linguistic dependence that we had on European cinema in general. . . . For us, the film's author-protagonists, cinema was an instrument through which we would also clarify our ideas. And*

Figure 10: Cover of *Hablemos de cine* 43–44 (September–December 1968). Rather than a publicity still, the image here shows the exhibition space for *La hora de los hornos* (Argentina, Solanas/Getino, 1968) at the Mérida Film Festival. Courtesy of the Filmoteca PUCP *Hablemos de cine* Archive.

> *that is how the film was written, constructed and filmed—all at the same time—starting with the original premise. We were developing the work this way to such a point that the editing was modified six or seven times, the narrative structures dozens of times, the script kept getting deeper, etc. And as we filmed, we studied, we debated, we read, etc. We made notes on film as if the film was a notebook and the camera was a pen. Many times, we even filmed scenes that we didn't know where we were going to put them, but we knew they expressed desired themes or situations.*[31]

Compare this account with the French published interview with the same director. Whereas *Hablemos de cine* was interested in the actual production process (particularly as the Peruvian situation was very similar to the Argentine in terms of access to raw materials), *Cahiers du cinéma* exclusively pursued the more theoretical aesthetic concept of "militant cinema." In his article and accompanying interview of Solanas, Louis Marcorelles shows how the French were affected by this film: "In the cinema, there is a revolution: we cannot remain neutral, we are compelled to react."[32] His questions, while also directed toward the genesis of the film, attempt to connect the Argentine project to other cinemas from Latin America, insisting on the similarity to the Brazilian Cinema Nôvo: "It is the same concern the Brazilians have. . . . *Cinema Nôvo* has created an absolutely autonomous cinema concerning the cultural landscape, independent of European models."[33] For the French, *La hora de los hornos* was particularly important because of its success at using a politically militant filmmaking aesthetics to accompany its radical ideology.

For the Latin Americans, however, the European accolades proved this type of cinema was a model that could attract international attention. Because Peruvian cinema was still in a nascent stage and national filmmakers might want to consider this model, González questioned Solanas about his experiences *prior* to making this film, providing a narrative on Latin American filmmaking unlike those published in the European journals. As such, the tone of Solanas's responses reflects a sentiment of camaraderie, from one Latin American to another:

> [A.G.N.:] *Before* La hora de los hornos, *we knew nothing about your work. Could you tell us a little about this?*
> [F.S.:] *I am self-taught. I had wanted to make films since I was thirteen or fourteen years old but I was very inhibited by the film journals, by the grand communities, by books about cinema. They spoke of geniuses, of monsters,*

of untouchable things. Above all, we have to demystify and humanize things. In 8mm, stupendous things can be accomplished and in 16mm, superb things. . . . In film . . . there is also the problem of dependency, of believing that what is abroad is always better. To learn film, one necessarily needed to study abroad. In my twenty years, I lamented not having a few more pesos to go study in Paris or Italy because, for me, a great film was one that has a little bit of the sense and language of those great masters.[34]

Solanas continued by relating his formative experiences attending a great number of movies, directing for the theater, and advertising and acting in movies before actually attempting to create his own film. In the end, "it took us almost three years to make the film and, although we still have to make the third part,[35] we believe that *La hora de los hornos* shows that revolutionary cinema is possible and that there are no excuses for not making politically committed cinema, even though the methods are more precarious."[36]

Though these two interviews are similar in many aspects, the different foci are primarily due to the different audiences for which each one was writing. Both publications demonstrated interest in the New Latin American Cinema but had different agendas for doing so. The French were more attracted to the militant aesthetics that echoed on the screen what the Europeans were exhibiting in the public forum following May 1968. The shock upon seeing such political cinema in Pesaro was a call to arms for the European critics: in spontaneous ecstasy, the European viewers carried Solanas through the streets.[37] Solanas's film, in fact, would provide a basis for Pascal Bonitzer's seminal article "Film/Politique" in 1970 and arguably might be the first time *Cahiers* looked beyond Brazil to the new films from Latin America. During the mid-1970s, *Cahiers* would also develop a considerable interest in the Bolivian director Jorge Sanjinés and particularly the Chilean exiled filmmakers such as Helvio Soto and Miguel Littín. It is significant that this kind of adulation came from the Europeans, including the French. As Solanas himself stated to González, the film benefited from following a period of intense political unrest throughout Europe: "Of course, it was very important that the climate within the festival matched the student fervor that came down from France and Germany and was already reverberating in Italy."[38] The *Cahiers* article therefore appears almost as an explanation of why such laudation was so richly deserved.

That the film premiered in Pesaro before Mérida is purely coincidental. Nevertheless, the European acceptance validated the film for the Peruvian—and arguably, the wider Latin American—reading audience. For Solanas, the Pesaro festival "was an enormous experience because it was the first time I had contact with Brazilian and Cuban directors."[39] The occurrences at Pesaro in 1968 constituted the first major recognition of Latin America *outside* the region following the Viña del Mar festival. If Viña del Mar brought together filmmakers and critics from around Latin America to showcase the similarities of their situations, the first success following that encounter created a positive synergy that indicated other regional productions might also find such international acceptance. In a way, the European festival validated the entire regional "movement." For the local audience, Solanas came across in this article as virtually one of their own: a struggling filmmaker from outside the dominant cinema production machine who spoke Spanish and whose country was experiencing familiar political jostling. González's question even seemed to contain a tone of camaraderie: "What can you tell us about the experience with your film's screening at Pesaro?"[40] González's reference to "*us*" despite the presence of only one interviewer can refer to *Hablemos de cine*, Peruvians, or the journal's now multinational reading public. The questions concerning the filmmaker's origins are clearly intended to stimulate a sense of Latin American solidarity with other Latin American filmmakers in similar situations.

Detachment: Viña del Mar 1969

For the remainder of the journal's publication run over the next fifteen years, *Hablemos de cine* published an article about Latin American cinema in nearly every issue, apart from all the articles about Peruvian cinema. In some cases, they examined a particular national cinema; in others, staff members interviewed key figures within particular national movements, or reviewed a series of films that had come to Lima as part of a national cinema retrospective. At the beginning, articles were written to introduce and explore the current trends in other national cinemas. The first two explored, Cuba (vol. 34) and Brazil (vol. 35, 36, and 37), were vanguard industries that had a major presence at both the festival in 1967 and in the international film scene. By publishing considerable information about continental cinema, *Hablemos de cine* acquired a certain cachet as a regional publication as much as a Peruvian one. Even though most of the films discussed within its pages could not be seen in local theaters, the cine-club audiences that were the primary readership for the journal were still interested in what was happening regionally.

The screening of *La hora de los hornos* at Mérida, Venezuela, in 1968, however, was one of several feature-length films that collectively altered the timbre of Latin American cinema. These films were geared toward a more militant aesthetics, actively challenging through theme and the camera the predominant filmmaking techniques of European and American cinema. The Mérida festival announced a call to arms, to use "a camera like a gun" to combat what was seen as neocolonialist filmmaking practices in Latin America.

Though more efficiently organized (Francia says in his history that the mistakes in funding and organization made in the first Latin American festival were corrected for the second one), the Viña del Mar Film Festival of 1969 is primarily remembered today for solidifying more internationally the ideals of militant cinema. Even the poster for the film festival features a camera pointed directly out from the poster: though it is definitely a 16mm camera, it also strikingly resembles a pistol and a viewer looking at the poster would have to confront the "barrel" of the camera. This interpretation, however, was appropriate given the films screened, which included several significant Cuban films commemorating ten years of the Revolution, such as Tomás Gutiérrez Alea's *Memorias del subdesarrollo* (Memories of Underdevelopment, 1968) and Humberto Solás's *Lucía* (1968); Bolivian filmmaker Jorge Sanjinés's first major feature-length films *Ukamau* (That's the Way It Is, 1966) and *Yawar Mallku* (Blood of the Condor, 1969); Uruguayan Mario Handler's *Liber Arce* (1969); several major Brazilian features, such as Glauber Rocha's *O dragao da maldade contra o santo guerreiro* (Antônio-das-Mortes, 1969) and Walter Lima's *Brasil ano 2000* (Brazil, Year 2000, 1969); and a centerpiece screening of Solanas and Getino's complete three-part version of *La hora de los hornos*, which lasted four and a half hours. Though all of these films were fiercely nationalistic in expressing the situations within their own countries, a similar rejection of traditional filmmaking qualities and values—whether deliberate or simply because such equipment was painfully hard to come by throughout the region—permeated nearly all of these productions. As if to reinforce this way of thinking, participants elected Cuban documentarian Santiago Álvarez to preside over the Latin American filmmakers meeting and Che Guevara was named (in absentia) honorary president.

Bolstered by a large contingency of forty students from the Santa Fé film school, the Argentine presence and the ideas of Cine Liberación dominated much of the proceedings, particularly during the forums held among the filmmakers. Many left the festival even more firmly convinced of the benefits of militant cinema. For example, on the plane ride returning from the festival to Lima, Isaac León chatted with Colombian critic and filmmaker Carlos Álvarez, who had presented his short film *Asalto* (Assault, 1969). In the published interview that followed, Álvarez reaffirmed what he considered to be the only viable form of cinema:

> *I believe that the only possibilities for coherent Latin American filmmaking that can appropriately work against the dominant distribution system are the films being made by our comrades Mario Handler, the Venezuelans, and the [Argentine] group Cine Liberación. Their films are characterized by the use of 16mm film stock, very low budgets, and distribution in relatively small, marginalized circuits distanced from the commercial system.*[41]

Though *Hablemos de cine* presented Álvarez as the first Colombian filmmaker the journal had ever interviewed, he was not necessarily representative of national filmmaking in that country in general. Later encounters with other filmmakers, in fact, countered Álvarez's perception. Nevertheless, his position mirrored that of many filmmakers coming out of the festival, strengthened in their quest to break with dominant cinema.

A vocal minority, however, found the discussions at Viña del Mar 1969 to be frustrating owing to the decreased attention to film in favor of politics. One of the more celebrated directors of the festival, Raúl Ruiz, caused a major stir by articulating significant early dissent from the host delegation, Chile. At the 1967 festival, though Chile had showcased all of its talent through a variety of short films, the effort still had not revealed a significant film presence. This changed by 1969 when five local features were screened at the festival, three of them having made a significant impression: festival director Francia's *Valparaiso, mi amor* (Valparaiso, My Love, 1968); Miguel Littín's *El chacal de Nahueltoro* (The Jackal of Nahueltoro, 1968); and Ruiz's *Tres tigres tristes* (Three Sad Tigers, 1969), which had won a prize at the Locarno film festival and thus gave both the film and filmmaker a relatively high profile.[42] Upset and unnerved by the continuous emphasis on militancy with little regard for cinema in early discussions of the festival, Ruiz's speech, though quietly expressed, disrupted early proceedings:

> *My voice does not project well, as is true for 80 percent of Chileans. The declamatory, vague, and parliamentary manner in which things are being discussed goes against the way of being Chilean. We talk about things in a different way. Here, common ideas about imperialism and culture that can*

> *be read in any magazine are being repeated. Now Fernando Solanas comes to show us* La hora de los hornos, *which we all saw last night. We're going off to the side now to talk about film. Those of you who wish to want to do the same can join us. Oh, and we also don't like your joking with us concerning Che Guevara* [tampoco nos gusta que nos tomen 'pa'l fideo' al Che Guevara]. *That is the same as the Spanish who place a statue of San Juan Bosco on the table at all their meetings on film.*[43]

The Chilean disturbance was marked with a very nationalist tone—particularly in Ruiz's use of the Chilean expression "tomar para el fideo," meant to mean "to poke fun at somebody"—at what was intended to be a pan-national encounter.[44] The Chilean journal *Ercilla* noted that, while this incident was significant, the filmmakers eventually returned and discussions stayed more focused on issues of cinema. Ruiz's concern nonetheless echoed that of the Peruvian critics and uses virtually the same terminology as the name of the journal itself: "We're going off to the side now *to talk about film*" (*para hablar de cine*).

Ruiz's open dissatisfaction with the way events proceeded gives some indication about the direction *Hablemos de cine* would take. While the summation of the festival events in volume 50–51 (November 1969–February 1970) does not mention Ruiz's reaction, the journal also did not unequivocally embrace the ideals of the festival in the way it had in 1967. From both Francia's and the journal's accounts, there were no Peruvian films presented at this festival, but the conference was attended by three members of the journal: editor-in-chief Isaac León; Antonio González Norris, who had exclusively attended the Mérida festival; and Francisco Lombardi, the publication's newest and youngest member, who had just returned from the Santa Fé (Argentina) film school and had not yet begun to make his own films. The critics recognized the importance of a number of the festival entries and generally gave positive reviews to these films while noting the impact of their political valences. Lombardi's review of *La hora de los hornos*, for example, while noting that even at the festival only the "completely politicized aficionados" could sit through the entire length of the film, extolled the virtues of the film as being "truly new in that it does not underestimate its possible spectators . . . but rather respects, if with some difficulty, their intelligence."[45] Of the numerous Cuban films, González wrote, "Without a doubt, Cuban cinema, after ten years of revolution (and existence), has striven to succeed and has achieved its goals."[46] Only with Sanjinés's entries did the journal become critical of politics interfering too much with the narrative. Lombardi's review of *Ukamau* and *Yawar Mallku* predicted a dubious future for the Bolivian director: "[*Yawar Mallku*] ends up as demagogic as any American propaganda film as it is not supported with any wisdom and completely leaves out any aesthetic achievement. . . . From this perspective, the future work of Sanjinés should be seriously questioned. Unfortunately, the political intentions that he pretends to possess are not even remotely effective, cinematographically speaking."[47] The tone of uncertainty and disappointment with the events of the festival that can be identified in Ruiz's speech was also clearly articulated in the introductory remarks to the festival summary and the accompanying essay "Latin American Cinema in the Hour of Truth," both written by Isaac León. While the introduction provided an overview of festival activities and was generally favorable, León also pointed out how many issues raised in 1967 that the Peruvians had felt were important were now being neglected in favor of a political mentality León described as "belligerent," "radical," and "monopolizing." The following passage from the introduction is quoted at length to note both the extent of the frustrated expectations of the Peruvians as well as the tentative language used in an attempt to simultaneously associate with and obtain distance from the militant context:

> *It must be noted that on the level of theoretical debates, the results were quite useful but completely left aside the important question of distribution and circulation of Latin American films, themes that were covered in marginalized conversations. In addition, if the excitement and enthusiasm imparted on most of the interventions justify the attention received, the primary insistence on direct and exclusively political cinema might be questioned (even if all good cinema made in Latin America must be more or less political, even if it doesn't wish to be). We must take into account the concrete possibilities, the specific situations, and even the individual formulations of each Latin American director in his own context. Of course, this does not indicate any ideological disagreement with the dominant political ideology in Viña, but simply a more open form to calibrate the possibilities of our cinema in accordance with the realized experiences and the obtained results.*[48]

If the experience at Viña del Mar '67 left the Peruvians embarrassed over their position relative to the New Latin American Cinema, Viña '69 found them equally confused about whether or not they should even be part of such a movement. On the one hand, they greatly admired most of the films they witnessed at the festival, particularly when the films were measured against commercial Latin

American cinema that catered to the lowest common denominators of comedy and melodrama. The New Cinema was an exciting movement to be a part of; nonetheless, like Raúl Ruiz, *Hablemos de cine* began to suspect that perhaps the ideals of the New Cinema were a little too extreme to suit their particular concerns.

León's essay, which followed the summary, more explicitly delineated the concerns of the journal with regard to the films and events witnessed at Viña '69. Once again, the ambivalent tone indicated an unwillingness to completely reject the ideals of militant cinema. In assessing the roots of such cinema, however, León alluded to why the Peruvians would have a harder time accepting this particular mode of cinema:

> *We should note that while Cuban cinema, within the framework of a socialist state, develops in consonance with the objectives and goals of the Revolutionary Government, Brazilian Cinema Nôvo grows in tension with a politically adverse structure, and the Argentine Grupo Liberación, in its own way, is completely belligerent with the governing system of its own country. . . . In the expressions that search for an authentically national* way of being, *the individual cultural elements, tensions, and immense contradictions . . . open up the most significant range of cinema in this part of the Third World.*[49]

León proposed a logic in which militant cinema emerged either as a propagandistic vehicle for an already militant state or as a reaction to an oppressive governing entity. This dichotomy overlooks issues of political aesthetics as separate from the political realities that have inspired them; even so, such an explanation explains why Peruvian filmmaking—and its criticism, perhaps—were not really committed to the same issues as the New Latin American Cinema.[50] Whereas the filmmakers in Bolivia, Brazil, and Argentina—and later, after the fall of Allende, in exile from Chile—worked against their respective governments, in Peru, the kinds of filmmakers who opposed the Velasco government in 1969 were not interested in militant aesthetics. The few features made in 1968–1969 were popular comedies starring television personalities such as *El embajador y yo* (The Ambassador and I, Oscar Kantor). This film, as previously mentioned, was primarily impressive for showcasing the cosmopolitan nature as well as the new infrastructure of Lima during the Belaúnde administration. Velasco's government, however, was outwardly more interested in the oppressed, native populations of Peru, whose stories would have been more effectively communicated through the guerrilla filmmaking methods espoused by Cine Liberación. The military government of Peru in the late 1960s and early 1970s already held a political perspective somewhat similar to that of the militant filmmakers. The type of filmmaking that would work against that current political situation would have been closer to a polished Hollywood-style production. The contemporary Peruvian production situation therefore could not work in conjunction with revolutionary filmmaking as it was being formulated to produce the types of films embraced by the movement.

As we have seen in the introduction to the articles on Viña 1969, the journal did not necessarily dislike or fail to recognize the value of these militant films. Rather, much like some of the Chilean contingency at the festival, *Hablemos de cine* called for a plurality of film techniques and possibilities: "We do not believe that there is one single path. In principle, all valid forms will contribute to a cultural and political sensibility."[51] León avoided approaching in the article how Peru would fit into this vision of continental filmmaking. Statements such as this should not be considered a manifesto so much as an attempt to work out reasonable parameters of the Latin American film scene within which the Peruvian directors and critics could function. The political opposition that stimulated this cinematic activity in Argentina, Bolivia, and Chile would not manifest itself in Peru; in fact, it is under the Velasco military regime that the first significant law to stimulate national cinema was passed in 1972. Ironically, because Peru was not so politically unstable as its neighbors, neither its cinema nor its critics felt the impulse to resort to militant aesthetic or thematic tactics.

Hablemos de cine's write-ups of the later two festivals—Mérida in 1968, Viña del Mar in 1969—are not only significant in the material they write about, but also in what they overlook: the Peruvian presence. The articles would have the reader believe that, following the disastrous presentation of *Forjadores de mañana*, no Peruvian films were sent or invited to these festivals, but such was not the case. At both of the later festivals, Manuel Chambi and other members of the Cuzco school attended and screened a number of short documentaries, including *Estampas del Carnaval de Kanas* (Scenes from the Kanas Carnival), the short-film festival winner from back in 1965.[52] The eliding of a Peruvian presence is significant and may have been caused by any number of reasons. For one, both of the later festivals were dominated by the presence of feature-length films and few short films (other than the Cuban ones) were mentioned in the summaries. As shall be highlighted in the next chapter, Peruvian cinematic output at this point was almost exclusively in the form of short films. The shorts screened at the festival may have also been overlooked because they had already been seen by Peruvian audiences, but this is unlikely given the journal's previous reexamination of *Forjadores de mañana* following Viña del Mar 1967. The most probable—albeit disturbing—revelation is that the journal ignored the other Peruvian films because they came from Cuzco. The journal's staff had been particularly damning toward the Cuzco school's sophomore feature effort *Jarawi* (1966) and that film's box-office and critical failure led to no further filmmaking efforts from primary director Manuel Chambi.[53] As such, the editors likely viewed these older films as attempts at Peruvian filmmaking that were no longer part of the vanguard of Peruvian cinema. Lacking another presence or possibility for a more *limeño*-oriented filmmaker, the journal continued what may be seen as its somewhat racist tendency (characteristic of elite white society in Lima). While subtle at this point in the journal's publication trajectory, this racism would become more pronounced with the feature releases of *limeño* Francisco Lombarda and *cusqueño* Federico García in the late 1970s.[54]

The stance articulated by *Hablemos de cine* marked the beginning of the publication's isolation from the rest of the region's cinematic activities. Part of this dissociation was due to the volatile nature of the political and cinematic movements within Latin America. For example, though a third encounter of Latin American filmmakers was planned for Viña del Mar, economics and politics resulted in the festival's tentative move to Santiago and a postponement until 1973. By the time work was under way to bring back the festival to Viña in December 1973, Augusto Pinochet had taken over the Chilean government, and the festival eventually migrated permanently to Havana in 1979, where the major Latin American film festival continues to exist.[55] Thus, between 1969 and 1973, no major encounter was held between filmmakers on Latin American soil—and by then, many were exiled in Europe and were now meeting one another and making films there, some of them permanently. Although Peruvian filmmakers had started to flourish following the cinematic law of 1972, neither films nor filmmakers traveled outside Peru. Even if they had, Peruvian filmmaking during this period never truly reflected the aesthetic or thematic concerns embraced by the more revolutionary—and thereby recognized—Latin American filmmakers that achieved a certain international status. While Federico García's work in the early 1980s (such as *Laulico*, 1980, and *El caso Huayanay*, 1981) is reminiscent of Sanjinés's work, no Peruvian film was seen to have the politicized filmmaking techniques or themes that characterized much of the New Latin American Cinema until 1984's *Miss Universo en el Perú* (Miss Universe in Peru, Grupo Chaski).[56]

Latin American Cinema Beyond the Festivals: Responses to Cuban Cinema

Though Peruvian cinema itself was somewhat isolated from the goings-on in the rest of the region, *Hablemos de cine* continued to be interested in Latin America. Because *Hablemos de cine* remained in print nearly fifteen years following Viña del Mar 1969, it had the unique opportunity to observe the progression of New Latin American filmmaking over an extended period of time. The journal's longevity allowed it to establish trajectories of various cinemas and revisit filmmakers to compare situations over a period of time. Nearly every issue from March 1967 to the final issue in 1984 contained at least one important article discussing some aspect of Latin American cinema. In addition to devoting space to the "major" continental producers of Argentina, Brazil, and Mexico, significant articles also concentrated on Bolivia, Chile, Cuba, Colombia, Uruguay, and Venezuela; there is even one small two-page article in volume 63 (1972) that proclaimed "Paraguayan Cinema exists!"[57] The journal made its commitment to Latin American cinema clear in the introductory comments to an interview with Cuban cineaste Alfredo Guevara in volume 34 (March-April 1967):

> Hablemos de cine *begins here a section the long omission of which has concerned us greatly. We have always considered it a priority to report on filmmaking in our neighboring countries that—paradoxically—we know little to nothing about. Only the opportunity to attend Viña del Mar and afterward travel to Argentina, Uruguay, and Brazil has allowed us to give this the full attention it deserves. This section will be made up entirely of primary source material: interviews, exclusive articles by our correspondents or from colleagues (usually the most respected critics in their individual countries), etc. Our readers can therefore continually observe the singular and common concerns from cinema from the tumultuous continent to which we belong.*[58]

Although Peru and its film culture developed differently from other Latin American countries, the journal's status as a significant regional publication grew, thanks to the extended coverage of other cinemas in the region. The constant comparisons with film situations at home also broadened the cinematic knowledge of readers in Lima, who would be otherwise unaware of these regional trends.

Following the festival, *Hablemos de cine* paid significant attention to Cuban cinema, the only Latin American cinematic tradition given more coverage in the journal than the Peruvian. Reactions to Cuban cinema contrast with writings in another major Latin American film journal, *Cine cubano*.[59] There are a number of significant differences between the two journals, starting with funding. Whereas *Hablemos de cine* was an independent publication almost entirely dependent on subscriptions and sales of individual copies, *Cine cubano* was founded (and funded) as the official publication of the ICAIC (Instituto Cubano de Artes e Industrias Cinematográficas), itself an official cultural arm of the Cuban government. A sample issue—volume #103 from 1982, for example—includes statements by Gabriel García Márquez denouncing the judges at the Cannes film festival for not selecting the Cuban (and sole Latin American) entry *Cecilia*, directed by Humberto Solás, for any prize; an interesting study of what Cuban audiences actually like watching onscreen; and an essay defending the entire "New Latin American Cinema" project as not being redundant, written by Ambrosio Fornet.[60] This last piece in particular demonstrates the interdependence between the motivation and ideals of the New Latin American Cinema and Cuban cinema in particular; ensuring that the ideals of the continental project would not be lost while maintaining the relevance of local, Cuban production.

Hablemos de cine chose to start with examining Cuban cinema primarily because the short film *Manuela* won the top prize at the 1967 Viña del Mar festival. Following the festival notes and an interview with festival director Francia, volume 34 continued with an interview with Alfredo Guevara, the president of the ICAIC. Although fully aware of the impact and implications of the Cuban Revolution itself, editors Isaac León and Federico de Cárdenas seemed ignorant of more specific aspects of the ICAIC. Such unawareness was common in many of these first explorations of Latin American cinema, which were investigatory in nature, striving to learn about cinematic contexts with which the editors had no previous contact. Their questions demonstrate a curiosity about Cuban cinema before the Revolution to establish what basis there might have been for a historical trajectory, but Guevara dismisses any notion of pre-Castro national cinema.[61] (This deprecation might be compared with *Hablemos de cine*'s constant referral to the 1960s as the "beginning" of Peruvian national cinema, completely overlooking the efforts of Amauta Films and others in the late 1930s.) Guevara instead spends a large portion of the interview talking about the contemporary state of film and how the ICAIC and their films fit within the overall social and political mechanism, both in terms of creating films as well as distributing them. Guevara discusses the importance of *El mégano* (The Charcoal Worker, 1958), a short documentary about a group of farmers who became coal miners: almost all the major contemporary players within the Cuban industry were involved in making the film including future directors Julio García Espinosa, Tomás Gutiérrez Alea, and Santiago Álvarez.

The journal published a more complex treatment of Cuban cinema at the occasion of a retrospective screened in Lima in 1970, commemorating (a few years late) the tenth anniversary of the Cuban Revolution. *Hablemos de cine* devoted more than half of the contents of volume 54 (July–August 1970) to the wide variety of films screened for the Peruvian public. The published retrospective featured different types of articles that were commonly used in the journal's examinations of other Latin American cinemas. Each film was reviewed by one of the Peruvian staff members and was accompanied by either an interview or an article by the filmmaker that was reprinted from another source. The reprints were taken from other respected publications: in this case, *Cine cubano* (Alfredo Guevara's "Cuban Cinema at Age 10," Tomás Gutiérrez Alea's "*Memories of Underdevelopment*: Working Notes," Enrique Pineda Barnet's "*David*: Method or Attitude?") and the Spanish journal *Nuestro cine* (Pablo Mariñez's interview with Humberto Solás). The remaining interviews were written by the Peruvian staff members, conducted overseas during the previous year: while studying in Europe, de Cárdenas had interviewed Jorge Fraga and Manuel Octavio Gómez in Pesaro, Italy; León had interviewed Octavio Cortázar on a trip to Santiago, Chile.

The introduction reiterated the significance of the event for local Peruvian audiences as well for the identity of the journal itself:

> *The recent display of Cuban cinema in Lima has cleared up the unknown, satisfied curiosities, and filled the expectations of film aficionados, political militants, and aficionado-militants in some way. . . . Made with a collective sensibility, [Cuban cinema] has struggled and continues to struggle to find a new public and to create a conscience that is both revolutionary and cinematic. To that end, as the Cuban filmmakers themselves say, film plays a double role as an active participant in the process of transformation as well as a reviewer of that process. Thus, the general popular perception of film has changed as they discover many possibilities that cinema can offer, particularly as it documents the first historic stage, observing the most immediate possibilities and resources.*[62]

Note that in the above passage the emphasis is still on the cinematic, but now the journal notes the connection between the cinematic and the political and that, at least with the Cuban question, the two can coexist. As a whole, the journal found merit in virtually all of the films screened at the retrospective. Isaac León called Humberto Solás's monumental triptych *Lucía* (1968), which chronicles the life of three women in three different periods of Cuban history, "the most expressively ambitious Cuban film . . . for its longitude covering three storylines, for its attempt at different styles, and for its historical breadth."[63] Jorge Fraga's historical encounter *La odisea del general José* (General José's Odyssey, 1968), which revisits the story of a revolutionary who fought in the jungle during the struggle for independence from Spain in the 1890s, received lavish praise from Nelson García, who said the film "successfully accomplishes its task [of vindicating the past as part of the Revolution] with dignity and simplicity."[64] García also extolled the virtues of the three short documentaries by Octavio Cortázar shown in Lima: *Por primera vez* (For the First Time, 1967), about a community just being introduced to cinema by the *cine-móvil*, or mobile cinemas; *Acerca de un personaje que unos llaman San Lázaro y otros llaman Babalú* (Concerning a Person Some Call St. Lazarus and Others Call Babalú, 1968), about a religious figure worshipped both within the Cuban Catholic and the Afro-Cuban religious cultures; and *Al sur de Maniadero* (To the South of Maniadero, 1969), recording a hunting expedition for crocodiles meant for the national zoo. In his summary, García called Cortázar "a filmmaker who renews and adapts himself with each successive film."[65]

For different reasons, the more enlightening reviews were Juan Bullitta's opinionated reaction to all the Cuban films shown in the retrospective-revealed in his review of *Memorias del subdesarrollo*-and Desiderio Blanco's examination of *La primera carga al machete* (The First Charge by Machete, Manuel Octavio Gómez, 1969) and *David* (Enrique Pineda Barnet, 1967). As he was the elder statesman, always well versed in international critical trends, Blanco's relating the use of mise-en-scène in two films to a larger context should come as little surprise:

> *According to the latest theories espoused by* Cahiers [du cinéma], *this would be a way of destroying the* impression of reality *produced by the nature of the film image, impregnated with bourgeois ideology and an alienating force. Nevertheless, we can see in* David *that this method accentuates the* impression of reality *of the world. . . . In* La primera carga al machete, *on the other hand, some stylistic concerns emphasize the* impression of reality, *while others destroy it completely. . . . The incorporation of these novelties gives Cuba a distinctive profile within Third World cinema, but has not managed to bring it all together into a creative whole.*[66]

Blanco's analysis of these two films acknowledged contemporary French criticism's interest in the militant nature of stylistic elements in "new cinema." For *Cahiers*, the emphasis on larger political implications of the film medium began with a shift of focus away from mainstream cinema, a shift announced as early as 1968.[67] While he recognized their attempts to comprehend a universal aesthetics of Third Cinema, Blanco's criticism disagreed with the universality implied by such theories, reflecting the journal's overall sentiments following Viña del Mar 1969.

At the opposite end of the spectrum of reviews lay Juan Bulllitta's assessment of *Memorias del subdesarrollo*. Though it had not yet received the international attention that would follow the U.S. government's refusal to allow Gutiérrez Alea to receive the National Society of Critics' special prize in 1974, the film had already garnered substantial praise from its premiere at the Pesaro film festival in 1968; hence, its status as an important film merited the placement of its review at the beginning of the journal's section on Cuban film.[68] As such, Bullitta's comments were the first to be presented in the journal's coverage of the retrospective. While none of the other individual reviews in the retrospective were overtly negative, in order to praise Gutiérrez Alea's film, Bullitta first examined what he considered to be the several missteps in experimental filmmaking in Cuban cinema. After postulating that "[*u*]*rgency* and *participation* would be the most accurate words to characterize the efforts of the last ten years of Cuban cinema," he continued by criticizing what he considered the overblatant political nature of the films' aesthetics:

> *This urgency particularly denotes—or, better said, determines—a dangerous accumulative character of various experimental forms, whose automatic and precipitous appearance is obvious to even a minimally impartial observer. This is exemplified in the stylistic diversity and treatment of an important production such as* Lucía, *whose three successive explorations of women in Cuban history do not begin to justify . . . the true meandering and stylistic dabbling that . . . condemns the narrative to lose its unity, to depreciate its overall merit by schematizing reality according to brilliant but questionable ideals . . . and to make superficial the value of the experiments in and of themselves by merely presenting them in rapid succession.*[69]

Bullitta's negative perspective (this is not the only time that Bullitta would vocally proclaim himself in disagreement with the rest of the group) at the beginning established the mistaken impression that the journal was at odds with the Cuban cinematic project; indeed, the remaining reviews were positive. Nonetheless, the relationship between the Peruvian and Cuban ideals was fairly uneasy, even marked by skepticism. Despite the leftist political climate of 1970 following the 1968 coup by General Alberto Velasco, the Cubans regarded the Peruvian journal with some misgivings, perhaps because the Peruvians were not so firmly committed as other cinematic publications to the ideals of militant "new" cinema.

Eleven years later, in July 1981, the recently formed Cinemateca de Lima screened a series of films in conjunction with the Cuban embassy, providing another opportunity to discuss and compare that country's cinema. The public reception of these films in Lima, however, was significantly cooler. The journal faulted the Cinemateca for screening the films in two large movie theaters, the Bijou and the Conquistador, when one of the smaller auditoriums used by other cine-clubs might have been a better option. Though seven films were screened, the retrospective only takes up seven pages of volume 75 (May 1982), which amounts to less than 10 percent of the total issue. (Compare this with more than thirty-five pages used in volume 54.) None of the films screened were recently produced, most of them being from five or seven years earlier: along with Gutiérrez Alea's *La última cena* (The Last Supper, 1976) and *Los sobreviventes* (The Survivors, 1979), the retrospective screened Sergio Giral's *Rancheador* (Rancher, 1977) and *Maluala* (1979) along with Sara Gómez's *De cierta manera* (One Way or Another, 1974) and Pastor Vega's *Retrato de Teresa* (Portrait of Teresa, 1979). León noted the timing of the screening in Lima "coincided with a fallow period in Cuban cinema, both in terms of volume and what could be called the accomplished results."[70]

Elsewhere in the same issue, a surprisingly in-depth examination of Venezuelan cinema—including interviews with directors Roman Chalbaud, Carlos Rebollado, Mauricio Wallerstein, and Uruguayan exile Mario Handler, who was now working within the Venezuelan system—highlights the decreased attention given to Cuban cinema. The marked difference in the reception of these films from that of nearly a decade earlier, however, introduced bigger questions about the continental project a whole: "Unlike the earlier retrospective [of Cuban cinema], this one did not encounter the expected reception, which has had the effect of putting the Cinemateca de Lima in serious [economic] debt. It also makes you ask yourself whether the 'boom' of Latin American cinema is already over, and whether Cuban cinema . . . no longer has the lure of the prohibited or the revolutionary aura that it had at another time."[71] For the first time, *Hablemos de cine* seriously questioned the longevity of the New Cinema, a movement the journal had embraced (along with most other Latin American critics) upon its "discovery" in 1967. By this point, however, the movement was losing its vibrancy. With a vested interest in communicating with their Latin American compatriots, the Cubans seemed most attuned to the stylistic diversification called for by the Peruvians in order to interest audiences abroad. Unfortunately, the scant number of films produced in Cuba in the early 1980s exposed signs of economic and artistic stagnation within that country.

The issue also provided an interesting interview with Manuel Octavio Gómez, who had also been interviewed by *Hablemos de cine* in 1970 in Pesaro. Though he did not have a film presented at the retrospective, Gómez was accompanying the films and granted an interview to Federico de Cárdenas and Isaac León in Lima. His first interview concentrated on questions about his most recent film, *La primera carga al machete*, but also provided considerable insight about how Cuban filmmakers came into their own:

> *Before the triumph of the Revolution, I was part of a cine-club. It was a minor group that was a subsidiary of a larger group: the "Nuestro Tiempo" [Our Time] cine-club, associated with the Socialist Popular Party, the Cuban Communist Party of the time. . . . Once the Revolution succeeded, a whole group of the cine-club became part of the Ministry of Culture of the Rebel Army, which organized activities such as mounting theatrical works, designing book covers, and making movies. That is how I became an assistant director, making some of the first documentaries to be made in Cuba.*[72]

In the "reencounter" twelve years later, while they still asked about his work, the editors relied on Gómez for broader information about the current state of the Cuban industry, beginning by asking how national cinema had changed in the three years since they had last spoken with Cuban filmmaker Manuel Pérez.[73] After Gómez listed the ICAIC projects in production at the time, the questions turned to the industry in general. By this point, however, Peru had begun to develop its own slate of films and filmmakers and, while their success was achieved in a completely different political and economic situation, the Peruvians' questions compared the two industries. For example, in 1982 Peru was still producing a great number of short films thanks to the Film Law of 1972. It was only natural that they asked about the production of short fiction films in contemporary Cuba. Gómez replied that, while newsreels were still being produced, "the fictional short has been left behind. It's strange, but it never really took off. There was a moment when it was needed to promote new filmmakers . . . but then it seems that the short had no outlet, not even on television."[74] Though this may have been the case in Cuba, it was not so in Peru, where experiments with short fiction film were limited, or in Colombia, whose more successful experience had already been documented by the journal.[75]

The interview with Gómez concluded with two questions concerning how the stature of Cuban cinema seemed to have declined considerably by the early 1980s. Gómez defends his position within the cinema, but also admits that the traveling Cuban retrospective of ten years earlier was not even being organized at home:

> —*Someone should do a retrospective of these last 20 years of Cuban cinema . . .*
>
> —*But it hasn't even been done in Cuba. All the material is carefully under lock and key, it's not as if there is any danger that this cinematic history will be lost. . . . Without a doubt, it would be interesting to make such a retrospective. I think that there are films that age better and worse than others. For example, Tomás Gutiérrez Alea's* Death of a Bureaucrat, *which has just played very well in the United States but when it was originally released did not obtain the attention it deserved.*
>
> —*In that sense, don't you think that Cuban cinema resonates less vibrantly during these last few years as compared with the 60s?*
>
> —*No, I don't think so. Cuban cinema has pushed forward and has made some impressive accomplishments. It's true that you can't untangle the problems that our cinema faces from the problems that our country has. As such, the quality of production has gone down somewhat. What also occurs—and it just has to be said—is that certain critics, slaves to fashion, pay less and less attention to Cuban cinema, going so far as to bury their previous engagement with it.*[76]

This last line is somewhat barbed and possibly directed toward the *hablemistas* themselves, who, as Latin American critics, had stepped back from their veneration of the Cuban paradigm. It is significant that, while *Hablemos de cine* covered a number of international film events in Europe throughout the late 1970s and early 1980s, it chose not to publish any information about the burgeoning Havana Film Festival, started in 1979 and quickly coming to international prominence over the course of the 1980s. The growing importance of the festival combined with an increasing number of international films shown on local screens was a fantastic boon for Cuban cinematic culture; nonetheless, Cuban films from this period had neither the intense revolutionary nature nor the comparably high quality of their predecessors. Michael Chanan notes that the rest of the region's successful attempts at filmmaking assured that Cuban cinema "would be judged in the direct and often highly challenging light of films coming from all over Latin America."[77]

Taking the three issues' treatment of Cuban cinema as a trajectory, *Hablemos de cine*'s coverage therefore fairly accurately represents the declining international influence of and interest in Cuban cinema. Gómez's last comments nevertheless highlight how *Hablemos de cine* may also have contributed to this decreased stature. Emphasizing a newer trend coming forward from a minor national cinema—as the emphasis on Venezuelan cinema in volume 75 may indicate—over the historically important yet dwindling Cuban cinema is precisely what Gómez criticizes in his interview. In doing so, *Hablemos de cine* confirmed its own status as a major arbiter of Latin American regional filmmaking, functioning as an international barometer of reception during an important, fertile period.

CHAPTER 5
FOR A FEW MINUTES
Considering the Short-Film Industry

> *The method of learning the practice of filmmaking in our country has been exclusively the short film, which is the medium where all of the feature filmmakers of today have come from.*
>
> —FEDERICO DE CÁRDENAS AS PART OF A ROUNDTABLE ON PERUVIAN CINEMA, IN *HABLEMOS DE CINE* (JUNE 1981)

At the dawn of cinema, all films were "short," no more than ten minutes or the length of one reel. The short film was simply another part of an entertainment program descended from vaudeville that also featured newsreels, cartoons, and live performances. Eventually, narratives lengthened to cover several reels to become the "feature film" and short-film exhibition was relegated to exhibition on television and at elite film festivals.[1] In the process, film criticism has given almost exclusive attention to the feature-length film, roughly regarded as anything longer than seventy minutes. There is no obvious answer as to why this is so, perhaps stemming from film criticism's origins in literary criticism, where an author's larger written works (novels, plays, and the like) are still privileged over shorter writing. Short writing has generally been regarded as a vehicle for experimentation, an alternate to the assumed canonical complexities of larger works. Nevertheless, the short story is still recognized as a genre in and of itself, a type of fiction that requires different talents from the novel and has its own set of prominent craftspeople, such as Katherine Anne Porter, Raymond Carver, and Julio Cortázar.[2]

While literary studies has created a space (if marginalized) for the study of shorter works, cinema studies has largely ignored the short film.[3] Indeed, by the time cinema studies came into being in the 1960s, the short film had already long been seen as little more than a supplement to a feature presentation. Someone reads a short story for the sake of the story itself, even if it is packaged as part of a collection or featured in a magazine; rarely does a spectator enter a theater for the sole purpose of screening a single short. Because most filmgoers are paying an entrance or viewing fee to watch films, a short film might be seen by the general viewer as too small or too experimental of a narrative for the money. Nevertheless, the short has often been an important first step for directors in the filmmaking process, precisely because its length renders financing its production less prohibitive.

The funding issue has enabled the short film to become key to the development of emergent national cinemas worldwide. Such development occurred in Peru when the Film Law of 1972 spawned a small, lucrative industry devoted exclusively to shorts. It is worth noting here that I have up until this point used the phrase "Peruvian film *tradition*" while avoiding the more commonly used "Peruvian film *industry*." Douglas Gomery notes: "in most of the world cinema is first of all organized as an industry, that is as a collection of businesses seeking profits through film production, film distribution, and the presentation of movies to audience."[4] Within this definition, the issue of *collectivity*, the notion that a group of film-production businesses together form a sustained economic grouping, prevents us from talking about a Peruvian film *industry*. Put quite simply, there has never been enough feature film production to sustain any collection of film-oriented business on feature films alone; if any have succeeded in remaining solvent for a period of time, these businesses have tended to operate independently and literally from film to film, generating neither sufficient product nor profit to be considered a viable "industry." Short films, however, are a completely different story: following the Film Law of 1972, literally hundreds of film companies sprang up to produce films that they knew would make a profit, thanks to a circuit of "obligatory exhibition" that every film was subjected to.

Though it eventually cannibalized itself by the early 1980s through sheer numbers and a lack of quality control, the short-film process allowed several directors to begin their craft and develop their confidence so that substantial feature film production emerged as early as five years after the law's inception. The group of directors that started making films during this period have been called "the Lombardi generation" after the most recognizable and influential feature film director this experiment produced. As a legitimate, serious film publication, *Hablemos de cine* did not initially regard short cinema as a valid medium for study, devoting only a few early articles to the format. The massive amount of product resulting from the Film Law of 1972, however, left the journal with no choice but to seriously consider short films[5] within the context of a nascent Peruvian cinema.

Hablemos de cine and the Short-Film Contest of 1965

Early on, *Hablemos de cine* studied short films made in Peru as an important step in examining the concept of national cinema. One of the first major cinematic events that *Hablemos de cine* participated in was a local short-film contest and festival sponsored by the Casa de la Cultura del Perú in July 1965. The publication was still only a few months into mimeographed publication and the editors were still considered little more than "young upstarts" without any real credentials (this explains why they were not involved in either the administration or the judging of this contest). Though it was hoped that the contest would spark activity and interest in filmmaking within Peru, the contest was an isolated event that had little impact on national cinema development. This interaction was nevertheless one of the few times that the journal chose to focus on the short-film format and reveals why examining short films is relevant when looking at developing national cinemas.

Coverage of the contest occupied most of volume 12 (July 31, 1965), complete with an editorial emphasizing its importance, reviews of some of the films screened, and an interview with one of the winners. In retrospect, the event is presented through the writing as something much bigger than it was: as *Hablemos de cine*'s authors readily observe in the editorial, other local press did not cover the contest, nor was it greatly advertised. The films themselves were not prime examples with exceptionally high production values, resulting in a lukewarm reception from the local audience. Evidence for this can be found in the convoluted phrasing used in some of the reviews, where the inexperienced editors painstakingly searched to find good things to say. For example, about Wenceslao Molina's *Ayacucho and Holy Week*: "A documentary that achieves the goal set in the title, though somewhat conventionally. Its vision is cold, contrasting with the fervent and sometimes jarring regionalist narration we heard."[6]

This lack of experience also contributed to a somewhat skewed, incomplete, and subjective coverage of the festival. The journal admitted to having not caught the first day of screenings (which was apparently not advertised) and tried to excuse their naïveté by noting that the films were shown back-to-back, with little time for anyone to take sufficient notes. (The end of the section of reviews mentions that they believed their reviews to be more "informative" than "critical.")[7] Nevertheless, the four editors[8] recognized that the festival, as the first of its kind to be held in Lima, must be shown support if local filmmaking were to begin in earnest in Peru. For them, attendance at the festival signified support for a larger project that this festival was meant to inspire: "A good phrase to summarize our impression of the festival would be 'Peruvian cinema in the works.'"[9] The journal *did* recognize, particularly as there were no feature films to write about, that short films indicated the first steps toward future, larger projects. Throughout the summaries of the festival, the editors stressed the nationalist aspect of the event: "We promised to attend the festival as, without a doubt, it meant taking the pulse of and confronting the current state of *our* cinema."[10] Though few of the films showed the beginning of national cinema, the participants had hopes for both the contest ("we applaud the idea of repeating this event next year") and the expected industry to follow ("It is not too optimistic to trust that 'in the future, Peruvian and Brazilian cinema can and will be at the forefront of Latin American cinema,' to quote César Villanueva, director of *Kukuli* [1961] and *Jarawi* [1966]").[11] Such expectations were overconfident: the festival did not return the following year, nor did Peru ever develop an industry even close in stature to the Brazilian.

Among other things, the journal recognized the importance of establishing relationships with the other filmmakers at the festival. The festival winner, *cusqueño* César Villanueva, who made *Estampas del Caranaval de Kanas* (Scenes from the Kanas Carnival) along with co-director Eulogio Nishiyama, granted a lengthy interview that *Hablemos de cine* indicated it would publish later, though this never occurred.[12] Instead, the festival notes were accompanied by an available interview with the second-place winner, Jorge Volkert, who had directed a short entitled *Forjadores de mañana* (Forgers of Tomorrow), which received a relatively glowing review from the journal upon its first screening. The interview with Volkert was equally amicable, which might be due to the fact that, as the introduction stated, he was "more than a stranger, but rather a friend of *Hablemos de cine*."[13] The staff also admitted that there were very few "good" films shown at the festival, so that it was relatively easy for both the judges and the staff to agree on the winners.

Choosing to focus on *Forjadores de mañana* becomes fortuitous for the journal in that it happened also to be the only film that would eventually travel to the Viña del Mar film festival in 1967. There, filmmakers from around the region were exposed for the first time to each other's work and the situations in which their films were made. Viewed alongside other, more sophisticated films, however, *Forjadores* was seen as a disaster that left the Peruvians ashamed. Villanueva's boastful statement that Peru would "lead the way with Brazil" in the arena of Latin American cinema proved to be a gross overstatement by the editors.[14]

Semilla

Hablemos de cine did not review or even discuss short films for another two and a half years. The next short discussed, however, was a major undertaking: volume 38 (November–December 1967) featured a large article called "Chronicle of a Film Shoot: One Million Eyes (Men on the Lake)" (*Crónica de rodaje: 1,000,000 de ojos [hombres del lago]*)." The article is an in-depth investigation of the day-to-day activities of Pablo Guevara's short film *Semilla* (*Seed*), a unique, personal retrospective of Third World filmmaking written by *Hablemos* editor, Juan M. Bullitta.

Filmed long before the rise of the short-film industry inspired by the Film Law of 1972 but following the journal's encounter at the Viña del Mar film festival in 1967, the film combined elements of documentary and fiction filmmaking in telling the story of a young boy and his father as he first prepares for a folkloric dance event, only to find out the truth about his mother's death.[15] Cited early in the publication run as the most eager of the four founding members to create films rather than just critique them, Juan Bullitta finally got his opportunity by acting as assistant director to Guevara on *Semilla*. "Chronicle of a Film Shoot" detailed his privileged, inside perspective on the making of this short. Somewhat verbose in his reviews, Bullitta's poetic writing style here accentuates the unique quality of this chronicle, offering a perspective otherwise invisible both to the *limeño* reading public and to filmmakers abroad. This writing exercise combined elements of a general travelogue, a filmmaker's diary, and instructions for making a film in Peru in the 1960s.

Bullitta began with a description of Puno, the locale chosen for shooting the film. A city high in the mountains, on the border with Bolivia at Lake Titicaca, this would have been a well-known geographical location for most *limeños*, though unlikely to have been visited by the reading public.[16] Trying to present an objective perspective, Bullitta wrote as both an eloquent tour guide ("The great monotony of this landscape, its horizontal straightness, its flatness, can drown a man born in the sensual and cynical cities founded by the Spanish conquistador near the pool of the Pacific") and a filmmaker-in-training ("Too much light [ideal, on the other hand, for our job]").[17] Informing the readers of the components of the filmmaking crew and then the differences between the nature of documentary and fiction films, Bullitta explored how this particular film could be viewed within the construction of New Cinema as seen at the Viña del Mar festival:

> *We insist that Peru should look to documentaries as a first step to more complex or ambitious productions in the field of narrative development. We find an example in [Brazilian]* Cinema Nôvo, *to cite one tradition particularly similar to ours. Such cinema will discipline our filmmakers. Their films confront a complex, fascinating reality that permits them to practice directing natural elements as basic vehicles in fictional cinema. In a new cinema like ours, necessarily tied to reality, we must avoid the external details of improbability that contribute to a false sense of cinema. I believe that instead we would prefer to be authentic. For example, César Miró's grandson turning into a ghettoized child, overstylized in Robles Godoy's* En la selva no hay estrellas.[18]

On one hand, Bullitta is never overcritical of either the filmmaking process or the film itself, naturally being too attached to it as a member of its crew. At the same time, his observations are colored and contextualized by his prior experience as a critic, taking a stab once again at the constant Peruvian auteur-in-the-worst-sense Robles Godoy.

Bullitta made several assertions based on his experience about the potential nature of national cinema. As noted above, he favored initial training in aspects of documentary filmmaking. (Colombian director Carlos Mayolo would later note in volume 72 [November 1980] that most Peruvian shorts that followed the Film Law of 1972 were indeed documentaries whereas the majority of Colombian films resulting from a similar law there were based in fiction: "I have noticed greater care [by the Peruvians] in narrative construction, more detailed scripts and production professionalism.")[19] Bullitta also commented on Peruvian geography as a valuable asset in the development of national cinema:

> *After having traveled and filmed in only one region of a Peruvian province, I can affirm that our cinema does not need studios with high-priced sets and scenarios. The chaotic, exuberant geography of the country constitutes more of a generous, rich variety of natural settings than we could possibly*

> *imagine. Peruvian filmmaking, taking advantage of the ever-advancing techniques of filming, must prioritize the external qualities, in the beauty of the Peruvian landscapes. . . . An earthy world that will shake the content of the first "greats" American cinema offers (Walsh, Ford, Vidor, etc.), still virgin to the world's cameras. We should be the first to reveal the physical nature of our fatherland. The ideal motto for national cinema should be: Peru as a film set.*[20]

Although *Hablemos de cine* was explicitly dedicated to criticism and not necessarily aspects of production, it is still somewhat surprising that this was the only production experience offered to its audience (particularly because potential filmmakers from Peru were also likely to be cine-club members interested in the critical perspective of the journal). For example, the journal does not go on set with any of the feature productions, including those of their colleague Francisco Lombardi. Bullitta's account remains one of the only first-person published perspectives of filmmaking practice in Peru—and in Latin America—in the late 1960s.

The fanfare attributed by *Hablemos de cine* to *Semilla* upon its release a year later was unprecedented for a short film, but not so surprising considering that both Bullitta and Guevara were *hablemistas* themselves. It is also no surprise to find that, when the film was eventually completed, the journal reviewed the film, breaking an unarticulated precedent of not writing about short films. César Linares's review in volume 45 (January–February 1969) was published under the section of reviews called "En pocas palabras" (In brief), where the longest reviews are only allotted a half-page of space. The tone of the review is naturally adulatory:

> *Pablo Guevara's* Semilla *widens the panorama of our meager, checkered cinema. In 1969, the film is most significant regarding future possibilities concerning how to* view *our situation. His film does not attempt to reinvent the wheel, but it demonstrates that it is possible to abandon the old, ingenious folklorism and esoteric formalism. . . . The film is, along with Chambi's* Estampas del Carnaval de Kanas *[*sic*], the best film made in Peru up until now—and that includes the features. And by saying that, I am neither exaggerating nor being a fanatic.*[21]

Although surely Guevara's colleagues at *Hablemos de cine* were proud of and excited by his accomplishment, Linares's comment that the film was the best that Peruvian film had to offer is not so outlandish, particularly given the examples of national cinema at the time. Since the journal's beginning, the Peruvian films made were either beset with overartistic auteurist characteristics (the first two films by Armando Robles Godoy), embarrassing co-productions (*Intimidad de los parques*) or, most recently, low-quality comedy vehicles for television stars (*El embajador y yo*).[22] As a member of the journal's staff, Guevara was aware of (even if he didn't necessarily agree with)[23] the ideas about national cinema that concerned *Hablemos de cine* and, in the process, the very cine-club audience to which the journal catered and before whom his film would eventually be screened. (The review noted that the film was screened at the Cine Arte club affiliated with the Universidad de San Marcos.) It is therefore logical that, in the journal's eyes, Guevara would produce *exactly* what the journal was looking for in a national film, even if such a film was not a feature.

Short-Film Production Following the Film Law of 1972

Semilla, *Forjadores de mañana*, and *Estampas del Carnaval de Kanas* were only considered at all by *Hablemos de cine* because they represented what the journal considered to be quality Peruvian filmmaking, a standard that features like *Jarawi* and *En la selva no hay estrellas* did not live up to. Even these very brief parlays into short films only further served to indicate that Peruvian films remained isolated events unconnected to a larger sense of "national cinema." Despite significantly more impressive technical and narrative abilities that were acknowledged by critics familiar with the cine-club scene, none of these shorts would or could be seen by enough Peruvian spectators to create a momentum of interest in pictures beyond the popular comedies that used their television stars to draw substantial box office.[24]

The Film Law of 1972 radically changed the landscape of Peruvian exhibition and filmmaking by mandating that every commercially screened non-Peruvian feature must be accompanied by a nationally produced short. In addition, each film (short of feature) would go through a circuit of "obligatory exhibition" (*exhibición obligatorio*), traveling through all theaters within Peru.[25] The law was sharply criticized by many (including, initially, those at *Hablemos de cine*) as placing too much of an emphasis on the commercial aspect of filmmaking, noting that the provision that stimulated the short-film industry only served to give money to the producers, not the filmmakers themselves. Nevertheless, the law suddenly guaranteed an exhibition space beyond the elite film festival or cine-club crowd that, at least in principle, was geared also to ensure future production. At the same time, it assured a market even for experiments in filmmaking, allowing many filmmakers to try something new and even fail with a film as part of a learning process. As such, the program functioned as a de facto film school in a location where none existed.

Although it provided for a regulatory commission (COPROCI, the Cinematic Production Commission), the law did not specify how films should be approved; nor did it make any provisions for quality or content of such films. Ultimately deciding to accept virtually all the short films produced in the first few years, this process unfortunately resulted in widespread corruption: the large majority of these short films were quickly and poorly produced and released to theaters while their profits were not recycled into the creation of more films, which is what the law was originally intended to support. Because a large amount of truly abysmal product went into the system, the public generally viewed short films as an annoyance, separate from—and always inferior to—the feature film experience; "quality" shorts therefore suffered by being associated with the negative stigma.

Though short-film production started to increase within the first year following the law's passage, *Hablemos de cine* did not immediately react to the beginning of the short-film explosion. In addition to the relative disdain for short films already discussed, the journal by this point was going through a number of economic and staff-oriented difficulties that resulted in its periodicity being slowed down to an annual rate of publication. Because the number of shorts produced per year grew so rapidly, it became impossible for the journal to track and review each individual film. Such delayed frequency in publication, however, did permit the journal to begin to track certain filmmaking trends and gave it a tremendous amount of product from which to choose their topics of general discussion.

Volume 67 (1974) exposed some of the problems with the general quality of the shorts as they pertained to both national cinema and a general Latin American identity. This topic also provided interviews with four of the best short-film directors (according to the journal) who had emerged over the two years since the creation of the Film Law of 1972: Arturo Sinclair, highly respected for making one of the first fiction shorts, *Agua salada* (Saltwater, 1974); Nelson García, former editor-in-chief of a short-lived competing film journal *Pantalla*, but now on the staff at *Hablemos*; Francisco Lombardi, another *Hablemos* staff member and one of the more prolific short-film directors; and Nora de Izcué, graduate of Armando Robles Godoy's film workshop and one of the first women to direct any type of film in Peru. Their films varied widely in theme and technique. García's *Bonbon Coronado, ¡Campeón!* (1974) was an experimental film using publicity and stock photographs to portray the life of an Afro-Peruvian boxer. De Izcué's first short, *Filmación*, was a "making-of" featurette based on her mentor Robles Godoy's *La muralla verde* (1970), but her most acclaimed medium-length film, *Runan Caycu* (1973), was a documentary based on the history of pro-agrarian reform insurgencies in and around Cuzco.

Because the filmmakers benefited from the law, their opinions contrasted sharply with those of the critics. As members of the journal's staff, García and Lombardi were asked to comment on the relevance of their lives as critics to the act of filmmaking in Peru. García responded that criticism offered "an opportunity to theorize and learn the craft of cinema [*el quehacer cinematográfico*]. Which is almost the opposite of actually *making* cinema."[26] By being a critic in Peru, Lombardi recognized that his films would necessarily be derivative of films from abroad as that was the majority of product he had been exposed to: "[To] some extent, it is somewhat castrating to have been a film critic in an underdeveloped country, which lacks a cinematic infrastructure and history. A good part of your cinematic stimuli are foreign and to some extent correspond to a different situation. . . . Having been a film critic simply makes you feel tremendously the underdevelopment that, in some way, we're all placed into."[27] Aware that the majority of short-film producers were generating and distributing shorts to take advantage of the Film Law, *Hablemos de cine* selected these four directors because they demonstrated a knowledge of both the Peruvian and larger Latin American communities, enough to attempt to place themselves within these contexts. Nora de Izcué's statements on the working class's lack of access to filmmaking could have come from any of the New Latin American Cinema practitioners:

> *The problem with Peruvian Cinema is found within the essence of our cultural structure. . . . Who has the possibilities of making films? What films do we see? Why are films made? Who holds the monopolies? Perhaps the key to the problem lies in knowing who in Peru is going to express themselves through cinema. Maybe only a few privileged filmmakers? Cinema continues to be an island, while other forms of communication are already more accessible. . . . Cinema continues to be closed to most, it continues to be the method of expression for very few.*[28]

Similarly, de Izcué doesn't see a place for auteurist cinema within Peruvian national cinema when asked about the films of Sinclair and Robles Godoy. She argues that such a concept "may work in another context, but not in ours" as, without much product to work with, even Robles Godoy could not be considered an auteur.

The Encyclopedia of Short Filmmaking

The short-film explosion did not wane: instead, it grew to a point of crisis when too many films were produced to guarantee their exhibition, creating a bottleneck situation where many completed shorts found their release delayed. With no money coming in from the shorts, and with the onset of an international recession of the 1970s, many short-film production companies went bankrupt. At the same time, the successful completion of several feature films in 1977 by filmmakers trained on short films forced the journal to reevaluate its opinion of the short format.

The publication of volume 70 (April 1979) demonstrated a significant ideological shift concerning short films with the first part of a "Diccionario del cortometraje peruano" (Encyclopedia of Peruvian short filmmaking), one of the only written records concerning short films made under the Film Law of 1972.[29] The most difficult task involved determining the judgment parameters for inclusion in the encyclopedia: not all films were of sufficiently acceptable quality for consideration, nor was it easy to figure out exactly who was responsible for a particular short. The journal's training in auteur theory (reminiscent of the French and Spanish journals) broke down; as the introduction states, the shorts "have often been executed by groups that piecemealed their material together . . . which lends a standard, opaque tone to a large percentage of the shorts and makes it difficult to find significant differences among many directors."[30] Naturally, the large number of films produced over the previous seven years made it impossible for the journal to cover every short film that had been produced. One criterion for inclusion was having produced two films following the creation of the Film Law of 1972, thereby critically assessing the effects of the law first and foremost on the question of industry.

In the history of *Hablemos de cine*, only the in-depth retrospective of American filmmakers (published in 1968 and 1969 in volumes 39 through 46) matched this serious, detailed exploration of the Peruvian short film. This attention is particularly surprising as such a comprehensive study was never attempted with the features (perhaps because all the features released at this time got their own individual reviews). The publication of the retrospective supports the notion that the short film was relevant to national cinema; in fact, it was the most prominent mode of cinematic production at the time, far more significant than the scant number of features.

All this is not to say that the critics were satisfied to examine shorts on their own terms. On the contrary, the editors still privileged the feature film: the retrospective tracked the fifty filmmakers that most showed promise to make the jump or had already started producing features. Discussions of the shorts within the pages of *Hablemos de cine* generally addressed the issue of progressing to feature-length films. Coverage of the short films validated their position as mere experimental "practice" for larger works. Here, the shorts cannot even be referred to as "calling cards" as the large majority were not created to attract funding. In a roundtable discussion in volume 73–74 (June 1981), the consensus among the *hablemistas* stressed the importance of the Film Law of 1972 in allowing budding filmmakers to make mistakes and learn, but Reynaldo Ledgard noted that "a system is needed to ensure the passage from short- to medium-length films and from there to features . . . as has occurred over the last few years." Though this progression had been a common path for directors (notably Francisco Lombardi), other staff members pointed out that these steps were neither guaranteed nor fostered by the Film Law. Federico de Cárdenas further commented that "the method of practical cinematic experience in our country has exclusively been the short film, which is the medium from which all the current filmmakers have emerged."[31] It is important to note that very few of the directors included in the retrospective went on to actually make features; nonetheless, a significant number of this group—including Felipe Degregori, Alberto "Chicho" Durant, Federico García, Luis Llosa, Francisco Lombardi, Kurt and Christine Rosenthal, Arturo Sinclair, Augusto Tamayo, and Jorge Volkert—did accomplish this goal, making this retrospective a valuable resource in expanding the critical trajectory of their work.

The "Diccionario" was split between two issues, with twenty-five filmmakers profiled in volume 70 (April 1979) and another twenty-five in volume 71 (April 1980), covering forty-six individuals and four "collective" groups who, for ideological reasons, chose to share or downplay individual authorship of their work. The individual entries/reviews were written by eight of the current editors.[32] Of the individuals profiled, eight were current or past members of the *Hablemos* staff (Bullitta, de Cárdenas, García, Guevara, Huayhuaca, Ledgard, Lombardi, and Tamayo), though the introduction to the retrospective clearly stated at the beginning that no editor would review his own work.

The journal made a significant effort to not merely pick the fifty "best" filmmakers, but to get a cross-section of short-film activity within Peru. Several names were obvious inclusions as they had already made features by this point: Armando Robles Godoy, for example, had taken a break from feature filmmaking to concentrate on shorts—though as Ricardo Bedoya's entry points out, the shorts served merely to encapsulate in smaller form "the same vices, the same pretensions, the same tired idea he postulates that montage is the essential element of cinematic language . . . montage which, of course, doesn't naturally signify [anything]."[33]

The summaries for the editorial staff included in the retrospective were brief but critical, providing a quick summary of various films' plotlines (if one existed) as well as technical information about form across all the director's short-film oeuvre, treating each candidate as a small auteur study. Often, the entries provided insight as to what other kinds of films were being produced at the time, such as Juan Bullitta's brief summary for Juan A. Caycho exemplifying what Bullitta called "folkloric cinema":

> *At the edges of cinema examining Peruvian folkloric themes, one of the most exploited as a result of the Film Law of 1972, a genuine national folkloric cinema exists. Its typicality, if we may call it that, derives from three elements: the intensity of the criollo, a primitive sense of both cinematic language and technical abilities that would make the Lumière brothers blush, and completely prosaic film imagery. Caycho's filmmaking functions as a perfect example of this genre in the worst of all possible ways.*[34]

Despite this fairly negative outlook, Caycho is not representative of the poor quality of most of the films produced; that honor went to W. S. Palacios, whose short films were underwritten primarily by the governmental tourism board COTUR. According to Isaac León, Palacios's work "reaped benefits for we're not quite sure whom. In any case, the films plague the Peruvian state or, more directly, the cinemagoer. . . . [These] shorts are notorious precursors to the archeological-folkloric plundering and foolishness to which we have been subjected over the most recent years."[35] Ernesto Sprinckmoller, who had been derided in the journal's discussions concerning the shorts, was cited as one of the biggest beneficiaries of the cinematic law without ever having produced a "quality" film. Reviewer Ricardo Bedoya called Sprinckmoller and his colleague Rodolfo Bedoya "*cortometrajistas 'salchicheros'*" (sausage-making short-film directors), for films edited together in a seemingly haphazard manner, compiled using ideas readily in agreement with the reactionary Morales Bermúdez government in place in 1975. Despite the lack of inventiveness, the Film Law nevertheless assured them a substantial sum of money.[36]

Several entries note the presence of various filmmaking situations that would otherwise have been even more marginalized in the growing industry. *Hablemos de cine* surprisingly labeled a number of collective efforts under their group names instead of by individual directors, undoubtedly much to the groups' pleasure, whose identities were solidified as a collective. These efforts examined included a number of leftist organizations (including Liberación sin rodeos and Marcha) producing shorts reminiscent of Cine Liberación, the famed Argentine collective that produced *La hora de los hornos* (The Hour of the Furnaces, 1967–69). Isaac León gave a favorable review to director Nora de Izcué, one of the only prolific female directors who nonetheless struggled to produce her films independently. Though de Izcué's shorts were mostly geared toward children, León noted that her techniques were experimental "in the best sense of the word, unlike those of her first instructor, Robles Godoy, from whom she has been lucky not to inherit any of his stylistic displays: the path from *Filmación* to her shorts in the Amazon effectively demonstrates this."[37] Likewise, although he had only made one film (*Facundo*) and hence was an anomaly to be included in the summary at all, Fernando Gagliuffi is commended by Nelson García for his work in animation, a truly underrepresented form in national cinema:

> *The animated film has had limited success in Peru, having been relegated almost entirely to the realm of advertising. Nonetheless, that is not to say that animation has been shamefully represented, but animators—almost all graduates from programs abroad [as few are offered here in Peru]—have had to completely reinvent the necessary specialized technical equipment like building the animation table needed to work. It seems to me that these efforts have sapped all of their creative energy. These initial endeavors are nonetheless paramount if there is to be a future for Peruvian animation.*[38]

García's comment was unfortunately prescient: only a handful of animated shorts have been produced over the thirty years since he wrote this entry, having largely returned to the realm of advertising; the sole feature animated film ever produced in Peru, *Dragones: Destino de fuego* (Dragons: Destiny of Fire, directed by Eduardo Schuldt and notably cowritten by Lombardi scripter Giovanna Pollarolo), would not be produced until 2006.[39]

A Parallel Context: Colombia

As the journal turned to other Latin American cinemas late in their publication run, it found that the situation in Colombia paralleled the Peruvian experience with short films. Both countries established laws in 1972 to stimulate the industry that involved mandatory exhibition of short films, a percentage of whose ticket sales would return to the production companies that made the films. In Peru, this was called "obligatory exhibition," while in Colombia it was called "surcharge cinema" (*cine de sobreprecio*). The principal apparent difference between the two countries' short films, as Carlos Mayolo noted in an interview in late 1980, was that the Colombians "developed the fictional short before the Peruvians. . . . But you are also getting to that point now in Peru. What particularly interests me is that both of our film laws have similar problems and deficiencies."[40]

Concurrent with the release of the second part of its short-film encyclopedia in volume 71 (1980), *Hablemos de cine* also published several interviews with Colombian filmmakers. Considering the Peruvians had not seen—and probably would not get a chance to see—the films that would be discussed in the article (a point of irritation for Isaac León, who wrote the introduction), publishing the interviews at this point invited comparisons between Peruvian and Colombian cinematic situations. However, while the Peruvians were shown to have embraced the system of "obligatory exhibition" by using shorts as trial runs for larger productions, *Hablemos de cine* selected the three interviews compiled for the Colombian section to represent several perspectives of the situation, each filmmaker finding his or her own way to work within the current cinematic climate in Colombia—even while criticizing it directly—instead of against it.

The documentary short team of Marta Rodríguez and Jorge Silva were known for two powerful short films depicting rural working conditions: *Chircales* (Brickmakers, 1972) and *Campesinos* (Peasants, 1975). Such socially conscious topics, however, would have to be compromised to fit into the *sobreprecio* system. Rather than do this, Rodríguez and Silva chose to maintain a distance by financing their films completely independently. Both filmmakers asserted that more than being merely "a type of official filter," the Colombian law (much like the Peruvian law) stimulated filmmaking that was not necessarily artistic, as it was purely artisanal: "People are making movies as if they were shoes. Sure, cinema is only a product, but one that can stimulate ideologies, right? In cultural terms, what has resulted from the *sobreprecio* has been absolutely miserable." Choosing to work outside *cine de sobreprecio* did not mean that their films did not find an audience: "Our films, sometimes referred to as marginalized, underground, or something else, are shown all over the place: universities, unions, cinematheques, etc. . . . We don't hide ourselves or make clandestine cinema."[41] Though there is little indication that Peruvians felt this way toward their own "obligatory exhibition" standards, Silva and Rodríguez served as viable examples for Peruvian filmmakers who might not have wanted to work within the system set up by the government.

Working effectively inside the law's parameters, Ciro Durán produced some of the more popular features of the 1970s. While perhaps not the most revolutionary filmmaker—León and other filmmakers criticized his *Gamin* (1979), a feature documentary concerning children from the streets, for being overmanipulative—Durán argued that "quality films" could still be produced under the *sobreprecio* system. Nevertheless, at the time of the interview's publication in 1980, the system was collapsing: the major distribution company, Cine Colombia, had decided to buy all the shorts at a fixed price and pocket the surcharge that was supposed to go to the producer. Though shorts were still being screened under the law, Durán acknowledged that the national focus had turned almost exclusively to the feature and that it seemed the development of an industry had stalled: "the distributors, as well as the importers of foreign product and the exhibitors who profit from it, have always been against the development of a film industry in Colombia. The recently created Cooperative [of Film Producers] was developed as a response to the degeneration of the short-film market when distributors and exhibitors took more and more money away from the producers."[42] Though the system worked for Durán to "reach the largest audience possible," he also recognized that the *sobreprecio* system had reached an impasse between development of an industry and satisfaction of a monopolistic distribution system that preferred the status quo.

Carlos Mayolo and Luis Ospina found a middle ground between these two positions on the Colombian model, working within the *sobreprecio* system while simultaneously commenting on it. They achieved this to great success with *Agarrando pueblo* (Conning the Public, 1977), which, as they put it, "tried to comment on the many types of documentary shorts made under the *sobreprecio* system" by showing that, when the subject wasn't depressing enough, the filmmakers would stage it to be even more depressing. Ospina noted, however, that the film actually "sparked increased feature film production. That's what the industry is like now. People have discovered that the *sobreprecio* system is not that great because the distributors purchase the shorts at a fixed price."[43] The situation within the country forced cinematic activity to turn to features—but though established filmmakers could do this, such action did little for creating an industry per se.

The Omnibus Film Alternative

For a very brief period, several Peruvian filmmakers experimented with another format: the omnibus film, which bundled several medium-length (usually 20–30 minutes each) films, each made by a different filmmaker, to make one feature-length production.[44] Because such films were neither shorts nor true features, *Hablemos de cine*'s varied responses to the three Peruvian anthology films demonstrate the confusion critics faced when encountering this particular format.

The review of the first omnibus film, *Cuentos inmorales* (Immoral Tales, 1978: fig. 11), was actually split into four separate reviews of the individual films written by four different staff members and published in volume 70 (April 1979). While providing the distinct reviews is logical—each part, after all, is a different film in its own right—in practice this was somewhat unprecedented. *Hablemos de cine* had encountered the omnibus film early in its publication run in volume 14 (September 1, 1965) when Federico de Cárdenas reviewed the Italian omnibus film *Alta infedelità* (High Infidelity, 1964), directed by Mario Manicelli, Elio Petri, Franco Rossi, and Luciano Salce. That review was not broken up into its different parts; rather, the film was written up as a single feature, although de Cárdenas broke down the merits of each segment separately. The impact of the short-film explosion, however, had an obvious impact on the method of reviewing Peruvian omnibus films, which were treated with more care than had been the French and Italian predecessors. Directors such as Fellini and Antonioni had other features that they had directed entirely by themselves and that were seen by other journals as significant works of cinema; thus their shorter films could be viewed as "minor" works. Peruvian cinema, however, did not have such a history and, except for Lombardi, none of these directors had previously directed a larger work, making these *mediometrajes* their most significant pieces to date.

Rather than view the four films together within a single constructed piece, each shorter film could also be configured into the trajectories of the individual directors. That three of the four—José Carlos Huayhuaca, Augusto Tamayo San Román, and Francisco Lombardi—were either present or prior staff members of the journal also supports the idea that the journal wished to assist in elevating their colleagues to the status of auteur. Constantín Carvallo's review of Huayhuaca's *Intriga familiar* (Familiar Intrigue) cited earlier declarations made by Juan Bullitta that "Huayhuaca's films have become a novelty for our market: the 'capacity to observe women with desire,'" as if Huayhuaca had an extensive history of filmmaking.[45] Likewise, Ricardo Bedoya's review of Lombardi's *Los amigos* (The Friends) starts by stating the film "is a clear step forward with respect to the partial achievements of *Muerte al amanecer*," thereby establishing both short and feature films as part of Lombardi's filmographic trajectory.[46] The film is a clear middle ground for the journal: the overall film's length elevated it to a

Figure 11: Poster from *Cuentos inmorales* (1978). Courtesy of the Filmoteca PUCP.

status whereby each short was given a substantial review of almost a page each, something only previously done for a short film with *Semilla* back in volume 45. Nevertheless, none of these pieces were considered to have the same value as a feature. Many of these reviews contain a line similar to Carvallo's close concerning *Intriga familiar*: "In reality, we should expect that [Huayhuaca's] initial attempt at storytelling, in which he has committed a number of sins, serves as a lesson of sorts and that *La pensión* (The pension), his first feature just announced,[47] demonstrates to the attentive viewer the best of what some of his [other] shorts have hinted at."[48]

The next omnibus film, *Aventuras prohibidas* (Prohibited Adventures, 1980), was treated differently by *Hablemos de cine*: each individual film was given a separate review, but there was also an introduction treating the entire film as a single work. A single author, Juan Bullitta, as opposed to different reviewers for each short, wrote all the parts of this review. While recognizing the opportunities of the genre, Bullitta criticized the "new national interest" in omnibus films, specifying that only the Italians had actually succeeded at this type of filmmaking:

> *It is not easy to maintain the unity in diversity; that is to say, to create a seamless product that satisfies the spectators. Most commonly, the final product results in imagery and narrative that tends to wander and ramble. This is surely the case with* Aventuras prohibidas. *In this case, the completely personal preoccupations and options of the filmmakers are made more obvious. The title only serves as a weak unifying element. And in the background, within the structure of the market in which these films are offered to the spectator, the episode film finds it very difficult to be put forward and reach mass acceptance.*[49]

From the perspective of the filmmaker, the opportunity to expand a narrative beyond the ten-minute limit prescribed by the Film Law of 1972 for shorts—but still with less risk than a feature—was a definite advantage. But the oversaturation of short films in the Peruvian market did not encourage spectators to want to pay to view more shorts, despite the potential draw of urban subject matter directed by proven short-film directors.

Bullitta's article continued to espouse that short- and medium-length films were seen as substandard to the feature-length film, arguing that in the Peruvian market where shorts were omnipresent and national features were finally (if slowly) being produced and released, the middle ground of the omnibus would get lost in the process. Bullilta noted that the Peruvian public's rejection of *Aventuras prohibidas* was unfortunate as Luis Llosa's film, *Doble juego* (Double Game) was technically advanced (if insipid in its narrative) and Huayhuaca's film was the most interesting urban film produced up to that time, comparable to Lombardi's work.[50] Huayhuaca's *Historia de Fiorella y el Hombre Araña* (The Story of Fiorella and Spider-Man) followed a coming-of-age story of two teenagers dealing with a possible pregnancy and the resulting illegal abortion, then visited them many years later leading very different lives. The first part of the film was edited in a very fragmented style, while the second was much more linear.

The Peruvian industry only produced one other omnibus film, 1981's *Una raya más al tigre* (Yet Another Stripe on the Tiger), with a short film each by Argentine-born Oscar Kantor, German documentarians Curt and Christine Rosenthal, and Peruvian Francisco Salomón. Considering that Kantor, the most accomplished of these directors, was known primarily for comedic features starring television personalities such as *El embajador y yo*, it comes as no surprise that *Hablemos de cine* was merciless in its review. Reynaldo Ledgard clearly stated that the problem with the film did not necessarily lay in the format but in the individual films themselves; that they did not relate to one another made it all the more inexcusable:

> *This would seem to be due to the marked erosion of the omnibus film as a genre: it is as if this way of composing a film brought with it a series of guidelines about what kinds of stories to choose, how they should be treated, etc. This seems to me to be a somewhat superficial interpretation: the problem is not in the format but in how it is used. A cinematic project in this country should have a reason for being, a specific purpose. The obsession to make films in whatever fashion and gain whatever kind of public creates a space that lacks cultural or social meaning—and in the long run also doesn't guarantee box-office returns, as the pathetic case of* Una raya más al tigre *indicates.*[51]

Only Salomón's *Short Saturday* (*Sábado chico*), an examination of machismo as expressed at work, home, and in a nightclub with a good performance by actor Tony Vásquez, received any credit from Ledgard at all. If the Peruvian omnibus films could be seen as a series, the critical and commercial failure of *Una raya mas . . .* ensured that the experiment would not be repeated.

Once the presence of nationally produced features was established within the Peruvian film system in the late 1970s, the journal shifted its focus and never looked at the short-film format again. The importance of the short film would not be readdressed until 1992, when the repeal of the Film Law of 1972 by Alberto Fujimori caused an uproar in the filmmaking community that would lead directly to the founding of the film journal *La gran ilusión*.[52] Nevertheless, in their unprecedented examinations of the short-film industry, the writers of *Hablemos de cine* demonstrated the idiosyncratic development of Peruvian national cinema, connecting the short films that allowed filmmakers to explore and experiment in the mid-1970s to the features that would more solidly define filmmaking in Peru in the years to follow.

CHAPTER 6
CREATING THE "LOMBARDI GENERATION"

The Rise of an Urban Cinematic Aesthetic

> *"National cinema" will be another tall tale, another limeño fantasy, only one that will undoubtedly be zealous and commercial.*
>
> —JULIO ORTEGA, INTERVIEWED IN *HABLEMOS DE CINE* (AUGUST 1966)

When *Hablemos de cine* covered a short-film contest in 1965, the editorial that opened volume 12 commented in passing that "it cannot be overlooked that the majority of films presented came from the provinces. *Limeños* seem to be less interested in film."[1] True enough: of the seven films reviewed from the festival, only Jorge Volkert's *Forjadores de mañana*, the second-place winner, was actually set in Lima. The editors loved the winner, César Villanueva's *Estampas del Carnaval de Kanas*, agreeing enthusiastically with the judging committee that the film deserved the top prize. In volume 38 (November–December 1967), César Linares included it as one of the two best works of any length made up until that point in Peru. An interview with Villanueva, also co-director of the only aesthetically successful Peruvian feature to date (1961's *Kukuli* with Eulogio Nishiyama), would have been quite a coup. It appears as if such an interview was conducted, yet never published.

If the journal was committed to the idea of "quality Peruvian cinema," why was Volkert's interview published, but not that of the festival winner, Villanueva? But then again, why was *Fojadores de mañana* selected to go to the 1967 Viña del

Mar Film Festival over Villanueva and Nishiyama's film? Did the selection committee at the festival choose Volkert's clearly inferior film over *Estampas*? Was the film from Cuzco considered for submission? Why didn't *Hablemos de cine* comment that Villanueva and Nishiyama's film would have been a better choice for the festival?

The journal never explicitly addressed questions such as these at the time, but we may wonder why *Hablemos de cine* felt it necessary to note the heavy presence of themes and images from the provinces in its editorial. Very quickly after Peruvian features started being released, the critical film community in Lima identified two types of films primarily based on narrative themes concerning setting: urban cinema (*cine urbano*) and peasant cinema (*cine campesino*). This partitioning reflected the division within Peruvian society of the "urban" realities of the wealthy coastal city of Lima, where most of the white population is located, and the impoverished existence of the mountainous Andean region, inhabited almost entirely by Indians.[2] In terms of land area, most of Peru remains even today an agricultural society with only one metropolitan city, Lima. As such, the capital is the sole location for transactions with most industries (business, finance, government, commerce, media, and so on) and boasts almost 20 percent of the entire country's population. But most of Peru has regarded its capital with a sense of uneasiness: while founded by the Spanish in 1535 as the powerful center of the southern part of their American empire, Lima has represented both opportunity and oppression to the ever-growing number of rural migrants to the capital. With jobs located on the lower end of the economy, the rest of the country lives well below established poverty lines. During the mid- to late twentieth century, the rural population swarmed into the capital, creating neighborhoods and shantytowns called *pueblos jóvenes* (young towns) that caused the city to grow exponentially. Nevertheless, though an overwhelming majority of the country is of native (or at least mestizo) origin, the separation between urban and rural parallels the racial divide between the whiter, European-oriented coast and the darker, native Andes. Families from other parts of Peru consistently self-identify with those regions as opposed to identifying as *limeño*, even after many generations have been born in Lima.[3] With such differing ideas concerning local and national identity, a debate on how national cinema should be constituted was bound to enter into questions of urban and rural, and therefore also into questions of race.[4] The editorial's throwaway comment in 1965 noting the difference between *limeño* and provincial filmmaking was simply the journal's first articulation of the uncomfortable privileging of Lima over the rest of the country specifically regarding film, film culture, and—most disturbingly if not surprisingly, given Peruvian demographics—the concept of national cinema.

The Influence of the Velasco Regime

The passage of the Film Law of 1972, which successfully stimulated film activity in Peru, was the result of a tremendous effort by many individuals over several years; the law had, after all, been initially proposed during the presidency of Fernando Belaúnde some years earlier. In the early 1970s, however, to embrace the indigenous was to support governmental directives espoused by General Juan Velasco, the current military ruler who outwardly "sought to impose a 'revolution' that would end what they viewed as the historical predominance of foreign economic interests and the local oligarchy in the political and economic life of the nation."[5] As such, the government quickly instituted a number of measures to appeal to the peasant class, highlighted by a relatively successful (if temporary) agrarian reform program instituted in 1969 and the adoption of Quechua as a second official national language in 1975. The nationalist program as defined by the Velasco regime reconstructed national identity to pointedly include native (specifically Andean) interests in all facets of Peruvian culture.

Many of the short films that immediately emerged because of the Film Law were narratively associated with the Andes, not the city, and it might be logical to assume that this was a result of catering to the new programs behind the government. As we have seen in the examples screened at the short-film contest of 1965, however, short filmmaking in Peru already tended to privilege the Andean over the urban, at least superficially. Examining those films closely and comparing them with the films produced in the 1970s reveal a major difference in how Andean subjects were treated: whereas the films shown at the contest in 1965 (excepting the winner, *Estampas del Carnaval de Kanas*) generally regarded areas outside Lima with something akin to a "tourist's" eye, short films ten years later were much more critical, tending to examine the realities of the Andean situation beyond the surface. Most of these later films were documentaries, but the narrative of these documentaries tended to be more ethnographic than archaeological in orientation, delving into everyday situations of Andean culture and proving the filmmakers more interested in going beyond the surface treatment of most short documentaries in the 1950s and 1960s.

Pablo Guevara was one of the more distinctive members of *Hablemos de cine*, primarily because he was older than most of the other staff members and already established as a poet when he joined the journal in 1967. Guevara never considered himself so much a critic, however, after also becoming a filmmaker. The release of his short film *Semilla* in 1969 made him the first staff member to produce a film.[6] Nevertheless, his presence as a staff member was not very conspicuous until the publication of a debate on the state of short-film production in Peru in 1975. In a roundtable discussion called "The Crossroads of Peruvian Cinema" with Ricardo Bedoya, Federico de Cárdenas, and Isaac León, published in volume 67 (1975), Guevara was committed to the ideal of a present-day, inclusive national cinematic identity. It is important to note that the journal listed the discussion as having been held in March 1975, which places it *before* the "bloodless coup" that ended in General Morales Bermúdez's becoming president. Therefore, this roundtable was still conducted during the presidency of Juan Velasco; hence Guevara's comments still concur with the ideology of the government in control at the time.

The debate began by immediately identifying the Film Law of 1972 as problematic, if not detrimental to the emergence of a national cinema. Federico de Cárdenas noted that the law was designed to stimulate an industry using financial incentives by returning a portion of the admission prices back to the producers. Though the law was instituted during the Velasco regime, its emphasis on the producers clearly demonstrated the influence of the procapitalist first Belaúnde government. Because the current powers favored a more socialist view of society, the law as designed was somewhat at odds with the contemporary ruling ideology. The law did *not* specify how the characteristics within the content of the films themselves might reflect what would be classified as "Peruvian cinema," nor really was it preoccupied with such considerations, instead emphasizing industrial development (that is, an economic consideration) over the nationalist.

Guevara saw the several acts of nationalization (oil, fishing, copper, and the press by 1975) instituted by the Velasco regime as evidence of a positive trend toward developing an interest in national identity through film. Using the Mexican and Argentine industries as examples, he noted that national cinematic personae developed along with certain radical changes in socioeconomic actions. Though this national-populist fervor at the governmental level was wavering considerably by 1975 (so much so that later that year the regime would fall out of power), Velasco's presidency was identified with major nationalist images centered around the popular; that is to say, not with the white oligarchic society that traditionally was seen to hold power and influence.[7] Guevara thus acknowledged the potential for Peruvian cinema to explore a more inclusive, multiethnic identity as similarly embraced at the highest level of political power:

> *We need a National Cinema where Peruvians can see themselves. It is important to discuss this idea because in the cases of the other national cinemas I mentioned earlier, their cinematic image has been constructed using either history or folklore, reaffirming the stereotypical vision already captured by commercial cinema. At this moment, Peruvian national cinema should examine the contemporary Peruvian reality using characters instead of historical figures, and from many different vantage points within its varied geographical boundaries.*[8]

Mirroring many articulations of "cinema as constructing a new national identity" common among several of the writings within the New Latin American cinema, Guevara spoke here about a broader definition of what constituted "Peruvian," one that ideally encompassed the myriad representations of Peruvian society. Though *Semilla* explored the realities of Puno, a town on the Bolivian border on Lake Titicaca, such a representation would regrettably remain isolated in how national film identity would actually be expressed.

Lombardi and García: Of *lo urbano* and *lo campesino*

In 1977, the release of four fiction feature films heralded the beginning of a somewhat more consistent production regime in Peru. Given that three of the four directors releasing films that year—Francisco Lombardi, Federico García, and Jorge Volkert—had produced only short films before this, the year was a triumph for both the Film Law of 1972 and the short-film industry. García and Lombardi quickly emerged as the first successful Peruvian feature film auteurs, earning this distinction by both the sheer number of films they produced (a third of the country's total over the next ten years between the two) and the favorable critical reception granted to them within Peru. Given that *Hablemos de cine* strongly identified with *Cahiers du Cinéma* and had previously demonstrated its interest in the primacy of directors through the *acercamientos* and even through its treatment of short films, the development of a critical mass of features that could elevate a local filmmaker to auteur status is significant.

Although the filmmakers of the Cuzco school (including Figueroa's contributions in the late 1970s) had previously produced films from the Andean region, it was not until Federico García's feature-length contributions that the critics started identifying the *campesino/urbano* division in print. As a whole, García's early work clearly represented the struggle of the *serrano* natives against more oppressive forces both from within their own communities and from afar. Born

Figure 12: Director Federico García standing with the poster from *Kuntur Wachana* (1977). Courtesy of Federico García.

in Cuzco, García was a major supporter of native issues and was in charge of cinematic activities of SINAMOS (Sistema Nacional de Apoyo a la Movilización Social/National System Aiding Social Mobilization), the social propaganda arm of General Juan Velasco's leftist-leaning military government.[9] García's first feature, *Kuntur Wachana* (*Donde nacen los cóndores/Where the Condors are Born*, 1977) (fig. 12), was to a degree a cinematic manifestation of the ideals of Velasco's government, centering on the successful attempt at agrarian reform in 1969. (The film was released, however, long after Velasco had been deposed by the reactionary Morales Bermúdez, who did not have the same interest in the peasants as his predecessor.)

Based on a true story, the film follows the travails of the Huarán hacienda when Saturnino Huillca tries to unionize it in the late 1950s, beginning a series of oppressive actions on the part of the *hacendados* and revolt by the *campesinos*. Following the assassination of both Huillca and another organizer, Mariano Quispe, the elders of the town invoke the legend of the determination of the condor, who fights against all possibilities to return to its native land. The peasants continue to revolt until the agrarian reform movement in 1969, when the hacienda is broken up and the peasants form the Huarán Cooperative. *Kuntur Wachana* was a politically militant narrative, unique in the trajectory of Peruvian cinema but calling to mind the works of Italian neorealism and of many participants of the New Latin American Cinema. Evoking the filmmaking style and techniques of Bolivian director Jorge Sanjinés from such films as *Yawar Mallku* (Blood of the Condor, 1969) and *El coraje del pueblo* (The Courage of the People, 1971), García insisted on verisimilitude through shooting on location on the Hurán hacienda, as well as employing members of the Huarán Cooperative involved in the actual events that inspired the film in both scriptwriting and acting capacities. The film's release in 1977, when the government of Morales Bermúdez was taking apart the agrarian reforms instituted by Velasco, was a critique of the current regime's actions but was seen as reminiscent of the "radical revolutionaries" of a few years earlier.

Having originally been a film critic for numerous *limeño* publications, including *Hablemos de cine*, Francisco Lombardi came to the making of feature films in an entirely different manner than García. Whereas García was weaned on short films made for SINAMOS, Lombardi made films for commercial distribution only after the Film Law of 1972 guaranteed their exhibition. His production company, Inca Films, was one of the few to funnel the money earned in short-film production into the creation of a feature-length film. Based on the actual 1955 execution of Jorge Villanueva Torres (known as the notorious "Monster of Armendáriz") for raping and murdering a young boy, *Muerte al amanecer* examines the many players and their actions during the evening leading up to the firing squad. The film focuses primarily on Lieutenant Molfino (Gustavo Rodríguez), the officer in charge of firing the bullet in the morning, who develops a moral conflict concerning his participation in the execution. The film itself is ambiguous about whether Torres is actually guilty or whether his position as a homeless black man allowed the judge to easily "achieve justice" for the murder. Although the first major effort of a young, relatively inexperienced filmmaker, *Muerte al amanecer* was both a critical and commercial triumph, showcasing a high technical quality unique among the other Peruvian films made at the time.

Isaac León noted in an assessment of the year's features in volume 69 (1977–78) that García's and Lombardi's films had more similarities than differences. Both films were looked upon favorably by *Hablemos de cine* and regarded as significantly positive national films that went beyond what the journal considered negative aspects of other Latin American examples: "*Muerte al amanecer* and *Kuntur Wachana* free themselves from stale, preconceived notions [of Peruvian cinema] that we have seen when they imitate the worst of Mexican cinema or try to tackle 'European' preoccupations and themes. . . . Taken together, these two films represent the point of departure of a 'non-colonized cinema,' a phrase that we use without its most 'ultra' sentiments which can only be attributed to the more clandestine and militant Third World cinema."[10] The division between urban and peasant cinema was understandably worrisome for *Hablemos de cine* and León's article was an early attempt to diffuse the inaccurate terminology being used by othe Lima-based critics. *Cine campesino* (literally, peasant cinema) was applied disparagingly to films coming out of the Cuzco region, including Luis Figueroa's *Los perros hambrientos* (The Hungry Dogs), released the same year. León found Figueroa's adaptation of Ciro Alegría's novel to contain the same negative and patronizing "indigenist" cinematic aesthetics exemplified by the films of the Cuzco school, an association made clearer by Figueroa's earlier participartion as co-director of 1961's *Kukuli*. Though highly political in its propagandistic embracing of Velasco's agrarian programs, *Kuntur Wachana* was seen as "a break in indigenism" and therefore an improvement.[11]

Despite these similarities and the nearly identical practical training by each director through their shorts, the two films were still seen by audiences and critics in terms of both setting and, in the process, plot: though there are very few shots in the city itself, *Muerte al amanecer* was a well-known story that concerned events that occurred in Lima, while *Kuntur Wachana* was set clearly in the agricultural mountainous area surrounding Cuzco. León's article takes great pains to avoid establishing this kind of dichotomy between the two films by addressing them in purely aesthetic terms, but the division was exacerbated by box-office results, which favored the more urban film, *Muerte al amanecer*. Such a reception would seem to emphasize the cultural and social divide between Lima and the rest of the country and confirmed the importance of Lima as the center of cultural activity concerning cinema. Here developed a paradox: Lima's status as the center of cinematic cultural power affected the content of the very films it found acceptable, thus only reinforcing the position of the *limeño* over the Andean representation of national identity. Though mandatory distribution meant that all Peruvian features would be shown throughout the country, most of those theaters were still concentrated in the capital,[12] and, despite the large population that had emigrated from rural parts of the country to the city, the large urban audiences seemed to prefer urban narratives.

The differences between the two films are more aesthetic than thematic and Lombardi's film was most likely accepted by the *hablemistas* because it used film techniques and a narrative structure more reminiscent of American movies. *Muerte al amanecer* does not attempt verisimilitude in its depiction of the "Monster of Armendáriz"; rather, the focus is on developing the psychology of the characters central to the film: the lieutenant, the judge, and the Monster himself. *Kuntur Wachana* was quickly associated with the testimonial filmmaking of Bolivian director Jorge Sanjinés, whose films also interwove textures of the actual situations that inspired the film's narrative, often through the use of actors who were also witnesses to these events. While the film does feature several striking frame compositions (particularly at the end of the film as the peasants rise up against the hacienda), it is also more interested in serving as a document of a true story rather than with the subtleties of how mise-en-scène works to tell the story. Lombardi's film stylizes the action in *Muerte al amanecer* (fig. 13), juxtaposing images of the two isolated characters (the anxious lieutenant and the alleged murderer) with those of the official dignitaries socializing throughout the evening. Even as it is a criticism of the death penalty, the film is also a subtle portrait of the Peruvian social structure with its many races, classes, and positions exemplified through acting and characterization.

In his article, León pointed out that the film "cannot disguise its Peruvianness. The commercial success in Peru and the failure of its exhibition in Venezuela [the film was a co-production] are good indicators of that."[13] Lombardi's film succeeded in Peru largely because the nature of a Peruvian reality was so subtly portrayed in a microcosmic fashion through its characterization. In contrast, García's film comes across as the more "obvious" example of "Peruvian-ness," with its native characters reclaiming agency both within the narrative from the landowners and in the realm of national film history from previous incarnations of "indigenous" portrayals: after all, García himself said in an interview with Juan Bullitta published in the same issue that "our militance on the cinematic front forms a part . . . of the great process of national liberation in which the masses are the protagonists."[14] Interestingly enough, García himself did not come up with the idea for *Kuntur Wachana*: inspired by an experience while filming Nora de Izcué's medium-length documentary film *Runan Caycu* (1974), the inhabitants of Huarán themselves proposed the idea to García when he visited the cooperative while working under SINAMOS, hoping to show their situation as a positive nationalist example.[15]

By 1981, the division between the two directors became even greater. Lombardi's newest feature, *Muerte de un magnate* (Death of a Magnate, 1980), though considered a step down from his earlier effort, once again succeeded fi-

Figure 13: Cover of *Hablemos de cine* 68 (1976), featuring an image from *Muerte al amanecer* (Lombardi, 1977). Courtesy of the Filmoteca PUCP *Hablemos de cine* Archive.

nancially while neither of García's latest films, *El caso Huayanay: testimonio de parte* (The Huayanay Case: Partial Testimony, 1981) and *Laulico* (1980), found a large audience. Once again, both directors' films were political in their own ways. García's *El caso Huayanay* examined the case of Matías Escobar, a functionary who committed a number of atrocities against members of the Andean village of Huayanay before being killed, with the community taking collective responsibility for his murder. The film exposed the failure of the legal system to meet the needs of the community. As with *Kuntur Wachana*, García employed the assistance of the community of Huayanay to tell this particular story. Lombardi's film, on the other hand, reveled in exposing the chaotic debauchery emblematic of the upper classes of Peru, leading to the inevitable death of a fishing magnate on New Year's Day, 1972. Again, though the film was based on a true story, the events are stylized instead of filmed for their veracity. In their own ways—García's film by privileging the native voices, Lombardi's film with its grotesque depiction and eventual demise of a white character—both films fit nicely within the ideals of General Velasco's leftist government, which thereby functioned as a criticism of the reactionary regime of Morales Bermúdez in 1980.[16]

The members of *Hablemos de cine* postulated that the real reasons for the financial success of Lombardi's films had little to do with their urban settings. In a roundtable discussion published under the title "Peruvian Cinema Between Reality and Desire" in volume 73–74 (June 1981), Juan Bullitta reaffirmed the impetus behind the mainstream, Americanized "look" of Lombardi's cinema, evidence of a "dominant style":

> *I think that there has been an effort to release a successful product, with the goal of bringing in a guaranteed public. [*Muerte de un magnate is*] a film similar to foreign [non-Peruvian] films from a technical perspective. If the public overwhelmingly likes it, it is because they perceive this [foreign] standard: clarity of expression, codified maneuvering of language, a level of quality similar to the type of film [the public] is familiar with. This is the first time that a large public has recognized these [characteristics] in a Peruvian film and it has therefore turned them on to our cinema.*[17]

Discussion of the failure of the "peasant cinema" to reach a significant audience was more problematic. Reynaldo Ledgard believed the answer lay in the public's palpable distaste for the rural, though Isaac León countered by pointing to similar rural cinemas in other countries:

> R.L.: *It goes without saying that there is a predominantly urban cinematic public in this country, a public which determines a film's financial solvency. The paradox is that peasant cinema must depend on this public in order to become solvent, which forces a film to use a series of other methods—be they political, ideological, or based on a literary source—to gain that public. Of course, the [*limeño*] public does not always accept such coercion, as demonstrated by the poor performance of* Laulico.
> IL: *But if we return to examples from other countries, we see how these issues can play to their advantage. The western, for example, is the national American genre and there are pictures of the Brazilian Northeast or the ranchera* mexicana*—all embraced by a large part of metropolitan spectators. I think that the lack of acceptance [here] can be tied to the type of rural cinema that has been offered, not only the composition of the public.*[18]

By paralleling these mythological genre ideals of the pastoral (the American western, the Mexican *comedia ranchera*, and the like) with García's Peruvian peasant films, León entirely ignored the disparate realities of both countries' treatment of a "rural setting" and the native peoples who populate those areas. He faults the Peruvian films for simply being inferior in quality (implied in the comment "the *type* of rural cinema that has been offered") but the very racial tensions that are apparent in García's films as being historically prevalent—and therefore largely taken for granted—are only confirmed by León's comment. The genre films León references codify the rural area in a particular way, using the western landscape to signify the freedom and opportunity for man to tame the countryside and the immensity of possibility. García's films do not use the setting in this manner at all, privileging instead the Andean faces and voices over the meaning granted to the setting through mise-en-scène. The discussion also marked the conspicuous absence of Pablo Guevara's position from volume 67's roundtable:[19] the participants at this discussion were all *limeños* with little vested interest in the depiction of the Andean Peruvian beyond purely academic and blindly critical standards.

Ledgard's comments specifically reference the cultural preferences of film audiences where national films were concerned. If it is true that many *campesinos* were coming to Lima and were not identifying as *limeños*, the numerous "rural" films being produced in Peru should still have found an audience even in the capital. There are many hypotheses, however, as to why this did not happen. For one, if residents still identified with traditions from the provinces, such a rural lifestyle clearly did not incorporate the movies: the large majority of theaters could only be found in cities and most of the populace had no means of getting to venues, much less paying for admission. Conversely, those who were trying to assimilate into *limeño* society might have chosen to distance themselves from the "indigenist qualities" identified in the films by the Cuzco school and the large number of poor "anthropological" shorts that had been distributed since 1972. The rejection of these films might also have had nothing to do with the subject matter but rather with the recognition by both critics and audience of these shorts as inferior quality films. While the films of the Cine-Club de Cuzco were truly innovative in the late 1950s and early 1960s, critics in Lima were greatly displeased that neither filmmaking nor narrative techniques improved from picture to picture.

Similarly, as a technically proven director, Lombardi might have intentionally chosen urban narratives, recognizing what would generate a favorable audience response. But this choice might have also been a conscious reaction to a lack of realistic urban cinematic narratives within most Peruvian filmmaking. In other words, if most Peruvian imagery seen on film focused on the Andean, then an urban *limeño* narrative would allow Lombardi to stand out. Such a scenario within literature propelled Mario Vargas Llosa's novel *La ciudad y los perros* (*The Time of the Hero*) to international—and then national—acclaim in 1963. Though *Muerte de un magnate* clearly had a wealthy white main character, Lombardi's next film, *Maruja en el infierno* (Maruja in Hell, 1983) focused on a poor neighborhood in Lima with a mixture of racial characteristics.

Whatever the reasons, the success of these urban films and the failure of the country films threatened to stimulate solely urban narratives; after all, the latter generated the significant profits that maintained a film industry. Moreover, as Ledgard astutely pointed out in his response to this problem, peasant films could not depend on the rural audience for financial success but rather had to appeal to metropolitan viewers. The journal failed to make explicit the eventual stratification of the industry should this trend continue, fashioned around the demands of the *limeño* audiences, further supporting the capital as the ideological center of cinematic activity. Such an effect would nullify steps being made to generate a truly national cinema, instead exposing the "national" cinematic tradition for what it really had always been: a *limeño* film tradition, in which the editors of the journal had become complicit.

Filmmakers, producers, and exhibitors did not actively consider expanding film literacy into the very rural areas of Peru. In Cuba, for example, a portable cinema called a *cine-foro*, with a screen and projectors packed into a small truck, traveled far into the countryside to bring films to locations that had never been exposed to cinema before. In volume 52 (July–August 1970), *Hablemos de cine* reviewed Octavio Cortázar's *Por primera vez* (For the First Time, 1968), a short film about the *cine-foros* shows, in Lima at a 1970 retrospective. The interest in expanding media literacy, however, was not made a priority in Peru, leaving exhibition locations exclusively in more urban settings.

Hablemos de cine focused its attentions on the growing divide between the urban and the peasant as depicted on the screen and behind the cameras through the remaining three issues of the journal. In what appears to be an attempt to more fully address the problematics of *cine campesino*, the section devoted to Peruvian cinema in volume 75 (May 1982) concentrated exclusively on an in-depth examination of director Federico García. José Carlos Huayhuaca's essay, "The Dilemma of Language or Compromise: The Films of Federico García," began by distinguishing how the term "peasant cinema" had been used: "I would like to note that, as opposed to 'urban cinema'—that which we can call cinema *of* the city—*cine campesino*, at least as we know of them today, is not a cinema *of* or *by* people of the country but rather *about* them. This perhaps explains the folklorism and the fascination for local color that entrap and endanger the majority of these kinds of films."[20] In contrast, García's films maintained a consistent emphasis on the plight of the disenfranchised *serrano* population. Probably the most important statements made by García during his interview regard his relationship with other filmmakers to whom he had been compared. The first was the much-maligned Cuzco school, a natural comparison particularly given that, while he was not an originary member nor did he participate in the filming of *Kukuli*, his experience with film began with the Cine-Club de Cuzco in the 1960s. Whereas a contemporary, Luis Figueroa, continued this aesthetic tradition, García saw the need for a break:

> *I do not deny recognizing the valiant achievement made by [Manuel] Chambi, Figueroa and [César] Villanueva, who had notably projected the image of the Indian on Peruvian screens for the first time. But [filmmakers like myself] do not start from the same place as they did. We start with a political assumption: we understand cinema as a medium to transform society. This is ultimately our goal. It is by chance that everything that is folkloric is not the focus of our preoccupations. [The filmmakers associated with the Cuzco school] come from a cinema, if you will, that is indigenist or neo-indigenist; ours is not an indigenist cinema—speaking of indigenist in a sense that is a little pejorative in the way in which it lends itself to the idea that is concerned*

> *with the problem of the Andean peasants—but rather a political cinema. In a way, we have more of an affinity with the Bolivians Sanjinés and Eguino than we do with the Cuzco school.*[21]

While this statement rejects an essentialist anthropological identification by geography or upbringing by affiliating himself with Sanjinés, García later in the interview distanced himself from the Bolivian director by affirming his identity as both *cusqueño* and *serrano*:

> *You previously mentioned Sanjinés [*sic*],*[22] *whose films I appreciate and admire but . . . I have some problems with the films he makes because his is a cinema previously codified from outside, with a political proposition and the utilization of a much more conventional language which can be explained by, to give an example, the fact that Sanjinés does not speak Quechua. He is not Andean, yet he has assumed the identity of Andean cinema with an absolutely clear political position. It is a cinema made by an intellectual politically committed to his people [*pueblo*], but still implying an outsider's form of expression. To put it in more graphic terms, I am a type of little Indian [*indiecito*] who has started to make films.*[23]

This affirmation aimed to establish a greater credibility and validation for himself as a Peruvian through identity politics, though once again it should be noted that the primary audience of *Hablemos de cine* were *limeños* who would not necessarily identify with García either ethnically, socially, or geographically. Likewise, García's elevation of the political influence on his films above any stylistic aspects runs contrary to the core opinions of the editors (and, theoretically, the journal's readers). Near the end of the interview, Huayhuaca argued that his fellow critics have traditionally "postulated that all reality in film . . . is mediated by language." The language Huayhuaca is referring to is naturally the journal's emphasis on structuralist *style*, referred to by the journal in their discussions on mise-en-scène; García does not see a contradiction between this assertion and how his films should be viewed, a standpoint that Isaac León challenges:

> F.G.: *We do not renounce language. There is simply a difference in points of view, a qualitative difference, we might say. I think that your position stems from language, while ours does not; rather, it comes from a political nature, of political effectiveness.*

I.L.: *There's a problem here. I do not agree with you. I don't believe that our vision comes from language as a kind of end in itself. Films communicate through [mise-en-scène]; therefore when we critique a film like yours in such a formal manner, it is not done in the name of a type of language, but rather it is grounded in how adequately that language you have used relates to the goals you have established. If not, our method of critique is wrong and not only with your film but with any other. It cannot come from a pure, abstract, ideal model.*
F.G.: *I see your point and it seems to me completely correct, but what I would like to make clear is that for us, the handwriting is not so important as the content of the note and that it can be understood by the public to which it is directed.*[24]

For García, what a film says is more relevant than how a narrative is told. In some ways, this echoes the concept of an "imperfect cinema," formulated in 1969 by Cuban filmmaker and theorist Julio García Espinosa, that "is no longer interested in quality or technique." García Espinosa claims specifically, however, that cinema should counter the ideals of the film critic, recognizing their stranglehold effect against innovative structures and themes: in his view, imperfect cinema is only concerned with "how an artist responds to the following question: What are you doing in order to overcome the barrier of the 'cultured' elite audience that up to now has conditioned the form of your work?"[25] Federico García's articulation is not nearly so militant, offering a conciliatory stance toward the *hablemistas'* perspective; moreover, his statement contradicts the fact that, as he confirmed earlier in the interview, his primary method of relating these stories is through the testimonial, a conscious stylistic decision in presenting the material.

The final issue of *Hablemos de cine*, volume 77 (May 1984), heralded 1983 as yet another banner year for national filmmaking with six feature films being released, including yet another success by Francisco Lombardi, *Maruja en el infierno* (fig. 14). Lombardi's film once again provided the focus for the section devoted to Peruvian cinema, but the journal treated the director as a representative of a different kind of filmmaking from that of García. Their questions required Lombardi to address some of the issues brought up during the conversation with García in volume 75. The introduction to the section proudly announced the more confrontational tone of the interview, perhaps in response to claims that the journal was much easier on the films of former staff members, particularly those former members like Lombardi who still maintained friendly relation-

Figure 14: Still from *Maruja en el infierno* (Lombardi, 1983). Courtesy of the Filmoteca PUCP and Francisco J. Lombardi.

ships with the current staff: "Neither we nor he had conceived an encounter with easy questions and predictable answers, nor of course a simple informative interview."[26]

The most heated comments came from a disagreement about the reception of *Muerte de un magnate*, which Lombardi thought was judged by a journal that had lost its interest in mise-en-scène and had shifted its focus to concentrate more particularly on content. Given that the journal seemed so interested in the urban/rural dichotomy, his interviewers never ventured to get Lombardi's explicit opinion one way or another on the topic. At a relatively calm moment in their discussion, however, the director postulated that the bench mark in creating film is neither the message nor the method, but rather the necessity of reaching as large an audience as possible:

> *I consider that here films should generate great interest, appealing to the sensibilities of a considerable number of people. I always have this in mind*

> *whenever I write a story. Without a doubt, this is a limitation and challenge, but I find it stimulating, inspirational. Filmmakers who wish to discuss very personal issues directed to a small audience should hold their projects for better times when the national or foreign markets . . . can accommodate them. That said, I think that films can be made with a something of a personal touch even when directing them for a larger public.*

Following the ideological considerations of both García and the staff at *Hablemos de cine*, Lombardi's discussion of markets seems almost out of place. Yet his preoccupation with finding the largest possible audience for his films says something about his filmmaking style and his choices for narrative: while he remains the most versatile of Peruvian directors, his films are directed to appeal to a large audience. In Peru that means directing toward the cosmopolitan nature of Lima, clearly not for an audience in the Andes, where theaters were scarce. Lombardi's viewpoint alters the consideration of the Peruvian cinematic identity: whereas García believed in a balanced representation of the ideal Peruvian, Lombardi's interests are more realistic and market-driven, based on obtaining a large box office, which, by sheer numbers, meant directing his efforts towards Lima—and, extending Lima's cosmopolitan tastes, toward possible foreign distribution.

Confirmed by his films and filmmaking style both prior to and following this interview, Lombardi's position as a successful director financially and critically not only solidifies the dominance of "urban cinema" but also his own status as the preferred model of "Peruvian auteur." Having committed to notions of auteurism through the practice of examining mise-en-scène in nearly every aspect of the journal's activities and having been disappointed in early attempts at Peruvian features, *Hablemos de cine* embraces Lombardi not only as one of their own (literally, as he had begun his career writing for the publication) but also as a filmmaker whose genre-driven, *limeño*-oriented style and narrative themes constituted a viable model. These very reasons also allow his films to travel across borders fairly successfully, making Lombardi's films attractive to film festival programmers and audiences overseas.[27] Lombardi himself also recognized the importance of establishing an air of auteurism around his own work; note in the passage above that a "personal touch" is essential to his work. As he grew to become the only recognizable name outside Peru through foreign distribution of the films produced in the 1980s and early 1990s—*La ciudad y los perros* (The City and the Dogs, 1985), *La boca del lobo* (The Lion's Den, 1988), *Caídos del cielo* (Fallen from Heaven, 1990), and *Sin compassión* (No Mercy, 1994)—Lombardi's techniques and themes would be only slightly modified by other directors such as Felipe Degregori (*Abisa a los compañeros* / Down with the Comrades, 1980), José Carlos Huayhuaca (*Profesión: Detective*, 1986), Augusto Tamayo (*La fuga de Chacal* / The Flight of the Jackal, 1987) and Alberto Durant (*Alias La Gringa*, 1991), enough that later critics would refer to all of these filmmakers as "the Lombardi generation," a moniker that refers not only to a time period but also to aesthetic and narrative trends.

In what amounted to the journal's most serious article concerning the national cinema, Isaac León started the section on Peruvian filmmaking with an in-depth analysis titled "Preaching in the Desert?" He charged that articles written about Peruvian cinema tended to be more informational than analytical:

> *Until now, Peruvian cinema has been treated by critics—and* Hablemos de cine *is no exception—either through an analysis or commentary of each individual picture or through a limited focus or summary offering data, figures, techniques for evaluation, and future projects. A little of everything, which is fine as undoubtedly such criteria is useful, but there exists an ostensible deficit concerning analysis of the tradition as a whole. This theme is almost always mentioned in passing or with a sideways glance but it is nevertheless the most important in establishing an ongoing relationship between films and audience.*[28]

In this recognition of the place of the film journal within the context of Peruvian cinema, León immediately addressed the division between urban and rural cinema, which he stated was a false, arbitrary dichotomy. Though he once again emphasized the urban/rural divide through its two major directors, Lombardi and García, León warned that this situation masked an inability and insecurity among critics to categorize either the filmmakers or the films:

> *Unlike the classifications critics usually make with other cinemas that are based on modes of genre or style with various generalizations or attributes assigned to individual directors, in our case these have counted less if at all. This is perhaps because defined genres could not be determined, styles were not sufficiently profiled and, since Armando Robles Godoy left the feature film scene, nobody has insisted much upon auteurist concerns and on film as an instrument of personal expression. The directors' concerns have instead centered on the thematic and narrative material and on the reception by the*

> *public. Because of this, even when we could have been speaking with the same or more correct sociological nomenclature of "the films of Francisco Lombardi and Federico García," to give as an example two men who have produced the most and the most varied work, it has not been done this way.*[29]

León affirmed that Peruvian cinema cannot and should not be divided merely by location, that doing so obscured the similarities between the films and maintained the ongoing partition between city and country that permeated Peruvian cultural identity and ideology. He yearns here for a return to assessing film primarily through mise-en-scène, but he also recognizes that Peruvian filmmakers may not concern themselves with the same issues as critics.

In a long interview published in volume 75 (May 1982), Federico García noted that the testimonial nature of his films was the most authentic way to relate the narrative from the perspective of the community itself. Reynaldo Ledgard contested this statement, noting that García was as much an outsider to the native communities he was filming as the *limeño* viewer would be:

> *If you take to its inevitable conclusion the idea that you must renounce the most conventional codes to reduce yourself to a type of documentary observer, a little transparent or testimonial, then the films would be different. We would not be able to distinguish in them a series of sequences that respond to the issue of conventional, generic film language. And why is that? Because perhaps in these films, your point of view is not entirely Andean and, maybe unconsciously, at the moment you are filming you're introducing elements of "urban cinema" or you're thinking of a hypothetical urban public that also understands that kind of language.*[30]

Though García did not agree with this, other staff members concurred: Ricardo Bedoya reiterated that although the film was the story as told by the people of Huarán, it was still filtered through García's lens, through the eyes of someone who is not part of their community. Though the filmmaker insisted that as a *cusqueño* "my fundamental cultural origin is Andean and my vision of the world expressed through film does not appear as anything but Andean," Federico de Cárdenas came closest to the actual issue when he refers to García as a "semi-urban" filmmaker.

The interview does not continue this thought process, but de Cárdenas had exposed for a brief moment the conflation of Cuzco as representative of all of rural cinema, when in fact it is the second-largest city in Peru and as such is "urban" in its own way. While Cuzco is a much smaller city than Lima and is characterized as being poor and unquestionably Indian (much like the rest of the mountainous region of Peru), there are nonetheless issues of urbanity within the Cuzco identity that are overlooked after the more glaring *urbano-campesino* contrast with Lima. For all the theoretical discussion of how Peruvian cinema should reflect a cultural diversity, in practice, Peruvian filmmaking was limited to these two cities and their surrounding areas. In this discourse, Cuzco acted as a representative for all "rural filmmaking"; thus many other geographical and cultural regions were overlooked entirely. The Andean city of Cuzco is very different from other Andean cities such as Arequipa, Huancayo, Cajamarca, Huaráz, and Puno; neither Lima nor Cuzco exemplified coastal areas like Tumbes and Trujillo to the north or Tacna, Ica, and Chincha to the south. The debate represents a conventional dichotomy between the coast/Lima and Andean—in a country that culturally identifies not with two geographical regions but three, as in the common phrase used by Peruvians to describe national geography: *costa, sierra y selva* (coast, mountains, and rainforest). The Amazon region is completely overlooked in the journal's discussions about Peruvian filmmaking and therefore Peruvian national cinematic identity.

The dismissal of the other Peruvian rural cultural realities in this debate relates partially to Cuzco's marginalized but nevertheless noted position within the Peruvian cinematic culture, particularly as the location where the Cine-Club de Cuzco made their films. It should be remembered that post–World War II Peruvian filmmaking traces its roots not to anything that emerged from Lima but to 1961's *Kukuli* and the shorts the Cuzco collective produced in the late 1950s and early 1960s, which traveled internationally and brought attention to Peruvian filmmakers in the first place. From the perspective of the *limeño* critics, however, the problem with the Cuzco school's films were that they did not advance, either technically or in terms of narrative construction. (This criticism extended to the work of Luis Figueroa, the only director in the collective who then went on to do feature work on his own.)

To indicate "*limeño* critics" above, however, is to be redundant: a principal reason for this reading of *cusqueño* filmmaking in the 1970s is that film culture in general concentrated in Lima, certainly from a critical standpoint. Whereas the Cine-Club de la Católica naturally developed *Hablemos de cine* as a written forum for the most active, outspoken members, a similar critical outlet did not develop from the Cine-Club de Cuzco outside of the actual films. Moreover, the very few Cuzco-based cinephiles interested in other aspects of film culture were, for various reasons, lured to Lima: founder of the Cine-Club de Cuzco Manuel Chambi came to Lima to help found the Universidad de Lima's film school in 1968 and the only critic affiliated with the Cuzco school was José Carlos Huayhuaca, who came to Lima and eventually joined *Hablemos de cine* in 1974.

Paradoxically, Cuzco's "incredible achievement" as a "rural city" in producing any films at all developed its cinematic identity to the detriment of film activity developing elsewhere. Filmmakers have come from other parts of Peru—Lombardi, for one, is proud to note that he was born in Piura, a northern coastal city, not Lima—but they make films in Lima or (less frequently) in Cuzco. Even the films that are made in the underrepresented regions generally do not depict the everyday realities there, resorting instead to show how *limeños* function outside their habitat. Such was definitely the case with Armando Robles Godoy's *En la selva no hay estrellas* (In the Jungle There Are No Stars, 1966) and *La muralla verde* (The Green Wall, 1970), both set in the jungle, but also with several of Lombardi's later films set outside of Lima, most notably *La boca del lobo* (The Lion's Den, 1989) and *Pantaleón y las visitadoras* (Captain Pantoja and the Special Services, 2000). Lombardi's *Bajo la piel* (Under the Skin, 1994) is a police thriller (again, a genre film) set in the arid northern coast, revealing a reality outside both Cuzco and Lima. The serial killer/film noir plot is inextricably linked to ancient Moche cultural traditions from the region; while the female protagonist is a Spaniard, the remaining characters are all meant to be from the area.[31]

To this end, we must recognize that *Hablemos de cine* did not discuss "rural cinema" (*cine rural*) as an overarching whole, but rather "peasant cinema" (*cine campesino*), as tied to the geographical/ethnic/cultural Andean component—particularly as embodied in the major city of that region, Cuzco—that, along with the criollo, constitutes the primary and erroneously dichotomous contribution to discourse on general Peruvian identity. This tunnel vision does not reflect an oversight just on the part of *Hablemos de cine* as a journal in and of itself, so much as a common cultural perception within the national identity as a whole that continues to struggle to recognize and exalt its native Andean characteristics even as it overlooks others. Even during the "enlightened" identity-formation period under Velasco, the government instituted Quechua as a national language, but not Aymará, the third major language spoken by a large population in the Southern Andes.[32] The small but significant presence of Afro- and Asian-Peruvian populations is also generally elided in the criollo-*campesino* dichotomy. This is not to say that Peru does not recognize the cultural achievements of its many other regions, but that such achievements tend to be perceived as artisanal and anthropological, not within the realm of the modern art of cinema. *Hablemos de cine*'s exclusive focus on Lima and Cuzco confirmed that national cinema, whether defined through its *limeño* or *cusqueño* representatives, would necessarily be exclusively urban; hence, its perspective could never be entirely "national." We might therefore question how cinema—tied as a modern art form to the city, with its critics and practitioners that seem to speak exclusively from the city—has also been granted the opportunity to assess the representation of "the national," however incompletely, through its explicitly urban perspective.

Rejecting the New: Politics and *Hablemos de cine*

The journal's 1982 interview with Federico García noted that the rightist government of Fernando Belaúnde Terry, ousted by the populist general Velasco in 1968, had returned to power in 1980. Within the article, the journal expressed surprise that elements of the Film Law of 1972 had not been repealed:

> *Fernando Belaúnde's return to the presidency after twelve years of military administration was not necessarily received well by [local] cinephiles, given that the current government might look unkindly toward cinematic legislation drafted during Velasco's regime, particularly a law that was so transparently protectionist. Although maintaining the law was not guaranteed, much to our surprise things have continued along in the same vein for the past two years. . . . That is to say, the new political conditions have not changed the advancement of Peruvian film for better or for worse.*[33]

This governmental shift to the right contrasted sharply with García's overtly political perspective from the left; the mere mention of this political stance at this time within an interview with the director only served to emphasize García's new position as a somewhat controversial figure. Rather than address or confront these perceptions, the introduction to the interview instead specifies the journal's desire to demystify the aesthetic nature of his films for viewers, thereby also refusing to participate in a political debate:

> *Until now, the figure of Federico García has been the object of various controversies, from those on the right who see in him little more than a cinematic agitator, to various sectors associated with the left who have accused him of*

> *opportunistic ploys. In the sustained dialogue that follows, García brought up the various political charges levied against himself.* We have omitted almost all of them. *We are neither prosecutors nor judges and we do not intend to contribute to a political debate of accusations and denunciations that affects the environment of Peruvian cinema, as it does many others.*[34]

I would argue that this last line—that the journal did "not intend to contribute to political debate of accusations and denunciations that affects the environment of Peruvian cinema"—is false. To not respond to—or, within the article itself, even mention—the blatantly political nature of García's filmmaking for the seemingly higher-valued aesthetic view is a political stance in itself. In refusing to engage with García's films on the socially conscious level that he wished them to be viewed, *Hablemos de cine* established itself as the publication whose cinema would not be driven by a politics that was anything but aesthetically oriented.

In context with the rest of the continent's filmmakers and critics, this political stance engendered a relatively unique, yet ultimately isolating, primary Peruvian film aesthetic. The militant cinemas of Argentina, Bolivia, and Chile of the late 1960s and early 1970s brought international attention to their daring style, which revealed heretofore unknown and unseen realities within those countries; by being not nearly so radical, Peruvian cinema of the period was easily overlooked by those European and American film critics and publications in the early 1970s who were actively searching for and embracing revolutionary ideals. At the same time, such explicitly activist cinema inspired significant disapproval from the governments of these countries, which at best exiled many protesting filmmakers and halted development of national cinemas in those countries. The many filmmakers that emigrated to Europe also came into direct contact with the politically conscious cinephiles of the late 1960s and 1970s writing for European publications; hence, the plight of exiled filmmakers had the unintended effect of drawing attention to the cinemas of their countries of origin, specifically to how such national cinematic traditions had been broken and disrupted.

In contrast, cinema in Peru continued a slow but steady development from the early 1970s through the 1980s. A large part of this can be attributed to the simple fact that most Peruvian filmmaking generally did not explicitly critique any Peruvian government. The twenty-year tenure of the Film Law of 1972, started under the Velasco regime, survived through the governments of Velasco, Morales Bermúdez, Belaúnde, García, and the beginning of Fujimori's first turn in office. These five governments operated under completely different ideological perspectives;[35] yet the Film Law of 1972 was never associated with any political party. If anything, the law's emphasis on funding can be most closely associated not with Velasco but with the first Belaúnde administration, which was when Armando Robles Godoy started discussing the prospects of a more effective film law with government officials. With governmental support for the creation and distribution of national films at home, filmmakers had no need to go into exile.

The same lack of interest in militant filmmaking characterized *Hablemos de cine* and, in the process, ensured its longevity. The journal's explicit and exclusive allegiance toward a focus on aesthetics and mise-en-scène also ensured that the journal remained outside the purview of the Peruvian government. The very politics that instructed the journal's everyday concerns also protected it from the legislative powers. From interviews with other filmmakers from around the continent at the film festivals at Viña del Mar and Mérida, *Hablemos de cine* was aware of a disgruntled leadership's drastic impact on filmmaking opportunities in the region. This is not to say that the Peruvians were neutral where other Latin American filmmakers encountered political problems: for example, they called for the release of Cinemateca Uruguaya president Walter Achugar in volume 64 (April–June 1972) and the Chilean filmmakers imprisoned under Pinochet in volume 66 (1974).

Whereas nothing quite this drastic on a human rights level was occurring in Peru (or at least not to members of the filmmaking community),[36] there was a conspicuous lack of attention paid to significant events in Peruvian politics that did (or had the potential to) alter national filmmaking and film-viewing practices. This inattention was only unusual because each change in government had significant effects on the local cinematic community. When *Hablemos de cine* began in 1965, moderate rightist Fernando Belaúnde Terry was president. After his removal in October 1968 by Juan Velasco Alvarado, who supported a leftist model favoring the peasant communities of Peru, an effective film law was passed in 1972. In 1975, Velasco was quietly overthrown by Francisco Morales Bermúdez who, though also a military ruler, demonstrated his reactionary positions by removing many reforms instituted during the previous regime. Despite this abrupt turn in political ideology, the Film Law of 1972 remained untouched. Under international pressure, the government returned to a democracy in 1980 with the reelection of ousted president Belaúnde. As a sign of new freedoms, one of the first acts of the second Belaúnde administration replaced state censors with a ratings board. This change allowed many films that had been banned over the last fifty years finally to be viewed, include in such diverse titles as Leo McCarey's *Duck*

Soup (1933), Luis Buñuel's *Los olvidados* (The Young and the Damned, Mexico, 1950), Bernardo Bertolucci's *Last Tango in Paris* (1974), and Pier Paolo Pasolini's *Saló o le Centoventi Giornate di Sodoma* (*Salo; or, the 120 Days of Sodom*, Italy, 1975).[37] Peruvian exhibition practices also changed with the removal of censorship; an influx of previously banned pornographic films drew a significant percentage of the already male-oriented *limeño* movie audience. Stimulated by the immense profits, many movie palaces converted permanently to pornography.[38]

Hablemos de cine did not comment on any of these changes in government, and only once, in volume 72, did it refer to a governmental action: when the censor board was disbanded in 1980. While it can be argued that Peruvians themselves might not need to be reminded of the situation they experienced every day, by the mid-1970s the journal had subscribers from overseas who might not be familiar with the contemporary situation in Peru (contrast this with *Butaca sanmarquina* in the late 1990s and 2000s, which commented extensively on many similar issues of local cinematic concern as they have occurred).[39] *Hablemos de cine*'s omission of the context of these particular political events could therefore be read as an effort to avoid the attention of political entities.

The possibilities of political action on the journal were most clearly demonstrated in 1973 when the government nationalized the general press (including all newspapers and magazines), largely in an effort to control *El Comercio*, the major *limeño* daily newspaper, which had grown critical of the Velasco regime.[40] As a specialized publication and not a general one, such as *Caretas* or *Oiga*, *Hablemos de cine* probably did not have any reason to fear being taken over by the government. Nonetheless, the journal avoided even mentioning this governmental action, much less judging it. *Hablemos de cine* only critiqued official governmental policies when they strictly affected film in Peru, be it in the areas of exhibition (censorship), distribution (the call for a national cinemathèque) or production (the need to reform the Film Laws of 1962 and 1972). Even these critiques, however, were not specifically directed to, critical of, or accusatory toward the government; rather, they were simple comments that "something needs to be done."

One of the few times *Hablemos de cine* spoke explicitly about governmental actions or policies concerned the Film Law of 1972, although this subject was only given scant attention by the journal immediately following its implementation. Mentioned in passing in the editorial of volume 63 (January–March 1972), the entire text of the law was published in the following issue (April–June 1972) but without any further comment. It is unclear why the journal waited almost three years to have a serious discussion concerning the new film law, perhaps because they assumed that the resulting films would be as insignificant as those that followed the Film Law of 1962. By volume 67 (1975), the journal realized the immense impact of the new law and devoted nearly thirty pages—almost half the issue—to the current state of Peruvian cinema, which was at that point being swamped by the explosion of short films made for obligatory exhibition. This marked one of the few times the journal articulated ideas that went beyond the aesthetic and the purely cinematic.

The political timbre of the law was broached by a very long debate among four of the major editors at the time: Ricardo Bedoya, Federico de Cárdenas, Isaac León, and Pablo Guevara (director of the short film *Semilla* [Seed, 1969]). The comments made at the beginning of the debate indicate a considerable ideological shift stimulated by both the current political situation and exposure to other Latin American cinemas; significantly, however, this shift is only expressed by Guevara:

> *If we compare the Peruvian films we have already seen, which ones reflect us as Peruvians? The work that shows a capitalist society or one marching toward socialism? Every nation is trying to figure out how to identify themselves cinematically. Cuba, for example, searches for the essence of the Cuban through nationalist songs and a new cinematic aesthetic, in art and in culture. It is more difficult to be nationalist in the sciences, because technological advances are no longer marked by nationality. The ownership of patents does, but not the science itself. The arts are the venue where that identity can still be recovered. A society can be transformed based on personal qualities grounded in geographic or territorial methods. What films have we seen where we can find this? Maybe [Francisco] Lombardi is the only director who takes a good look at Peru, but his look is only a glance, nothing more. He doesn't explain it, interpret it, or look for causes.*[41]

I shall return to this comment on Lombardi later in this chapter. For now, I shall point out that Guevara articulates both the place of the arts in establishing national identity and the direction in which the contemporary Peruvian cinematic tradition should be heading: given that the "Peruvian revolution" of the Velasco regime was changing the face of what was traditionally valued as Peruvian, cinema should have reflected a similar ideological shift. Guevara cites Cuban cinema as a viable example of how cinema contributes to establishing a national identity—and significantly more than does the Argentine example of "Third Cinema" espoused by Cine Liberación and Fernando Solanas, which he finds to be too much a "manipulating cinema of the superstructure." Isaac León agreed that the key was to ensure that contemporary cinema reflect the ideals of the nation as it is; under Velasco, this meant working toward socialism:

> *The national always functions within a concrete social formation that looks toward certain superstructures that in turn supply a reflection of "the national." Cinema reflects something of this. This idea of "the national" is reevaluated based within certain contemporary historical parameters. Perhaps we should examine in other cinemas, how in a particular historical moment the vision of "the national" corresponds to an ideological vision that reevaluates past artistic or folkloric endeavors.*[42]

As Federico de Cárdenas pointed out, however, these nationalist perceptions of cinema were at odds with the law meant to stimulate it: "There is a conflict between a law prepared during one set of conditions, the parliamentarianism of Belaúnde, and the current set of conditions. We have a cinematic law that is fundamentally oriented around the private sector."[43] The Film Law of 1972 was a nationalist law that, while successful in the short term of stimulating genuine production, lacked the ideological grounding to confirm its purpose as nationalistic. De Cárdenas highlights that this legislation stimulated an industry purely through financial means in the form of giving back to producers money earned from the obligatory exhibition of each film, an action seemingly contrary to the ideals of the Velasco regime. The law nevertheless resulted in *exactly* what *Hablemos de cine* and local filmmakers had desired for a long time: a relatively self-sufficient *consistent industry*, necessarily based on economic precepts—with the catch that the most fruitful and prolific area of this fledgling national industry occurred in the arena of shorts, not features. The passage and administration of a capitalist-oriented law during a leftist regime confused the editors, who were now as well versed as their European contemporaries in basic Eurocentric Marxism. Beyond Cuba, Guevara also cited the Cultural Revolution in China as being instructive in how cinematic cooperatives could effectively create legitimate national cinema instead of relying on the economic formula familiar to the film industry:

> P.G.: *Privatized cinema bases its existence upon a sacred triangle: producer, writer, actor. Even the director is only an intermediary. The one in charge is*

> *the producer who puts down the money. . . . A true national cinema therefore not only must change the content but also the form of production. One of the greatest lessons of the Chinese Revolution is that the growth of productive forces is just as important as granting greater power to the masses. We must break with the way cinematic production is currently conceived. . . .*
> R.B.: *What you are proposing is the configuration of a new cinematic law, not a reformation of this one, as nothing can be done with this one with its origins in the private sector.*
> P.G.: *No, but something can be done to bring in the fundamental ideologies of Peruvian revolution.*
> I.L.: *But this is a question of differences in political practice.*
> P.G.: *I think the possibilities are not that far off. It merely concerns establishing laws that consider cooperative forms and public cinematographic property. The sectors to be covered are already established: private, state-owned, and public. It is the public sector of cinema that should be implemented.*
> I.L.: *What you say is true: the theoretical attitude of the [current] government would permit the initiation of these new forms of production, but a change in superstructure would be necessary. Despite the changes, everyone would still overvalue the traditional forms under the preponderance of the director-star.*[44]

The staff of *Hablemos de cine* had never considered merely the act of filming in Peru as classifying the film as intrinsically "Peruvian": note the early rejections of Manuel Antín's *Intimidad de los parques* and all of Robles Godoy's films as having insufficient national flavor. With volume 67, however, national film production became part of a neo-Marxist argument concerning the structure of the fledgling industry itself and that the "national" nature of the film did not derive from its being filmed in Peru, nor from the citizenship of its makers, nor even from a Peruvian-themed script. Rather a film's ideological positioning would determine its sense of nationalism.

During this debate, the clearest view of how much this neo-Marxism differed from the journal's original assessments of Peruvian national cinema can be found in its examination of the short films of director Arturo Sinclair. His *Agua salada* (Saltwater, 1974) would later be considered by the same staff one of the best shorts that resulted from the Film Law of 1972. At this point, however, Sinclair was faulted not for his technical skill but for his failure to create an ideologically appropriate Peruvian short:

F. DE C.: *The major problem that I see in Sinclair is that his pictures don't have anything to do with the Peruvian contemporary situation. They might as well be set on Mars.*

P.G.: *But he can say that they are Third World films because they are made here.*

R.B.: *But that brings us back again to the problem of national cinema. This [film] isn't Peruvian because it's filmed here but because it would be impossible to imagine it placed elsewhere. What matters is reading the singularity of the Peruvian reality.*[45]

Although the roundtable discussion at *Hablemos de cine* concerns national cinema and the effects of the current law are laced with Marxist terminology and thought, it does not reference any of the primary nationalist, socialist thinkers that came from Peru, specifically early twentieth-century Peruvian Marxist José Carlos Mariátegui or Victor Raúl Haya de la Torre, the founder of the APRA political party. Both socialist thinkers also embraced ideas of a more inclusive Peruvian society, primarily the elimination of class structures in an attempt at a nationalist identity. Overlooking either of these thinkers cannot stem from ignorance; *Hablemos de cine* had reprinted some of Mariátegui's writing on film in an earlier issue.[46]

This debate showed a degree of corroboration with the ideals of the Velasco government. Such support might have been dangerous, particularly given the bad timing of publication: the article was printed in 1975, the same year that Morales Bermúdez quietly overthrew Velasco before plummeting the country into a more repressive, reactionary rule. Perhaps realizing this, a debate concerning Peruvian national cinema at the governmental level did not occur again until well into the 1980s. Notably, although he remained on the staff roster for quite a long time following, the journal's most radical member, Guevara, did not participate in a discussion like this again.

Had the journal actually published its seventy-eighth issue in 1986 as expected, the editors would undoubtedly have covered Lombardi's long-awaited adaptation of Mario Vargas Llosa's 1963 novel *La ciudad y los perros*. *Hablemos de cine* reported in 1966 on a failed effort made by Mexican producer Antonio Matouk and director Luis Alcoriza. According to the brief note, the film had been derailed "not because it was impractical but because the film would inevitably trouble the interests of a very powerful caste in our country that would censor the film for the same extracinematic reasons as *Morir en Madrid* and *Battleship Po-*

temkin."[47] The adaptation of *La ciudad y los perros*, recognized as the novel that sparked the Latin American literary "boom," would have achieved instant recognition and distribution overseas, but the novel's obvious critique of the military as a fiery microcosm of Peruvian class structure unnerved many in power.[48] Any further opportunities at filming such a critique would also have been thwarted in the 1970s under the Velasco and Morales Bermúdez military regimes. With the return of Belaúnde in 1980, the censorship board was disintegrated and conditions became amenable to film the adaptation. Vargas Llosa gave his blessing to Lombardi after hearing the director mention during an interview for the release of *Maruja en el infierno* in 1983 that filming *La ciudad y los perros* would be a dream project. The film became a major critical and financial success in Peru and for many years one of the only Peruvian films to receive distribution in the United States outside of the film festival circuit.

Despite the financial incentives still in place under the Film Law of 1972, however, it is almost inconceivable to imagine any other Peruvian director taking on this project—and if one had, it is most likely that such a picture would have looked very similar to Lombardi's finished piece. By the time of the film's release, Lombardi had become the standard of Peruvian filmmaking, one that exemplified a cinematic perspective that followed the aesthetic, narrative, and ideological frameworks put in place by *Hablemos de cine* over the previous twenty years. In fact, even without the film journal in place to debate the quality and level of "Peruvianness" of the films of the 1980s and 1990s, the large majority of Peruvian feature films released over the fifteen years following the demise of the journal all looked remarkably similar. The directors all had similar backgrounds, of course having been trained on the short films made throughout the 1970s. Still, it must be noted that, as part of the *limeño* cinephilic culture, these directors had all read the debates in *Hablemos de cine* concerning the questionable and fluctuating nature of national cinema. The "Lombardi generation," as twenty-first-century Peruvian critics call them, created films that were both critical and financial successes in Peru, occasionally winning international recognition abroad. Politically sensitive themes were more often cloaked by "technically perfect" (to play on García Espinosa's "imperfect cinema") filmmaking that emphasized linear narrative structures with a slight twist of what might be termed "local flavor." Much as *Hablemos de cine* "safely" presented itself to avoid problems with perhaps unsympathetic political administrations, Peruvian filmmakers learned to do likewise. (Note Pablo Guevara's comment above that Lombardi's vision of the contemporary Peruvian reality was "not a look, but merely a glance.")

The conservative, safe political position of *Hablemos de cine*—and, by extension, of Peruvian filmmaking in general—meant that it did not attract the same kind of international attention that was lavished on the cinemas of other Latin American countries. Focusing entirely on aesthetic concerns throughout its publication run, the journal avoided the polemic issues that occupied other film journals during the period. While this unassuming position assured *Hablemos de cine* continued publication and discussions of all kinds of film long after many other journals had folded (from lack of interest or government interference), the Peruvian cinema it had helped mold had, by the end of the 1980s, seemed to stagnate. The result was a standard type of genre feature that often flirted with the possibility of not even being considered a "national production." It would be almost twenty years before major changes at both the production and critical levels would shift to revitalize the concept of Peruvian national cinema.

CHAPTER 7
THE CHANGING OF THE GUARD

Peruvian Cinema in the Twenty-first Century

> *A film journal? Yes, although appearing in Peru today seems almost like a contradiction.*
>
> —OPENING LINES OF THE EDITORIAL OF THE PREMIERE ISSUE OF *LA GRAN ILUSIÓN* (1993)

Peruvian feature films of the 1980s and 1990s suggest a distinct voice and vision that could not be identified as explicitly Hollywood, European, or even Latin American, despite being obviously influenced by all those cinematic traditions; they also do not look anything like Peruvian features of the 1960s. At the same time, by the time of its closing for economic reasons in 1985, *Hablemos de cine* had moved over the past twenty years from a highly derivative, insecure publication to the dominant, confident voice of film criticism in Peru—and, with subscriptions reaching internationally, in Latin America as well.[1] To a large extent, the ideas and prejudices of *Hablemos de cine* helped define Peruvian filmmaking of this period, even after its close. The journal protested strongly the overtly racist, broad television comedies such as *Nemesio* (Oscar Kantor, 1968), and myopic exercises such as Armando Robles Godoy's *Ganarás el pan* (You Will Earn the Bread, 1965) in an effort to prevent these extremely popular pieces from becoming the norm of national cinema. Writers at the journal also tended to favor productions with an eye toward audiences from Lima, thereby not supporting work coming from elsewhere in the country. As such, some of the most popular films of the late 1980s were sleek, stylish genre pieces that would undoubtedly have been praised by the journal for their use of mise-en-scène and narrative economy.

Cut to 2003. Much as in 1977, local cinematic activity experienced a surge of interest and activity. Ten locally produced films opened in Lima; the Universidad Católica announced its seventh annual international film festival in Lima; and, after several years where new megaplexes were only being built in the very affluent parts of the capital, the Chilean company CinePlanet opened a new theater in Los Olivos, a lower-middle-class suburb far from Miraflores, San Isidro, and downtown Lima, the traditional centers of Peruvian cultural power. The conversion of single-screen theaters to the multiplex became advantageous for local productions as exhibitors were more likely to risk a small number of screens for a Peruvian film instead of having to chance a sole screen on a single local effort. While Peruvian cinephiles clearly owe a debt to the films, filmmakers, and critics of the 1970s and 1980s, the local cinematic landscape in the early 2000s is more strongly influenced by the advent of digital technology and the necessity of international funding, leading to a wider variety of styles and subjects.

Accompanying all this cinematic activity, no less than four specialized film journals published in Lima in 2003–2004: *La gran ilusión, Butaca sanmarquina, godard!* and *Abre los ojos*. All were weaned on *Hablemos de cine*, as is evident from each publication's attempt at serious evaluation of film, both local and from abroad. With growing, easy access to the Internet, however, cinephiles now no longer need depend on local publications for news and information about film in general. Peruvian cinema's newly complex identity has thus changed the relationship between local filmmaking and locally produced cinematic writing. The longevity of *Hablemos de cine* established a historical trajectory of contemporary Peruvian filmmaking that in turn allowed it to examine and reexamine particular issues, directors, and films to observe how each fit within the national question. At the turn of the century, Peruvian cinematic culture finds its voice diversifying with a new generation that challenges the ideals of how Peruvian cinema was originally written while affirming the place of the film journal as primary arbiter of "national cinema."

Hablemos de cine, Again: *La gran ilusión*

In order to talk about film criticism in the twenty-first century, we must first look to 1993, when the state of the Peruvian film community directly resulted in the creation of another Peruvian film journal later that year. Founded seven years after *Hablemos de cine* folded, *La gran ilusión* (The great illusion) was much different in appearance from its predecessor: published in book form as opposed to a magazine format, the first issue (fig. 15) featured a bright red, glossy cover with a photo still from Martin Scorsese's *The Age of Innocence* (1993). The collaborators, however, were very familiar. The editorial board consisted of Giancarlo Carbone, Rafaela García Sanabria, José Perla Anaya, and Isaac León Frías. The editorial staff included Augusto Cabada, Federico de Cárdenas, Rafaela García Sanabria, José Carlos Huayhuaca, Isaac León Frías, and Fernando Vivas Sabroso and was presided over by Ricardo Bedoya. The first masthead cites three additional collaborators: Guillermo Niño de Guzmán, Javier Protzel, and Enrique Silva. Of the twelve people involved in the production of this first issue, half (Bedoya, Cabada, de Cárdenas, de Guzmán, Huayhuaca, and León) had been staff members, if not significant editors, of *Hablemos de cine*. In its thirteen issues, the journal also saw the participation of former *hablemistas* Desiderio Blanco, Miguel Marías, and Paulo Antonio Paranaguá.

Because of the immense contribution of the former *hablemistas* and particularly because Ricardo Bedoya remained editor-in-chief, *La gran ilusión* has correctly been viewed as a continuation of the previous journal—albeit with several significant adjustments. The most important change was in the financial backing of the journal: whereas *Hablemos de cine* was entirely dependent on subscriptions and sales and the financial success of the Cine-Club de la Católica, *La gran ilusión* was officially a publication of the University of Lima, which had persuaded its faculty in the School of Communication to start a publication. While this backing meant less worry concerning funding sources, the new journal could not necessarily claim complete journalistic freedom. This funding structure made *La gran ilusión* more similar to a publication like *Cine cubano*, which was funded by the Cuban Film Institute (ICAIC). Nonetheless, the University of Lima is a private educational institution and the ICAIC may be more accurately described as a governmental entity; as such, the ideological implications of each sponsoring institution on its respective publication differ considerably.

The other major difference concerns the context of the journal's origin. *Hablemos de cine* came out of a period of intense cine-club activity and the personal desires of four young men determined to give their perspective on an art form they were passionate about. Though they expressed an interest in making films, there was no real filmmaking tradition in 1965. It is therefore logical to say that *Hablemos de cine* rose from intense (if relatively undirected) *spectator* activity, as opposed to a strong *production* background. *Cine cubano*, as has been mentioned earlier, was a journal produced by filmmakers as much as critics and

Figure 15: Cover of *La gran ilusión* 1 (1993). Courtesy of the Universidad de Lima Fondo Editorial.

was therefore involved in production from its inception. The young Peruvian critics were literally only that: young men fascinated by film with little established authority on the subject, apart from a few university classes and experience programming a cine-club film series.

In contrast, *La gran ilusión* emerged as a direct result of the *established* Peruvian film culture community reacting to a specific event: the 1992 repeal of the Film Law of 1972. Interestingly, though the first issue was published less than a year following the decision, the inaugural editorial did not even mention the repeal. The contents of the first issue nevertheless confirm the grave concern among Peruvian filmmakers and aficionados. *La gran ilusión* introduced humorous section titles based on significant films from the past, adopting *The 400 Blows* (François Truffaut, France, 1959) as the title for the section on film reviews and *Videodrome* (David Cronenberg, Canada, 1983) to acknowledge the growing influence of home videos on film viewing. Borrowing from Glauber Rocha's 1967 Brazilian masterpiece, the section on Peruvian film was called "Tierra en trance" or, in its English translation, "Land in Anguish," appropriately reflecting the new journal's feelings toward the state of its local cinema.[2]

The articles included within this Peruvian section of the first issue, taking up almost a third of the 167 pages, reflected a film tradition in "anguish." While the issue featured reviews of the two feature films released in 1993 (Felipe Degregori's *Todos somos estrellas* [We Are All Stars] and Danny Gavidia's *Reportaje a la muerte* [Report on Death]), the remaining articles emphasized the potential effects on national cinema caused by the removal of the Film Law of 1972. The introductory note to the section contemplated the possible outcomes that resulted from other historical doldrums of Peruvian film production: "Since the legal benefits that permitted more [national] shorts and features to be produced in the last two decades than ever before in history have been lifted, the time has come to reflect. Are we at the dawn of a new, prolonged recession of Peruvian cinematic activities, similar to what happened in 1931 and 1940, postponing an upward trajectory for our cinema?"[3]

The film community was most concerned about the complete removal of obligatory exhibition for all Peruvian productions. The action made the exhibition of locally produced features decidedly more difficult, but it made short-film distribution impossible. Short-film production companies (which assuredly had never budgeted appropriately to foresee this possibility) were left without funds to finish films already in the works; moreover, shorts that were already completed now had no locations to exhibit them. The remaining articles in this issue therefore discussed the fate of the short film—an ironic concern, considering the short film had been deemed a substandard form by *Hablemos de cine*. The section opened with Bedoya and León's "The Tribulations of Our Film Industry," an overview of the effects of the repeal on both short- and feature-length films. Javier Protzel's "The Short Film: Exploring Its Acceptance" proved in a quantitative study, conducted (surprisingly timely) in September 1992, that the majority (67 percent) of general audiences either didn't mind or enjoyed seeing short films before each feature.[4] José Perla Anaya detailed the effects of various laws on the development of cinema in Peru in his article "Film and its Right: Legal Aspects of the Emergence of a Cinema."[5]

The most significant article depicting the changing state of Peruvian filmmaking recounted a conversation among three staff members (León, Bedoya, and Fernando Vivas) and three short-film directors: Rosa Maria Álvarez, Aldo Salvini, and Augusto Cabada. Selected because each had won a prize at the most recent National Short Film Festival, the three directors had each been in the process of making another short film when the law was repealed, putting all of their productions on hold. Álvarez related how immediate the change occurred: "I remember I telephoned the lab technician to tell him that I had heard great things about his work. He replied that he had just been fired as a consequence of the elimination of the benefits from the law. Just at the moment when things were getting better. It's tragicomic."[6] By being active for twenty years, the Film Law of 1972 established an institutionalized training ground for new Peruvian filmmakers with guaranteed exhibition and therefore a secure income for production companies. The repeal caused a crisis among young or new filmmakers who, as Cabada noted, knew of few other viable local opportunities to make films other than through the shorts program: "I don't think that our generation of filmmakers realized that we grew up in a privileged time. We are not part of the group of filmmakers who had to fight for the passage of the Film Law—we inherited it as if it were a natural thing. In reality it was exceptional, above all if we compare the Peruvian film legislation with that of other countries in Latin America. Maybe this is why we reacted so late."[7]

Now one of the elder members of the editorial board, León asked the panel if they envisioned a historic return to the 1950s and early 1960s when filmmakers had to negotiate for exhibition with individual theaters, something that feature filmmakers—such as Marianne Eyde with her 1993 film *La vida es una sola* (You Only Have One Life)—were suddenly forced to do. Cabada noted first that he didn't think short-film exhibition was even possible without the mandatory law, followed by Álvarez stating, "Personally, I am not interested in making shorts that will not have the possibility of a wide distribution throughout the country, be it by law or by prior agreement with the exhibitors." Fernando Vivas then proposed, "Perhaps the experience of other countries that produce short films for cultural reasons can be practiced here."[8] Bedoya responded that the changed, modern situation into which Peru had entered over the last few years had altered both viewing habits and the change in cultural diffusion mechanisms, making the production of "films for culture's sake" impossible: "This only works in countries where cinema still remains at the center of cultural attention or possesses a strong economic influence. For example, I think that the production experience of the shorts made in Peru by the International Petroleum Company, which was making a cultural investment in Peru in the 1970s, is unrepeatable. . . . Film in the '90s no longer exists all over the country, whereas television does."[9] Bedoya's comments would also apply not only to the state of Peruvian filmmaking but also to *La gran ilusión* and Peruvian cinephilia in general: the decreased interest in cinema made it unlikely that a specialized film periodical would survive if it could not depend on the backing of a large institution with a vested interest, ideological or otherwise, in the promotion of culture.

The greatest fear of the short-film directors—and the new journal's staff members—was again not that the shorts themselves would disappear but rather that a necessary step to development as a feature-film director had been removed.[10] It would take a long time for any of these three young filmmakers to come into their own within the local cinematic production climate. Cabada became a significant screenwriting collaborator both with Francisco Lombardi and, in 2005, with Luis Llosa on the adaptation of Mario Vargas Llosa's *La fiesta del chivo* (The Feast of the Goat), one of Llosa's only nongenre ventures. (Filmed in English for international exhibition and starring Isabella Rossellini, Llosa and Cabada's picture was not released in the United States.) Of the three, only Saldini crossed over to features, directing *Bala perdida* (Lost Bullet) in 2001, nearly nine years following the repeal of the Film Law of 1972. Significantly, he was the only new Peruvian director—in other words, the only one who had not made a feature film in the period before 1992—to release a Peruvian feature until 2002.

In evaluating *La gran ilusión*, we should note that in the forty years since the first issue of *Hablemos de cine* was published, the critics associated with that publication became the establishment within Peruvian film culture. At the beginning of the twenty-first century, many of the *hablemistas* were still critics at general publications throughout Lima. Since 1985, Isaac León Frías wrote for *Caretas*, *Correo*, *La Crónica*, and the primary daily newspaper, *El Comercio*; Federico de

Cárdenas, for *La Prensa, El Observador*, and finally *La República*; Juan Bullitta, as the primary editor of the film page at *Correo* until his death in 1990; Ricardo Bedoya, for *Correo, Universal, Sí*, and *El Comercio*; Francisco Lombardi, for *Correo*; Melvin Ledgard,[11] for *El Observador*; Desiderio Blanco, Constantino Caravallo, Reynaldo Ledgard, and Guillermo Niño de Guzmán, for *Oiga*. Both Bedoya and Juan Carlos Huayhuaca also developed their own television shows involving film criticism. Many of the *Hablemos de cine* editors have also become professors of communication at the University of Lima (León, Bedoya, Augusto Tamayo, and Blanco, the last as vice chancellor of the university) or at Universidad Católica (Melvin Ledgard). In addition to their roles as academics, León and Bedoya have been particularly active in contributing to Lima beyond the university: León as the creative director for the Filmoteca de Lima and Bedoya as the historiographer whose meticulously researched books, *100 años de cine en el Perú* (1992) and *Un cine re-encontrado: Diccionario ilustrado de las películas peruanas* (1997), are two of the very few published resources on Peruvian film history.

Given this pedigree that can be attributed to nearly the entirety of the editorial and contributing staff, it may be somewhat surprising that *La gran ilusión* did not have anywhere near the impact on Peruvian cinematic culture that its predecessor had had. Having a variety of other venues where they were publishing more frequently, authors felt no sense of urgency to contribute articles to a specialized film publication such as *La gran ilusión*; indeed, they might have already published on more up-to-the-minute issues in their respective publications. The physical manifestation of the journal may have been daunting: unlike *Hablemos de cine*'s relatively disposable, magazine-like publishing format, *La gran ilusión* opted for a very large, bound volume with each issue running about 150 pages. The types of articles published also tended to be more academic than those traditionally published in specialized film publications; volume 6, for example, which celebrated the centennial of film in Peru in 1996, included large articles on the history of silent cinema in Latin America, a history of early exhibition in Piura, and a piece about the poetics of Andrei Tarkovsky. *Hablemos de cine* had featured this type of writing as well, but these essays were juxtaposed with writings on films that were very recently released; the volumes that needed to be compiled for *La gran ilusión* necessitated a very limited periodicity: originally aiming for release twice per year, the publication quickly became an annual and released only thirteen issues before folding in 2003. Therefore, although the articles in the abovementioned issue also featured more "standard" elements—such as an interview with Armando Robles Godoy and in-depth reviews of recent Peruvian films *Asia*, *el culo del mundo* (Asia: The End of the World, Juan Carlos Torrico), and *Bajo la piel* (Under the Skin, Lombardi) and American films such as *Seven* (David Fincher, 1995), *Mighty Aphrodite* (Woody Allen, 1995), and *The Player* (Robert Altman, 1992, released in Peru in 1996)—the large time gap between the release of films and publication of their reviews made the reviews themselves mustier than those in *Hablemos*. Coupled with this datedness was the relative inaccessibility of the volume: not only were issue prices relatively high (at one point almost U.S. $15 per issue), but the publisher, Universidad de Lima, increasingly only permitted the publication to be sold out of its own bookstore at its campus in Camacho, far from nearly all locales where cine-clubs were still running in Barranco, Miraflores, or downtown Lima.[12]

Concerning their relation to Peruvian cinema, a number of significant differences distinguished *Hablemos de cine* from *La gran ilusión* all the way back to their inaugural issues. For one, in 1965, there was no consistent local production to speak of; by 1993 a filmmaking tradition, if not an industry, was an established reality. Both were established out of a sense of urgent possibility concerning the cinema: a burgeoning, exciting art form in 1965; a desperate, probable death knell twenty-seven years later. However, whereas *Hablemos de cine* stated explicit interest in involving its staff in film production, *La gran ilusión* appeared willing to remain a critical journal *supporting* national film production. *Hablemos de cine*'s inaugural issue stated, "The ultimate goal that we have proposed is that of making movies in Peru, toward which we aim to create a favorable interest in the development of the art form of our time." Contrast this with *La gran ilusión*'s evident desire to establish its academic connections from the outset:

> *We are therefore on the right track in embarking on a new film journal project. And that the School of Communication Sciences has taken the initiative is a clear sign of the importance we give to film within the university environment. If it is true that the School of Communication at the Universidad de Lima—and its predecessor, the Program in Film and Television—already has a long history pertaining to the cultural aspect of the cinema, the last few years have also seen a significant increase in research and textual production of cinematic issues, particularly Peruvian. It is therefore within this context that this journal is situated.*[13]

In 1965, the first-person plural "we" in the editorial clearly refers to the Peruvian cinematic community writ large, including filmmakers, critics, and cinephiles; the "we" in the later editorial now seems more exclusive, more academic. This ideological distancing between critics and filmmakers within such a small cultural community actually signifies the growing sophistication and maturity of the filmmakers, no longer finding the critical voice necessary for their own validation as artists. Only two members of the original staff listing of *La gran ilusión* (Cabada as screenwriter, José Carlos Huayhuaca as writer-director) participated in actual filmmaking; the rest of the staff remained concerned solely with criticism. The two spheres were more closely aligned in Peru in 1964, when both sides were hungry for their own visions of Peru to be portrayed on the screen—hence, the critic-filmmaker. By the 1990s, the example of the French New Wave critics who parlayed their theoretical observations into filmmaking was a distant memory and filmmakers no longer chose to define themselves on the page.

Hablemos de cine, peruano: Peruvian Film Journals in the Twenty-first Century

The incredulous tone found in the quotation that opens this chapter might well apply to film writing in the early twenty-first century as much as it did in the 1990s. The situation concerning filmmaking in Peru only appeared to maintain a sense of status quo throughout the ten-year run of *La gran ilusión*: while several productions were filmed during this period, funding was largely unavailable for domestic projects. Passed during the government of Alberto Fujimori two years after the Film Law of 1972 was repealed, the Film Law of 1994 (D.L. 26,370) replaced obligatory exhibition (where a portion of ticket sales was funneled back to production companies) with a screenplay competition that would award seed money to the writers of winning scripts. On one hand, this new law more explicitly recognized the cultural value of cinema by establishing the program under the auspices of the Ministry of Education, instead of the Ministry of Industry, as had been established under Velasco. On the other hand, as Christian Wiener points out, the main problem with the new Film Law revolved around its complete dependence on the solvency and whim of the federal government. Following the first competition in 1996, only three additional "annual" competitions were organized over the next eight years; the winning writer-directors, however, faced more problems when the Peruvian government defaulted on this prize money. The Film Law of 1994 also did not make any provisions for exhibition; as such, even prize-winning short films were initially only screened at select film festivals such as *elcine* (Encuentro Latinoamericano de Cine/Latin American Film Encounter) held at the Universidad Católica. As elsewhere in Latin America, Peruvian filmmakers have necessarily turned from depending on governmental financial support for features to international co-production funding opportunities; likewise, instead of funding filmmakers directly, the Peruvian government elected to buy into the fund established by Programa Ibermedia, now the key funding source throughout the continent. Because of these and other international co-production schemes, Peruvian films have necessarily—if ironically—become "less Peruvian" to meet other nationalistic requirements put forth by these international entities. For example, the four films directed by Francisco Lombardi between 1994 and 2000 (*Bajo la piel* / Under the Skin, 1994; *No se lo digas a nadie* / Don't Tell Anyone, 1998; *Pantaleón y las visitadoras* / Captain Pantoja and the Special Service, 2000; *Tinta roja* / Red Ink, 2000) were co-produced with the Spanish production company Tornasol Films, S.A.—and each of these films features the conspicuous casting choice of a Spanish woman in a leading role. In each film, the presence of a Spaniard within the Peruvian context must be explained within the diegesis; such casting, however, allows us to interpret reverse colonialism into each of these plots, where the former colonizer Spain is now feminized, reversing a traditional view of the colonized as feminine.[14]

Compared to 1965, Peruvian filmmakers in the twenty-first century have a local feature film tradition within recent memory that reaches back at least to the "Lombardi generation" and has remained relatively consistent, if small. Until 2002, every Peruvian feature production was directed by someone who had been trained largely through practice within the short-film industry that flourished between 1972 and 1992; in 2004, the large majority of filmmakers were too young to have trained in that industry. As the "Lombardi generation" are still actively producing films, younger filmmakers have often worked and trained on these larger productions, sometimes simultaneously with their own separate projects: for example, Chicho Durant's 2004 feature *Doble Juego* (Con Game) was edited by Josué Mendez, director of *Días de Santiago* (Days of Santiago), and starred Fabrizio Aguilar, director of *Paloma de papel* (Paper Dove). At the same time, some of the newer filmmakers do not share the same connections to local filmmaking traditions. Álvaro Velarde (*El destino no tiene favoritos* / Destiny Has No Favorites) and Antonio Fortunic (*Un Marciano llamado deseo* /A Martian Named Desire) received their cinematic training from film schools in the United States (the New School and New York University respectively).[15]

Ten new features (some mentioned above) being released in a single one-year period also demonstrated a new diversity in both filmmaking techniques and topics. Several of these features have even made it out of Peru, thanks to co-production agreements and an increased Peruvian presence at international film festivals despite their breaking the mold of genre features. Moreover, although some of these films (generally the ones associated with the "Lombardi generation," like Durant's *Doble juego* and Lombardi's own *Pantaleón y las visitadoras*) are reminiscent of the 1980s type of filmmaking, most of these features attempted new narrative structures or styles that, while perhaps not innovative compared to what is happening in other cinemas around the world, brought a fresh perspective to Peruvian cinema. As a bright, colorful, metafilmic take on the world of making *telenovelas*, Velarde's *El destino no tiene favoritos* was a critical favorite for being an intelligently produced comedy. On the opposite end, Fortunic's *Un marciano llamado deseo* attempted a broad sex comedy in the story of a man who pretends to be a Martian in order to sleep with an American woman who is convinced that extraterrestrial life is about to descend upon Machu Picchu. Despite featuring super-hot *telenovela* actor Christian Meier in a nude scene, the movie flopped, but is memorable for inspiring the critics at *El Comercio* to expand their one-to-four-star rating system downward to include a new "white star" to signify something "below poor"; and for partnering with the national telephone company, Telefónica del Perú, to set up an alternate exhibition strategy in which large, outdoor screens were set up in poorer neighborhoods in an attempt to bring the film to a wider audience. Mendez's *Días de Santiago* (fig. 16), about a young man having problems adjusting back into society after returning from military service, was only the third commercially released feature to be shot on digital video; it won thirty-five awards at international film festivals in Buenos Aires, Lima, Rotterdam, and Valladolid (Spain), along with the Peruvian nomination for Best Foreign Film in 2003. *Paloma de papel* is perhaps the most traditional of this group; its story once again returns to the days of Sendero Luminoso and is set in the Ayacucho region. However, if *La boca del lobo* presented only the perspective of the young soldiers from Lima while representing the terrorists through panoramic shots of the Andes, Aguilar's film shows the reverse: focusing on a group of *senderista* terrorists as they take a young boy away from his family to train him to become one of them. Of these four films, *Paloma de papel* not only achieved international attention and distribution but also proved to be the biggest local crowd-pleaser as well.

Whereas film production has changed significantly, Peruvian film criticism at first glance seems very much the same as it was forty years earlier. As mentioned above, *La gran ilusión* ceased publication with its thirteenth issue in 2003; much as that publication continued the ideological trajectory of *Hablemos de cine* with

Figure 16: Still from *Días de Santiago* (Mendez, 2004). Courtesy of Josué Mendez.

a strikingly similar roster and critical perspective, *Tren de sombras* commenced publication in March 2004 as a near-seamless continuation of *La gran ilusión*. Unlike the case with *Hablemos de cine*, the decision to terminate *La gran ilusión* lay with disagreements with the publisher concerning sales and publication schedule.[16] The new publication is published out of rival private university Universidad Católica (PUCP) whose cultural institute in the wealthy suburb of San Isidro gained considerable momentum with its ongoing support for *elcine*, the international Latin American film festival founded in 1997. The founding of the new publication coincided with the move of the Filmoteca de Lima from the relatively impoverished Museo de Arte-Edubanco in Central Lima, consolidating a number of important serious cinematic activities under the auspices of Universidad Católica.

The elite aspirations of the new publication, however, were introduced with the very title, *Tren de sombras* (Train of shadows), as explained in the opening editorial of the first issue (March 2004):

> *In* Day for Night [La nuit Américaine, 1973], *François Truffaut compared a film shoot—and by extension, cinema itself—to the mechanics of a night*

> *train. . . .* Train of Shadows *is also the title of a notable Spanish film by José Luis Guerín [1997], but it is also an evocative image; we cinephiles see ourselves as curious people intrigued by the light that appears intermittently between the spaces of the shadows that move forward without stopping. Such is the impression that Maxim Gorky felt upon seeing a movie for the first time. And, starting now, with Guerín's and Gorky's permission,* Tren de sombras *will also be a quarterly film periodical.*[17] *It will be a publication dedicated to criticism and reflection and will strive to talk about cinema from all over [*estará atenta para hablar del cine de todas partes*]. And of course our own cinema, because we want films to be made in Peru, regardless of support, financing, or genre.*[18]

The editorial indicates that its readership consists of a preselected audience by referencing relatively obscure films (if Truffaut's is fairly well known, Guerín's is definitely one known only by cinephiles) and by hinting at the name of *Hablemos de cine* within the text. Perhaps unintentionally, the editorial separates the ideas of "hablar de cine" and Peruvian cinema into closely placed but independent sentences. The same is true of the publication itself: while a distinct section highlights writing on Peruvian films, standard American and European fare dominates the majority of the magazine. The magazine's layout is much glossier than the earlier incarnations with brightly colored block panels and many film stills accompanying the sixty pages of text.

The content, however, is composed almost exclusively of short, critical pieces on individual films that may be characterized somewhere between a review and an essay of around one to two pages in length. While this kind of writing was also characteristic of both *Hablemos de cine* and *La gran ilusión* (and of many other film periodicals from around the world), the difference here was a decided lack of anything else: lengthier, in-depth writing, which had characterized the earlier publications and established both as historical and cultural resources for cinematic fervor in general, are completely absent. Though the magazine opens with a ten-page retrospective of David Lynch reminiscent of *Hablemos de cine's* "acercamientos," there is no accompanying piece to tie individual reviews of his work together. As for coverage of Peruvian films, the first issue of *Tren de sombras* (fig. 17) demonstrates considerable breadth. If the first thirty pages are devoted to international cinema (primarily American product), the issue also contains fifteen pages of reviews of recent Peruvian productions. The selections are also not limited to fiction feature filmmaking, given that its lead article in the section

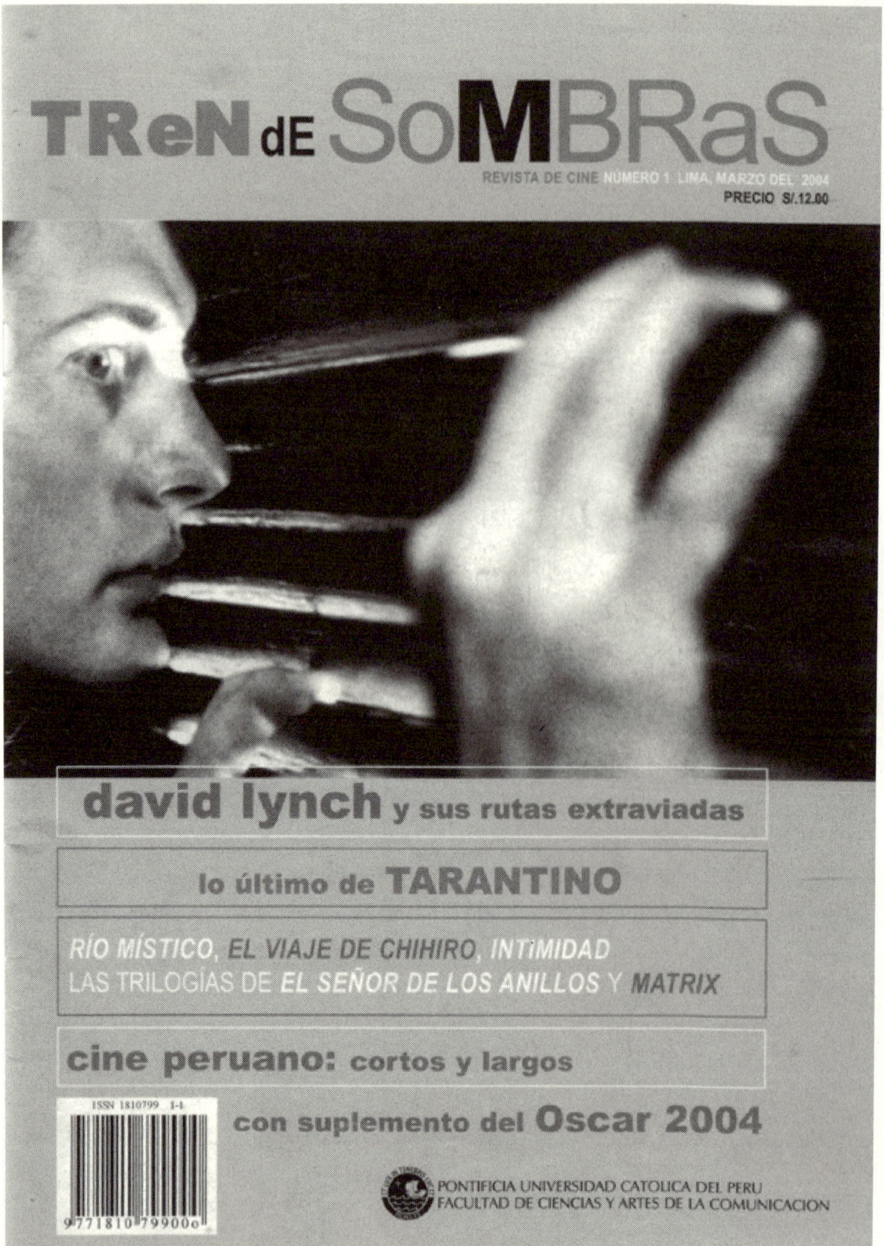

Figure 17: Cover of *Tren de sombras* 1 (March 2004). Courtesy of the Facultad de Ciencias y Artes de la Comunicación of the Pontificia Universidad Católica del Perú.

reviews Stephanie Boyd and Ernesto Cabellos's lauded feature documentary, *Choropampa, el precio de oro* (Choropampa: The Price of Gold), about a mercury spill at an Andean gold mine; a separate section also features reviews of ten recently produced Peruvian short films.

Overall, this inaugural issue lacks depth, coming across as a slight production. Its shallowness especially disappoints because it follows in the direct wake of its prior incarnations that had carried significant historical critical heft. Almost as a response to these concerns, the second issue of *Tren de sombras*, was released only five months later in August 2004 with a few additional sections of material. Though this issue still contains nearly twenty-five pages of reviews (including ten pages on Tim Burton), two larger sections provide greater space for academic concerns: one on exploitation cinema (*el cine trash*) and a much-larger dossier of articles on the state of film criticism in Peru. Though it is only hinted at in the articles, the reason behind the burst of energy concerning local film criticism comes primarily from the exuberant response from critics (including León, de Cárdenas, and Bedoya) in more commercial publications to Canadian director Atom Egoyan's 1994 film *Exotica*, which finally opened commercially in Lima in 2003. The accolades that that film received from local critics at first led to a bigger popular turnout for the film than expected; the film's relatively laborious narrative structure and provocative story (although set in a strip club, there is very little nudity) led to a noisy popular backlash from those who attended the film and were confused by it. These articles served to clarify what a critic is meant to do. Accompanied by responses from filmmakers Alberto Durant and Francisco Lombardi to local critics and a short article by younger critic Natalia Ames on "The Public and the Critic," this latter section features articles from familiar names: Ricardo Bedoya writes an opinion piece called "'Star' Wars" on what should be expected of daily reviewers, while Isaac León writes both the overview of the contemporary situation in "Proposal for a Discussion" and the more directed "Critics Facing Peruvian Cinema" (*El Crítico Frente al Cine Peruano*). In this last piece, León begins by noting: "there is no reason for the [local] critic to differentiate his position on Peruvian cinema from those of other cinemas. It's true that here we are better able to judge certain elements because, at least it is assumed, we know the history of our own cinematic tradition better—the films it has produced and produces."[19]

Not surprisingly, this defense of "brutal objectivity" when it comes to local cinema mirrors similar rhetoric that *Hablemos de cine* had published many years prior in an editorial concerning the first "candidate" for Peruvian cinema, *In-*

timidad de los parques: "We are convinced that you, Dear Reader, will be able to judge for yourself that if we are hard with a particular Peruvian film, it is only because: THOSE WHO LOVE YOU MOST WILL ALSO MAKE YOU CRY."[20] León continues, "To analyze the critical positioning in this country necessitates investigating its antecedents, and primarily analyzing the primary milestones achieved by publications like *Hablemos de cine*; in this way, one can see the influence that publication had on current efforts."[21] Neither León's article nor any of the others in this section concerning local film criticism provide details concerning their fellow critics, either at *Tren de sombras* itself or elsewhere.

I would argue that an individual critic, in reviewing an individual film, should be as objective as possible and ideally not be concerned with whether the film is Peruvian or not; to do anything less would be, as León clearly states, "insulting to the artist." That said, while the Peruvian critic does not have to *enjoy* the Peruvian film in question, he does have a responsibility to *write* about the film in the first place, precisely for the reasons León articulates above: because the local critic is most familiar with the history of both local production and criticism and can highlight elements that other critics may simply miss. In the twenty-first century, however, I would argue, an additional reason compels writers to write about and critique Peruvian publications: to establish their own relevancy as a local print publication within the global panoply of film criticism.

In the previous century, cinematic writing—short, critical essays on films already screened by readers—was invaluable for local readers eager to gain information to enhance their own cinephilic knowledge but with no other means to do so. In this respect, *Hablemos de cine* (and *La gran ilusión* after it) served the *limeño* cinephilic community well. By 2003, the nature of film writing worldwide had shifted from the "high period" of criticism in the 1960s and 1970s to a point where the very relevancy of film writing has been questioned. Susan Sontag's infamous 1996 essay "The Decay of Cinema" in the *New York Times* articulated a wistful, nostalgic elegy echoed by many contemporary critics who had lived through the earlier epoch: "If cinephilia is dead, then movies are dead too . . . no matter how many movies, even very good ones, go on being made."[22] In an essay for the alarmingly titled collection *The Crisis of Criticism*, J. Hoberman goes further: "The cinephilia of the sixties is over—it required not only the films of the sixties but also the social movement of the sixties." Hoberman couples this sentiment with a backhanded comment: "There is a sense in which print criticism is obsolete anyway."[23] In 1998, Hoberman was referring to television, reveling in Fellini's final film, *Ginger and Fred* (*Ginger e Fred*, 1985), which celebrated old cinema while showing television for the cheap thrill that it was. Certainly television's ascendancy was evident in the United States, where, by the early 1980s, *Siskel and Ebert at the Movies* became a syndicated program broadcast nationally, turning "thumbs up" and "thumbs down" into popular parlance while distilling film reviews into pithy statements designed for television segments. In Peru, however, owing to the dearth of new feature films and the lack of a large moviegoing audience, a similar television program could never have succeeded in the 1980s or 1990s.

Hoberman's comment about the demise of "print criticism" may nonetheless find resonance on a globalized level in the early twenty-first century with an eye to the role of the Internet and its role in radically altering both film reviewing and film criticism. Many newer critics in the first decade of this new century were simply not alive in the 1960s to develop nostalgia for the rabidly religious days of what might be termed "pure cinephilia"; instead, having grown up with VHS and DVD, newer critics think in terms of these technologies. Obviously this new cinephilia no longer requires so large a screen or so many simultaneous viewers as the old. And there are dangers with this new cinephilia: (1) with no one to immediately confirm and diffuse the pleasure, there is a greater chance that contemporary, home-video-format-based cinephilia could descend into the more pathological scopophilia that Laura Mulvey warned against in the 1970s; (2) with home videotapes and discs (and the bootleg copies of both) having become extremely inexpensive and therefore accessible to even the most financially limited, cinephilia can now be determined more by acquisition of objects (the movie, the disc) than by experiences per se.[24] Nevertheless, the Internet provides another possibility for the opportunity to share ideas about the films—what Paul Willemen referred to as "elbow-ribbing" when discussing a theatrical context—in order to replace and displace the community formation that had occurred in actual theatrical screenings.[25]

Likewise, film writing from around the world is no longer relegated to individual publications that can only be acquired at the local kiosk or cine-club—or, more relevant to this discussion, local film writing no longer provides the only or best source for cinematic information and/or cinephilic discourse. This change is especially evident in the Peruvian context: between 2000 and 2005, estimated Internet usage in Peru nearly doubled from 2.5 million to almost 4.6 million users, from 9.7 percent to 16.3 percent of the general population.[26] The surge in public Internet cafés, called "cabinas públicas," has led to something of a democratization of Internet and computer usage in Peru, indicating that access to Web-based material would not be so elitist as specialty film publications; access to the Internet to read articles published globally costs considerably less than the cheapest film journal currently published in Peru.[27] The nature of general Internet consumption in Peru, however, is not focused on locally produced media. Eduardo Villanueva Mansilla has noted that "the structure of content provision is similar in the Internet domain as it is in the media, with a high degree of concentration due to the presence of an oligopoly structure. . . . This creates a Web content sphere quite similar and not differentiable from the traditional media sphere, and the communicational practices of the public in the *cabinas públicas* reflect it."[28]

Given the state of globalized mass communication at the beginning of this century, it follows that cinephiles searching for cinematic discussion on the Internet will not necessarily look to Peruvian online publications for information about international cinema. The type of "light analysis" as practiced within the initial issues of *Tren de sombras* is readily available on the Internet from anywhere in the world from any number of other sources. By adhering to older ideas of what a film periodical should look like and how it should examine film, *Tren de sombras* risks becoming obsolete—except that it does present significant material on Peruvian product. The dominant and ever-more-accessible nature of globalized film writing actually highlights the importance of the locally produced film journal. Whether or not they choose to accept that particular mandate, local specialized film journals continue to serve the same two purposes that *Hablemos de cine* eventually realized throughout its publication run: (1) in the short term, the journal's reactions and opinions on the current cinema reflect, produce, and shape the local cinephilic culture, which may actually coincide with globalized reactions to these films; (2) in the long term, the importance of these publications lies in the historical reflections on the very culture that they are living in. In short, Peruvian film publications continue to maintain their relevance and establish their respective identities in the twenty-first century through their stated relationships with the question of local/national cinematic product, specifically Peruvian films and film culture.[29]

With the rise of an Internet presence and the demise of print criticism worldwide, logic dictates there would be less cinematic writing published in Peru by the beginning of this century—and yet, even counting *La gran ilusión* and *Tren de sombras* as the same publication, no fewer than four specialized film journals were publishing simultaneously in Peru from 2002 to 2004. Such a number indicates that a certain restlessness was felt among young critics ready to reject the positions of their forefathers from *Hablemos de cine*, much as the filmmakers of the early twenty-first century were not necessarily looking to the 1970s generation as immediate influences. Such diversity also signifies, as with the cinema, a certain "maturity" with regard to defining "Peruvian cinema." Filmmakers and critics recognize that Peru will never be able to support a feature film industry, yet neither at this point can Peruvian cinema be considered "nascent" or "beginning." Borrowing biological terminology, we might say Peruvian cinema has entered a "nymph stage": smaller and still largely undeveloped, but with more characteristics of a "developed" sense of national cinema.

The three other publications in fact have deliberately marked their positions with regard to the critics and criticism of the *hablemistas*; some offering homage, others openly caustic. As with *Hablemos de cine* in 1965, all these newer publications were written — if not also completely manufactured–by young critics clamoring to get a hold on the cultural capital invested within local film criticism. This demand invariably meant that each publication has had to define its position with regard to the concept of Peruvian national cinema as well.

The "New, New Guard": *godard!* and *Abre los ojos*

The aptly named *godard!*, beginning with its first issue in May 2001, most directly parallels the publication history that had characterized *Hablemos de cine* nearly thirty-five years earlier. Rather than expressing the hope for a new cinema, however, *godard!*'s stance at its founding can be expressed in a single sentence taken from the editorial in the second issue: "We do not believe in the current Peruvian national cinema."[30] The slight magazine, if more professionally published than the original run of *Hablemos*, was written almost exclusively by three young critics: Claudio Cordero, Sebastián Pimentel, and José Tsang. All three are graduates of the School of Communication at the University of Lima; thus much of their formal training comes directly from the *hablemistas* who teach within that program: Isaac León Frías, Ricardo Bedoya, and Augusto Tamayo. In a 2007 interview, Cordero relates that all three *godardistas* had read and even collected copies of *La gran ilusión*, but had grown progressively dissatisfied with both the criticism and the films released in the late 1990s and the subsequent decade.[31] In the premiere issue, the editorial attacks Lombardi for his latest film *Tinta roja* (Red Ink, 2000): "No prize from the Havana or San Sebastián film festivals will abate our anger directed at the most recent garbage thrown at us by Francisco Lombardi, whom we still haven't forgiven yet for his last two filmic incursions, *No se lo digas a nadie* [Don't Tell Anyone, 1988] and *Pantaleón y las visitadoras* [Captain Pantoja and His Special Service, 1999]." Rather than clarifying these statements, the first issue ignored discussions of national productions in the remainder of the issue, as if the films and the filmmaking situation were not even worth mentioning; instead, the magazine devoted the majority of its contents to commercial, Hollywood material, as opposed to the more explicitly "cinephilic" (read: art house) fare more typical of a serious film journal. The first issue sold out quickly, prompting the quick release of a second issue in September 2001 (fig. 18), a far quicker turnaround than that produced by *La gran ilusión*, which was by this point publishing annually.

This second issue, however, immediately followed the *elcine* film festival in August; in 2001, the critics' prize was awarded in a split vote to two Peruvian films, Augusto Tamayo's period piece *El bien esquivo* (The Elusive Good, 2003) and Aldo Savini's *Bala perdida* (Lost Bullet, 2001), besting more prominent films such as the Argentine *Nueve Reinas* (Nine Queens, directed by Fabián Bielisnky, 2001) and *Plata quemada* (Burnt Money, Marcelo Piñeyro, 2001) and the Uruguayan surprise hit *25 Watts* (directed by Juan Pablo Rebella and Pablo Stoll).[32] The festival organizers reveled in this achievement, stating that the simultaneous win signified "the rebirth of Peruvian cinema"; however, a number of other critics quickly contested this win. In his summary of the festival, Claudio Cordero reminded readers of the "not few spectators who booed and left in the middle of screenings of *Bala perdida*."[33] Other critics had even stronger words for *El bien esquivo*, which had premiered at the festival. José Tsang's essay on the film commends a negative review by Jaime Luna Victoria in the news magazine *Etecé*, a review that sparked much debate about the film in the popular press:

> *Why are other "slow" films not boring? Because those filmmakers try to entertain viewers with an appealing or interesting narrative structure, creative use of mise-en-scène, and/or some sense of dramatic intensity. Unfortuantely, Tamayo's film doesn't accomplish any of these feats in an interesting manner. For that reason the end result is unsatisfactory.*[34]

Luna's review, along with one by Alberto Servat, sparked vociferous defenses of the film by cinephilic mentors (and former *hablemistas*) León in *Caretas*, Bedoya in *El Comercio*, and Augusto Cabada in *Somos*. Tsang's argument, however, quite simply states that the film is not cinematic enough: "*El bien esquivo* may have many references—from literature, theater, photography, scenic arts, feuilleton, painting, architecture, costume design, interior design, etc. Everything except cinema."[35]

Figure 18: Cover of *godard!* 2 (September 2001). Courtesy of *godard!* Revista de cine.

In the final and third article on the concerns of *El bien esquivo* and the *el-cine* festival, Sebastián Pimentel accuses the critics of creating a stagnant version of contemporary cinema through a methodical linking of filmmaker to critical position:

> *Remember that we are talking about critics who, just like their forebears at that mythical French magazine, should have naturally continued on from criticism to directing. We only wish that such foundational work had been done, given that Peruvian film history still does not include any important or original films, or even any that can transcend universal boundaries (such as occurs occasionally, for example, in Brazilian or Mexican filmmaking).*
>
> *As such, perhaps it is therefore time to seriously judge the way with which some of the* Hablemos de cine *group, who include José Carlos Huayhuaca, Augusto Tamayo, and, of course, Francisco Lombardi. All of them have tried to adopt Peruvian themes to the molds and formulas derived from Hollywood. Hence, we get Huayhuaca's* Profesion: Detective *(film noir mixed with local comedy), Lombardi's psychodramas placed within stories involving police or criminal intrigue, Tamayo's* La fuga de Chacal *[Flight of the Jackel], whose police story featured a script co-written by Bedoya, etc. To this stream of mediocre products . . . we must add those who also took this mantle at a very early point: Luis Llosa, whom we may best remember for* Misión en los Andes *[Hour of the Assassin, 1988], and Alberto Durant (*Malabrigo *[1987],* Alias: La Gringa *[1993])—that is to say, more of the same.*[36]

I quote this passage at length to demonstrate how Pimentel damned both Peruvian cinema and the critics who he (correctly) claimed have helped create it by naming them individually. The essay exposes those who appreciated *El bien esquivo* for having bought too readily the promise of a national cinema unrealized. Given that much of Cabada, León, and Bedoya's remarks defend the nature of Tamayo's complex script, Pimentel reminds them that the script is not what they should be concerned about:

> *With* El bien esquivo, *it seems the time has come for this generation and its followers . . . to stop believing that a cinema made to ensure its perfection, a cinema obsessed with calculating on paper how to add national themes to generic formulas, can ever become great cinema. No. Until now, our film-*

> *makers have not taken any risks with their creativity. It seems as if they do not understand that films are made only once you start filming; films begin with mise-en-scène, with contact with life—and not with the script, with is always only a guideline. Any other way will only give us lifeless films.*[37]

As much as they critique their elders, these passages from *godard!* concerning national cinema first and foremost highlight the effects of *Hablemos de cine* even into the present century. For one, both Tsang and Pimentel confirm that, in defending the film, these "old school" critics only continued the notion that *their* type of Peruvian cinema, honed over a period of twenty years, should prevail. More telling, however, Luna and Tsang use the same logic and terminology that *Hablemos de cine* honed, demonstrating the elder writers' effect on Peruvian film criticism writ large and beyond the scope of the *hablemistas*-turned-popular-critics like Bedoya and León. Tsang and Cordero affirm their opposition to films that do not emphasize the creative focus on mise-en-scène. The verve with which these critics embraced Hollywood fare over European or national product almost echoes the preference for American genre films of both *Hablemos de cine* and the French *Cahiers du cinéma*, as if legitimizing this kind of cinema were a rite of passage for all young film critics. The rhetoric of cinematic terminology utilized by diverse Peruvian critics indicates that, while the "new new guard" may have wanted to separate itself from the *hablemista* way of viewing, they have nonetheless inherited the language of their forebears.

Initially, the problems associated with *godard!* mimicked the charges leveled against the early *Hablemos de cine* in 1965: youth and inexperience. The three young editors invariably overstepped their boundaries in their assessment of local films and sometimes hurt their credibility in their zeal to dismiss aspects of Peruvian film history. Though published elsewhere, comments written by Sebastián Pimentel about the history (or lack thereof) of Peruvian cinema were critiqued for inaccuracies by Christian Wiener in *Butaca sanmarquina* in 2002, accompanied by the a caustic reprimand, "It is essential that whoever calls himself a critic should at least be informed about what they write and, without intending to get personal, be able to back up what they write in black and white."[38] The magazine nevertheless remained, publishing with some regularity with higher production standards and a better appreciation and understanding of Peruvian films. Moreover, although the *godard!* group maintained an "outsider" attitude with reference to what they called "the official voice" of Peruvian film criticism, the group also gained a foothold within the very society they critiqued. Cordero reviewed films for the largest Lima daily, *El Comercio* (alongside *hablemista* Ricardo Bedoya), and Pimentel has likewise published in *Somos*, *El Comercio*'s weekly cultural magazine (along with Isaac León). When asked in a 2007 inter view why he did not consider himself part of the "official voice of critics," Cordero pointed out wistfully that "we are still a bit on the margins—after all, we have never been invited to be on the jury for the *elcine* film festival, which is something that everyone attends and would know about."[39] That said, in 2006, the same festival scheduled an official presentation within the program in honor of the magazine's tenth issue.

If *godard!* entered the cinephilic community through disrupting the general bonhomie among complacent film critics, a second, short-lived journal suggested a similar desire for a new direction in Peruvian criticism, one with smarter writing and fewer polemics. *Abre los ojos* (Open Your Eyes) only published two issues in 2002, yet created an indelible impression on the cinephilic community in the early 2000s. Like *Tren de sombras*, this journal was named for a 1997 Spanish film, although this one, directed by Alejandro Amenábar, was far more accessible; like *Hablemos de cine*, the title of the journal was a grammatically playful directive to its readers to pay more attention to cinematic elements. The stark, minimalist introductory pages were the antithesis of the brusque introductions in the first issues of *Hablemos de cine* and *godard!* Starting with a cover illustration derived from David Lynch's *Mulholland Dr.* (2001, notably *not* reviewed in the issue), the inside cover merely listed a series of last names of noted international auteurs; of this list, only one ("Ripstein," referring to Mexican director Arturo) is Latin American and none of the possible Peruvian candidates (Lombardi, Robles, García) are listed. The first page of the issue simply shows a relatively small photograph of Billy Bob Thornton from Joel Coen's *The Man Who Wasn't There* (2001) surrounded by ample white space, captioned with the line from the film, "You know what it is, Mr. Crane? You're an enthusiast." Also accompanied by much white space on page 3, the brief editorial—reprinted below in its entirety—recognizes the divisiveness stirred by the new presence of *godard!* among Peruvian cinephiles:

> *There are so many ways to view a film, just as many ways to view life. That is what makes us passionate: the diversity. And diversity is what defines us.*
>
> *If there is one thing that defines us as a film journal, it is the desire to not have a "single method." We have too many—or, perhaps, none. Instead of stretching the parameters of "how to write about film," we have at least tried*

> *here to open them up. In that way, we can embrace the contradictory mosaic that we are. No more, no less.*[40]

All of these references suggest the sophisticated reader whom *Abre los ojos* wished to cultivate, yet in many ways the approach is subtler and more inviting than earlier attempts; the very title, "open your eyes," comes across as more of a suggestion than the battle cry referenced by *Hablemos de cine*. This quieter, yet assured attitude could describe the editorial director, Mario Castro Cobos, programmer for the Cine-Club Arcoiris in the middle-class district of Jesús María. And, significantly, unlike the small initial staffs of both the other publications mentioned, *Abre los ojos* began with thirteen people on their roster, suggesting a larger collaborative effort at work even before the first issue was released. Much like *godard!*, the initial issue eschewed discussion of Peruvian cinema as a priority—note that nowhere in the prefatory material has anything regarding national cinema been mentioned—and instead provided a series of essays on a variety of international art-house fare. Rather than ignore Peruvian films completely, the three most recently released films—Salvini's *Bala perdida*, Tamayo's *El bien esquivo* and the Spanish co-produced documentary *La espalda del mundo* (The Back of the World, Javier Corcueca, 2000)—were featured briefly within a large section (nearly 40 percent of the forty-page total for the issue) called "Dossier 2001," along with sixty-seven other entries on other films released in Peru. In other words, these films were treated no differently than any other film. Castro's review of *El bien esquivo* found the film significantly flawed in much the same way as the writers at *godard!* but the tone, particularly in the final assessment, retained a gracious willingness to accept the film as a failed experiment:

> *The film loses its identity in not being able to find a plausible path between the genres of historical epics and adventure films. There are moments when the film seems like one genre or the other separately, but neither seems fully realized—and the moments when this does seem realized, everything stops instead. . . . What a shame. An elusive identity. Worth it for the effort.*[41]

As a whole, *Abre los ojos* distinguished itself perhaps by its pointed lack of interest in the expected norms of Peruvian cinematic culture, aiming instead for more esoteric material. Only two full-length articles on Peruvian film culture were printed during the journal's short publication run, both in the second issue and both exploring material not covered in other publications: cinephilic life in Trujillo, Peru's third most-populous city on the northern coast and traditionally not associated at all with national film culture; and an interview with Mauricio Hidalgo, co-director of the medium-length documentary *La década del silencio: La matanza de Barrios Altos* (The Decade of Silence: The Massacre in Barrios Altos, 2002). Given that there were at least three film journals with more established pedigrees publishing at this time in Lima, this small, young publication produced impressive original material, including interviews with Canadian documentarian Renny Bartlett, Chilean documentarian Patricio Guzmán, and Mexican cultural critic Carlos Monsiváis. Nearly all the *Hablemos de cine* contributors with whom I spoke in early 2003 praised the journal as the most promising new critical voice in film journalism; nonetheless, *Abre los ojos* never published a third issue. Significantly, by the middle of the decade, director Castro had started contributing to *godard!* as that publication also matured, demonstrating that publication's more open, if still somewhat confrontational, attitude toward national cinematic endeavors.

Hablemos de cine peruano: *Butaca sanmarquina*

As we have seen, the four Peruvian film journals of the early 2000s had very different stylistic, cinephilic, and historical concerns and personalities. *La gran ilusión* attempted to continue the tradition of criticism through mise-en-scène established by *Hablemos de cine*; *godard!* proposed a violent break with the films produced as a result of this criticism, even if their methodological approach remained similar; *Abre los ojos*, with its diverse, pensive approach failed to establish itself as a larger force perhaps precisely because it did not engage with the current polemical debates of Peruvian cinema writ large. The fourth publication, *Butaca sanmarquina* (fig. 19), is a fascinating amalgam of all of these traditions whose history reveals a publication that has developed into what I would argue is the true heir to *Hablemos de cine* as the prime publication of cinematic debate in Peru at the beginning of the twenty-first century.

Butaca sanmarquina's modest origins connect directly with the renewed cinephilic fervor within the Cultural Center affiliated with Universidad Nacional Mayor de San Marcos.[42] Originally founded in 1967 and a major hub of film-oriented activity for nearly three decades, Cine-Arte de San Marcos had gone relatively dormant in the mid-1990s. As the editorial for its inaugural issue clarifies, the journal was part of a restructuring process attached to the reorganization of Cine-Arte in 1998. As dryly related by founder Fernando Samillán Cavero, the goals for the journal were modest and largely pedagogical in nature:

Figure 19: Cover of *Butaca sanmarquina* 1 (July–September 1998). Courtesy of Dirección de Cine y Televisión of the Centro Cultural de San Marcos.

> *We have established the objectives and goals that we wish to accomplish in the short and medium term. Within these parameters, the publication of the journal should serve as a platform in order to:*
> - *Relate the thoughts and works of leading filmmakers;*
> - *Promote, through analysis and commentary, a critical appreciation for film;*
> - *Disseminate the accomplishments of Peruvian cinema through knowledge of filmmakers, their filmographies, their projects and aspirations; and*
> - *Learn about the activities undertaken by groups and persons working in film within Peru.*[43]

No matter their position on national cinema, all the other Peruvian film publications previously mentioned expressed a certain excitement about cinema — whether as art, as a mode of expression, as problematically expressed, and so forth — in their debut issue, as if they needed to defend the necessity of their published existence with energy or drive; perhaps this enthusiasm stemmed from the youth of the founding editorial directors of at least three of the ventures (*Hablemos de cine*, *Abre los ojos*, *godard!*). In contrast, the very name of this publication belies its unassuming attitude: rather than commanding spectators to participate within the cinematic experience or referencing the most experimental of the French New Wave filmmakers, the phrase simply refers to a theater seat (*butaca*) reserved for someone affiliated with Universidad de San Marcos (the adjective *sanmarquina*).

Far from participating in critical polemics and without articulating any aspirations to change or modify existing cinephilic practice, the first eleven issues of *Butaca sanmarquina* instead aimed to educate readers about current local filmmaking practices and provide some historical reference concerning national cinema. *Butaca* established an early identity through numerous interviews with local filmmakers and other local professionals, including actors, sound designers, directors of photography, and screenwriters. This interview breadth and attention to the local was a pointed rejection of the cult of the auteur. The magazine also deemphasized reviews, only once presenting more than five in a single issue. All reviews and most articles were handled by the young writing staff, identified in the first issue as all San Marcos students. As a publication explicitly sponsored and staffed by an institution, the journal also prominently featured events held on-site at the Cine-Arte location in downtown Lima, such as the awarding of the 1998 CONACINE awards.

Despite a regular, quarterly publication schedule, *Butaca sanmarquina* did not immediately gain significant traction within Peruvian cinematic circles. Geared for a younger audience, the tone of the periodical was more pedagogical than exciting, including the ever-present formal photograph of director Samillán printed on the editorial page. Samillán did not preside over polemical or provocative writing that could be found in other periodicals. His own pieces were almost exclusively personal historical accounts of older aspects of Peruvian media: most notably, two reflections on the death of producer Vlado Radovich. Even so, Samillán's writing seemed out of place juxtaposed with journalistic material about otherwise very contemporary figures. Finally, despite its association with an institutional entity called "Cine-Arte," the publication reserved space for articles on television as well—something very much in line with the educational program at San Marcos, but anathema to the cinephiles who reveled in "pure cinema" with *Hablemos de cine* and *La gran ilusión*.

Not adhering to the Cahierist traditions of cinematic writing, however, opened possibilities to more fluid definitions of "cinema" itself. This flexibility would be a distinct advantage in coping with the rapid changes that would affect Peruvian cinema in the early twenty-first century. With the already established interest in television, for example, *Butaca sanmarquina*'s interest in how digital video was being used in contemporary local filmmaking practices (September 2000) did not seem out of place, planting a seed for later discussions of how the Internet and video would also affect filmmaking in Peru.

The less discriminate understanding of cinephilia also allowed for Marco Avilés's fascinating "review" of Federico García's 1999 film *El Amauta* (The Wise One), which reads more like an essay about alternate exhibition practices held in Lima. Continuing his trend of biographical pictures concerning significant Peruvian countercultural figures (such as *Melgar, el poeta insurgente* [Melgar: The Insurgent Poet, 1982] and *Túpac Amaru* [1984]), this period piece explores the early life of José Carlos Mariátegui, an intellectual considered one of the main figures in Latin American Marxism. The problem, as Avilés notes quickly in his piece, was that García could not show the film in commercial theaters precisely because he did not have enough funding to make theatrical prints; the version he viewed at the Centro Cultural de España was, as he puts it, "a poor copy on video." The more nefarious issue—and what makes this particular "review" more compelling than most—was how the film had been denied funding by a variety of sources, including commercial television sales and CONACINE, which considered the film "a work that, for its questionable artistic level and commercial potential, was not deemed an appropriate choice to finance."[44] Instead of then reviewing the film, as was customary for this section of the magazine, Avilés instead chose to meditate on "the ways in which culture and market are intertwined in a country like Peru or, more precisely, what happens when art must also be profitable."[45] Avilés continued by restating the idea that both exhibitors and producers worked against developing a more "open" sense of national cinema, only rewarding films that will guarantee a good return on their investment and working against films with a political bent; he notes that in comments offered before the screening García made a joking reference to the recently released *No se lo digas a nadie* (a blockbuster directed by Francisco Lombardi), stating that "if Mariátegui had only been gay, surely this film would be on screens."[46] The conclusions that Avilés arrived at with this piece are neither surprising nor new—but that *Butaca sanmarquina* published a rather polemical piece on a film otherwise destined for obscurity highlights important distinctions. For one, definitions of "cinema" can be fluid enough to include this version shown on video tape in a nontheatrical setting; indeed, while his films have not been positively reviewed since 1977's *Kuntur Wachana*, García himself insists that his films are watched in many nontraditional formats, including screenings at community centers and union meetings and purchases from black-market vendors.[47] Thus, including a review on this piece invited readers to consider how this film might be included within a less concrete definition of "Peruvian cinema."

Although the organizational structure and types of articles and writing are consistent with the previous ten issues, *Butaca sanmarquina* 11 (April 2002; fig. 20) indicated a shift in focus through a major visual layout change. Cover design—which had consisted undramatically of a photographic film still encompassing the entire page with the title and cover lines (lines of text placed on the cover) superimposed on top of the photograph—now separated all text out into areas above (with black text on white background) and below (white text on black background) a large, colorful film still from Álvaro Velarde's *El destino no tiene favoritos* (Destiny Has No Favorites, 2002). The cover was far more striking and attention-grabbing than any of the previous had been, and served to separate the journal from other publications. Inside, a smaller font was used throughout the publication and often placed white text on black backgrounds as frequently as black text on white. The sleek, modern look achieved by the use of black instead of white to set off text brought a visual cohesiveness extending from the cover throughout the journal. The following issue (12, August 2002) also established an organization strategy for the content, dividing articles (much as *La gran ilusión* had) into distinct, recognizable sections, some of which were wittily named for other movies: "Interiors" (a play on the 1978 Woody Allen film title) for the

Figure 20: Cover of *Butaca sanmarquina* 11 (April 2002). Courtesy of Dirección de Cine y Televisión of the Centro Cultural de San Marcos.

section bringing together writings on national cinema, "Los olvidados" (literally, "The Forgotten Ones," though the English film title of the 1950 Mexican film by Luis Buñuel is *The Young and the Damned*) for the reprinting of historical film writing, and so forth. By the next issue (13), these layout changes were standardized so that later issues could be vertically associated with the new volumes.

As had the changes in the format of *Hablemos de cine*, the new look of *Butaca sanmarquina* 11 marked an ideological shift. Unlike the earlier publication's, however, this ideological shift was accompanied (and largely brought about) by a shift in personnel. Replacing Samillán as director was René Weber, a professor and filmmaker who had been an original member of the Grupo Chaski and whose writing provided a more provocative viewpoint for the previously otherwise nonpolemical publication. The editorial from volume 7 (September 2000) demonstrated the difference between the two directors: Samillán began the piece by congratulating Francisco Lombardi for winning a number of prizes at the Gramado (Brazil) film festival before briefly noting that the Peruvian government had, three years late, finally paid into the Ibermedia funding program. Rather than comment on the issue himself, Samillán ceded the space to Weber, who both highlighted the opportunities that participation within the program might bring and noted that the cinematic community must remain vigilant to ensure that defaulting on participation in the program did not happen again:

> *By finally submitting the $100,000 to the Ibermedia fund, our country can stop taking on the role of "ugly duckling" in the annual meetings among the Ibero-American film authorires. At the same time, the Peruvian representatives of CONACINE can also stop interacting with such a timid, notable low-profile manner against the government's unwillingness to fulfill a promise. . . . There is no time to let the ball drop on this issue; we must already begin the struggle to ensure the next annual payment gets paid as, after all, the governmental contribution comes annually.*[48]

Weber's writing is not necessarily polemical here but it is nonetheless firm on an issue of cinematic importance at the national level; notably, however, Samillán was unwilling to sign his own name to such rhetoric. The announcement in René Weber's editorial in volume 11, which declared that "starting with the next issue, *Butaca sanmarquina* will demonstrate some changes in structure and content," clearly signaled that the publication would no longer remain a mere pedagogical outlet.[49]

Within six months, *Butaca sanmarquina* began its transition to become, if not the dominant force in Peruvian film criticism, certainly the most important publication with regard to national cinema; it became the locus for virtually all debate concerning contemporary issues of Peruvian filmmaking. Many of its earlier supposed weaknesses became strengths as Peruvian cinematic culture slowly turned away from the traditional. For example, I have stated at many points thus far that *Hablemos de cine* as a journalistic entity benefited greatly from having Isaac León as the single, influential editor-in-chief who remained in that post for the entire run of the publication. Seen positively, his presence grounded the publication; taken negatively, his influence produced a singular form of criticism to a fault, causing Peruvian film criticism—and subsequently filmmaking—to become homogenized. *Butaca sanmarquina* benefited from the shift to Weber, who clearly wanted to stretch the possibilities of the publication by introducing more theoretical perspectives. Weber himself stated that one of the biggest changes in the publication was the appointment of an advisory board, establishing a diversity of senior-level writers. At the same time, many of the students who started with the journal—including Rony Chávez, Gabriel Quispe, and Carlos Zevallos—continued to craft their writing into a much clearer, mature style by incorporating more theoretical and historical perspectives. All three of these began by writing unremarkable reviews of Oscar-nominated films in the first issue; just five years later, in the December 2003 issue, all three wrote sophisticated historical pieces for a special collection of essays on film genres. It should also be noted that *Butaca sanmarquina*'s relatively regular and frequent release schedule—roughly every three months—allowed it to still review a wide range of contemporary releases in a more timely fashion than any of the other periodicals. Although the number of reviews published per article were generally fewer than at *Tren de sombras* (also publishing at this time), each piece was given two pages; the journal's more frequent publication schedule actually allowed it to assess more films over the course of the year.

Newer film practices in Peru also continued to be a priority in the pages of *Butaca sanmarquina*. Although the periodical quickly phased out its emphasis on television in order to concentrate on cinema, digital and Internet practices became hot topics, particularly as applied to a Peruvian context. For example, the June 2004 issue features an article by Claudia Ugarte on the Internet listserve called Cinemaperú. This article confirms that the most vibrant discussions about "Peruvian national cinema" have moved away from the pages of film journals to the Internet, where everyone can "read, learn about, get riled up about, respond, learn, teach, discuss, propose, are wrong, ask forgiveness—in other words, all use the Internet to elaborate the script of a contemporary debate: what to do with Peruvian national cinema?"[50]

The primary contribution of *Butaca sanmarquina* from the beginning was its emphasis on Peruvian cinema; while decreasing the more informational interviews with myriad filmmakers, the journal under Weber turned to more polemical issues that went beyond the pedagogical, but—uniquely—without alienating different perspectives. The October 2003 issue, for example, bought together seven articles on the current state of DVD piracy in Peru from a range of perspectives: from a report on a university cine-club that only shows pirated films, to the first-person "confessions of a pirate," to an interview with Martín Moscoso, the head of INDECOPI, the national copyright protection agency.

Long before *Tren de sombras* would address the topic, *Butaca sanmarguina* 13 (October 2002) featured "Critiquing the Critics (*Crítica de la crítica*)," prompted by a roundtable discussion between many of the critics currently writing and compiled by senior writer Christian Wiener. This piece summarized the history of film criticism in Peru while also exposing the faults of the majority of contemporary critics—and noting that the roundtable at one point devolved into "a useless and sometime personal interchange between the 'godfathers' of *La gran ilusión* and their apparently angry illegitimate children at *godard!*"[51] A side box provides self-perception from four critics of various ages, representing four publications: Emilio Bustamante from *La gran ilusión*, Mario Castro Cobos from *Abre los ojos*, Gabriel Quispe from *Butaca* and Jaime Luis Victoria from the news magazine *Etecé.* Notably absent from this group is *godard!* which may indicate what little regard Wiener and *Butaca* held for the maverick publication.

Given the animosity demonstrated in this story, one cannot imagine a debate about any aspect of national cinema in *La gran ilusión, Tren de sombras*, or *godard!* given the stated polemical positioning of both publications. Particularly in the second phase of its publication run, *Butaca sanmarquina* became the written voice for such discussions. The largest testament to this is that many feuding critics would meet on Butaca's pages, even when they had their own periodical as a platform. A key example is a rather lengthy, public exchange of letters printed over three issues of *Butaca sanmarquina* between critic and theorist Balmes Lozano and Isaac León Frías concerning the former's appropriation of auteur theory toward Peruvian directors and the latter's point that analogies between Hollywood and Lima as "industrial cinematic entities" are ruinous. The details of this debate are less at issue than the recognition that these two large figures within Peruvian criticism came together in debate within *Butaca.*

René Weber's editorial for volume 20 referenced the inaugural issue: "'We begin with a sense of modesty,' Samillán affirmed in the first issue. We have continued working with such modesty, but we have also set ourselves goals that are each time more ambitious, goals that preserve a critical and polemical spirit."[52] This particular issue tackled the larger question of the national within the global, political, and economic power structures as various directors, critics, and theorists debated Peru's place within UNESCO. Also debated were the World Trade Organization discussions in 2002 concerning cultural diversity and cultural exception, two concepts called for by France and Canada to protect their own film industries against the monopolizing force from the United States. Given the scope of this question, which involved much more than university-level cinephilic readers, as a final bid for "respectability" of a sort, the journal made a slight but significant alteration: the title dropped the word "sanmarquina"; following June 2004, the journal was simply known as *Butaca*. Internationally, this might cause some confusion as at this point there were at least three specialized film publications elsewhere in the world with this name. Locally, however, such a demarcation freed the journal ideologically from its institutional backing; as Weber noted in the editorial, it could now raise itself to "a higher professional standard." With contributions from many different political and ideological perspectives (even from rival periodicals), *Butaca* had, even before the name change, garnered respect as the premiere publication in which to discuss any aspect of Peruvian cinema. As the most valuable lasting resource of its time—precisely because of its ability to reflect the contemporary situation of "national cinema" in Peru and embrace and encourage new frontiers in how to define Peruvian cinema—*Butaca*, like *Hablemos de cine* before it, may prove itself further over the next twenty years not only to have chronicled what Peruvian films were produced, but also perhaps to have shaped Peruvian cinema writ large.

NOTES

Introduction

1. Unless otherwise indicated, all translations are the author's.
2. Throughout this book, I have used several Spanish nouns that denote the location where a person is said to be from, much like "New Yorker" or "Londoner" in English. The two most common used here are *limeño* and *cusqueño*, which in dicate someone from Lima and Cuzco respectively. Similarly, a noun form identifying writers at *Hablemos de cine* has been left in the Spanish, *hablemista*, a term commonly used by Peruvian critics and film historians.
3. Benedict Anderson, *Imagined Communities: Reflections on the Origin and Spread of Nationalism* (London: Verso, 1983), xx (my emphasis).
4. For this reason, governments also realized early the power and potential of cinema in fostering senses of nationalism and started funding the possibilities as a kind of "arming themselves" against Hollywood ideology/product. Extreme examples are Leni Riefenstahl and her Nazi propaganda films, Soviet cinema following 1917, Cuban cinema following the 1959 revolution, and the like.
5. Pierre Bourdieu, "The Field of Cultural Production; or, The Economic World Reversed," in *The Field of Cultural Production: Essays on Art and Literature* (New York: Columbia University Press, 1993), 35–36.
6. Núria Triana-Toribio, *Spanish National Cinema* (London: Routledge, 2003); Anna Everett, *Returning the Gaze: A Genealogy of Black Film Criticism, 1909–1949* (Durham: Duke University Press, 2001).
7. Alberto Elena and Marina Díaz López, eds., *The Cinema of Latin America: 24 Frames* (London: Wallflower Press, 2003). The book's introduction specifically

states that "the main criterion of this work has been the *representativeness* of the films under study" (2; my emphasis).

8. Mikel Luis, "*La boca del lobo*," in *Tierra en trance: El cine latinoamericano en 100 películas*, ed. Alberto Elena y Marina Díaz López (Madrid: Alianza, 1999), 360.

9. Isaac León Frías, "*La boca del lobo*," *Caretas* (December 12, 1988): 71.

10. León's review of *Misión en los Andes* for *Caretas* (September 7, 1987) might also apply to Lombardi's film a year later: "The film is no more than a mechanical succession of dynamic episodes that operate on the most superficial levels of storytelling. These are aptly supported by elements which would be OK in an American production, but which are new for one made here: the use of doubles and special effects, which provides us with the novelty of seeing extensive car chases on our roads, a car falling off a cliff or a fistfight on top of a train going over a bridge" (60).

11. José Carlos Mariategui, *Siete ensayos de interpretación de la realidad peruana* (Barcelona: Linkgua, 2006); Domingo Faustino Sarmiento, *Facundo: Civilization and Barbarism*, trans. Kathleen Ross (Berkeley and Los Angeles: University of California Press, 2004).

12. Angel Rama, *The Lettered City*, trans. John Chasteen (Durham, N.C.: Duke University Press, 1996).

13. It should be noted that the cinematic movement in Peru also began just after Mario Vargas Llosa's literary marvel *La ciudad y los perros* (*The City and the Dogs*) won the 1962 Biblioteca Breve award in Spain, marking the start of the Latin American "boom" of novels that gained international attention. Though the best-known text from this movement remains Gabriel García Márquez's 1967 novel *Cien años de soledad* (One Hundred Years of Solitude), the first works to gain traction (including Vargas Llosa's work and Argentine Julio Cortázar's 1963 novel *Rayuela* [Hopscotch]) were characterized by stylistically complex narrative structures that called attention to a postmodern style and notably urban settings, both also rejecting more "traditional" approaches to Latin American iconography in literature and receiving international attention for it.

14. Ian Hayden Smith, ed., *TCM International Film Guide 2008: The Definitive Annual Review of World Cinema* (London: Wallflower Press, 2008).

15. Ricardo Bedoya's *100 años del cine en el Perú* (Lima: University of Lima Press, 1996) is the most complete work to date. Outside of Peru, the country's cinema is discussed only fleetingly in several overviews of Latin American film as a whole. To offer some examples, one chapter in John King's *Magical Reels: A History of Cinema in Latin America* (London: Verso, 1990) devotes six pages total (246–250) to Peruvian cinema; Paulo Antonio Paranaguá's section of the

Spanish-language *Historia general del cine* (Madrid: Catedra, 1995) devotes three pages (10:369–371); Zuzana M. Pick's *The New Latin American Cinema: A Continental Project* (Austin: University of Texas Press, 1993) does not mention Peruvian cinema at all.

16. Pick, *New Latin American Cinema.*

Chapter 1. A History of the Peruvian Cinematic Tradition

1. I have relied heavily on Ricardo Bedoya's thorough and detailed history of Peruvian cinema, *100 años de cine en el Perú: Una historia crítica* (Lima: Universidad de Lima, 1996) for the information in this section, especially concerning historical information before 1965. In this history, I have also used Bedoya's *Un cine reencontrado: Diccionario ilustrado de las películas peruanas* (Lima: Universidad de Lima, 1997), an exhaustive chronological exploration of all films filmed in Peru from 1910 to 1997; José Perla Anaya's *Censura y promoción en el cine* (Lima: Universidad de Lima, 1991), an examination of legal documents as they pertain to cinematic production and exhibition from 1897 to 1991; Giancarlo Carbone's three volumes collected under the title *El cine en el Perú, 1897–1950* (Lima: Universidad de Lima, 1991), *Testimonios, 1950–1972* (Lima: Universidad de Lima, 1993), *El cortometraje: 1972–1992* (Lima: Universidad de Lima, 2007); and selections from *Contratexto*, issue 9 (December 1995). Isaac León Frías also wrote an early film history in 1970 titled "Hacia una historia del cine peruano" for *Hablemos de cine* 50–51 (November 1969–February 1970).
2. Ricardo Bedoya, "La formación del público cinematográfico en el Perú: El cine de los señores, *Contratexto* 9 (December 1995), 58–59. It is difficult to approximate today the class composition of other Latin American spectators: Emilio García Riera recounts that the first exhibition in Mexico of the Lumière cinematograph was held in the Grand Café where the public was "accommodated in plush theater seats," but says nothing of the class makeup of the patrons; *Breve historia del cine mexicano: Primer siglo, 1897–1997* (Mexico City: Instituto Mexicano de Cinematografía, 1998), 18. Likewise, Jacqueline Mouesca cites an anonymous 1896 review in Santiago, Chile, that focused on the dimensions of the screen and the images that passed on it, but overlooked the composition of the audience in the seats; *El cine en Chile: Crónica en tres tiempos* (Santiago de Chile: Editorial Planeta, 1997), 113–114. For a comparative overview of early Latin American cinema that includes Peru in its analysis, see Ana M. López, "Early Cinema and Modernity in Latin America," *Cinema Journal* 40, no. 1 (Fall 2000), 48–78.
3. Although the movie tents decreased as more sturdy (and less flammable) movie

theaters were built, the tents coexisted with the theatrical buildings until well into the 1930s.

4. Quoted in Bedoya, *Un cine reencontrado*, 97.

5. Unfortunately, few of the movies made by Amauta Films are available to view. The description of this film is summarized from Bedoya's *Un cine reencontrado*. One of the last films made by Amauta, *Cordero's Conflicts* (*Los conflictos de Cordero*; Sigifredo Salas, 1940) was restored in 2002 by the Filmoteca de Lima. This was the second complete restoration project for the Filmoteca, the first having been the silent film *I Lost My Heart in Lima* (*Yo perdí mi corazón en Lima*, 1929), restored in 1995.

6. This persona exists the world over under a variety of names. As detailed in a November 1938 review of the film in *Universal*: "France has its *gavroche* and *little man of Paris* [the *titi*]; Madrid, its *golfillo*; Chile, its *patacalata santiaguino*; Buenos Aires, its *canillita*. In all locations the childishness, combined with the striving for semi-manliness, demonstrates determined spirit and singular customs" (qtd. in Bedoya, *Un cine reencotrado*, 125).

7. I am avoiding here a discussion of the film's moral suggestion that it is better to remain in your own neighborhood/class than to try to get ahead.

A note should be made about the word "criollo." Ethnic studies have generally discussed "creole" as the intermingling of different racially and ethnically marked attributes into new attributes. Such is definitely true with what has been termed Peruvian criollo music, which indicates a blend of Spanish poetics with African rhythms that blended into Peru's most popular music on the coast. But the word "criollo" has a loaded, complicated significance in Peru. Originally used during the colonial period to distinguish white colonizers born in the New World from those born in Spain, the term has gained a connotation exclusively referring to the white, elite population, excluding all other racial identities. Intellectuals around the turn of the twentieth century who supported a more inclusive Peruvian identity, such as Manuel González Prada and José Carlos Mariátegui, spoke and wrote of criollo culture in derogatory terms.

8. Quoted in Perla Anaya, *Censura y promoción*, 63–64.

9. Emilio García Riera, *Breve historia del cine mexicano*, 120. Michael Chanan also notes in his entry on early Latin American film in *The Oxford History of World Cinema* (ed. Geoffrey Nowell-Smith [Oxford: Oxford University Press, 1997]) that concentration on Mexican filmmaking "was boosted again in 1943 when the United States, angered by Argentina's neutrality in the war and suspicious of its links with Fascism, took measures which included cutting off its supplies of virgin film stock in favour of Mexico" (433–434).

10. Paolo Antonio Paranaguá, *Le cinéma en Amérique Latine: le miroir éclaté* (Paris: L'Harmattan, 2000), 65.

11. Bedoya, *100 años de cine en el Perú*, 140.

12. L. Lunders, "Office Catholique International du Cinéma," in *The New Catholic Encyclopedia,* vol. 10, *Mos to Pat* (New York: McGraw-Hill, 1967), 655. Lunders notes that heightened cinematic interest in Latin America precipitated the opening of a regionally oriented office in Lima in 1963.
13. As a point of comparison, Scott MacDonald notes that New York's Cinema 16 cine-club featured nearly seven thousand members "at its height" between 1947 and 1963; MacDonald, *Cinema 16: Documents Toward a History of the Film Society* (Philadelphia: Temple University Press, 2002), 1.
14. Giancarlo Carbone, "Entrevista con Andrés Ruszkowski," in *El cine en el Perú: Testimonios, 1950–1972*, 38.
15. Pius XI, "Vigilanti Cura," in *The Papal Encyclicals, 1903–1939*, comp. Claudia Carlen (Wilmington, N.C.: McGrath, 1981), 520.
16. Pius XII, "Miranda Prorsus," in *The Papal Encyclicals, 1939–1958*, comp. Claudia Carlen Ihm (Wilmington, N.C.: McGrath, 1981), 363. This confluence of church and film was not unique to Peru: critic and historian Paulo Antonio Paranaguá has in fact noted that the easy embrace of Italian neorealism in Latin America was a "'historical compromise' [that] took place in the *cine-clubs*, a confluence of Marxists and Christians. . . . Both sides agreed that film has a messianic mission to fulfill: Marxists could project their desire for transparency onto Neo-realism while Catholics could see their own aspirations to immanence reflected there. We can consequently assume that the quasi-religious political films of the sixties have their origins in the debates unleashed in the fifties' '*cine-clubs*.'" See Paulo Antonio Paranaguá, "Of Periodizations and Paradigms: The Fifties in Comparative Perspective," *Nuevo Texto Critico* 21–22 (January–December 1998), 41.
17. For more on defining "art cinema," see Steve Neale's "Art Cinema as Institution," *Screen* 22, no. 1 (1981), 11–40.
18. See Carbone's interviews with Desiderio Blanco (60–69) and Juan Bullitta (71–88) in *El cine en el Perú: Testimonios, 1950–1972*.
19. Asked in an interview whether he was a founding member of *Hablemos de cine*, Blanco replied, "Yes, without actually being one. I sparked the *Hablemos de cine* movement. But they surprised me with the journal already completed. . . . One day they decided to publish [their opinions]. And I, coming back from a vacation, found that they had dedicated the first issue to me. It was a surprise" (qtd. in Carbone, *El cine en el Perú*, 62).
20. See chapter 6 for more commentary on Lima's reaction to the Cuzco school.
21. Ricardo Bedoya, *100 años de cine en el Perú*, 145 n. 7. In an interview, Manuel Chambi noted humorously that Sadoul not only referred to him as an "Inca" but also mistakenly called him "Jorge." See "Manuel Chambi López," in Carbone, *El Cine en el Perú: Testimonios, 1950–1972* (Lima: Universidad de Lima, 1993), 105.

22. Peruvians writing about the film laws established in 1962, 1972, and 1994 generally shorthand each law by referencing the law's number (in this case, 13936). A this referencing has little resonance outside Peru, I have chosen to instead refer to them by the year they became law (in this case, the Film Law of 1962).

23. See chapter 3 for a discussion as to how all of these films that took advantage of the Film Law of 1962 were evaluated and used as examples of "poor quality" cinema by *Hablemos de cine.*

24. See chapter 4 for an in-depth examination of the Viña del Mar Film Festivals, particularly with an eye to *Hablemos de cine*'s evaluation of Latin American cinema. See also festival director Aldo Francia's recollections of the festival in *Nuevo cine latinoamericano en Viña del Mar* (Santiago de Chile: CESOC Ediciones ChileAmérica, 1990).

25. "Towards a Third Cinema" was originally published in the Cuban journal *Tricontinental. Hablemos de cine* published it in issue 54 (July–August 1970), 49–55. In English the manifesto first appeared in *Cinéaste*, translated by Julianne Burton-Carvajal and can now be found in *New Latin American Cinema*, vol. 1, *Theory, Practices and Transcontinental Articulations*, ed. Michael T. Martin (Detroit: Wayne State University Press, 1997), 33–58.

26. Pick, *The New Latin American Cinema*, 23. Paulo Antonio Paranaguá notes that both Lombardi and Ruiz were students of the Santa Fé (Argentina) film school run by Fernando Birri, ironically one of the filmmakers that inspired Cine Liberación ("América latina busca su imagen," 336–337).

27. "Información: La sociedad peruana de cinematografía," *Hablemos de cine* 34 (March–April 1967), 30: emphasis in original.

28. Carbone, *El cine en el Perú: Testimonios, 1950–1972*, 188–189.

29. See Paulo Antonio Paranaguá's comparison of these three film laws in "América latina busca su imagen," *Historia general del cine*, ed. Carlos F. Heredero and Casimiro Torreiro (Madrid: Cátedra, 1996), 366.

30. José Perla Anaya, *Censura y promoción*, 181.

31. Ibid., 184.

32. The new boon of short films even attracted veteran auteur Armando Robles Godoy away from feature films to concentrate on developing his Film Workshop and directing films in the shorter format. Following the implementation of the law in 1972, the only feature he would direct again would be *Sonata Soledad* (Sonata of loneliness, 1987), which was never given a general commercial release.

33. Ironically, this was a review of Truffaut's *The Bride Wore Black* (81–82).

34. Bedoya, *100 años de cine en el Perú*, 249.

35. José Carlos Huayhuaca, et al., "Francisco Lombardi: 'Hacer cine en el Perú es para mi poner los pies en la tierra,'" *Hablemos de cine* 67 (1975), 30.

36. Federico de Cárdenas, "Una constación y una repuesta," *Hablemos de cine* 69 (1977–78), 21.
37. Isaac León Frías, "Cine peruano: La búsqueda de una voz propria en el largometraje peruano," *Hablemos de cine* 29 (1977–78), 17.
38. Federico de Cárdenas, "Una constación y una repuesta," 21.
39. In an article summarizing the events in national cinema over this period, Federico de Cárdenas acknowledged that the delay is attributable to "the always precarious economic situation of this publication" ("Una constación y una repuesta," 21).
40. Javier Proetzel, "Grandez y decandencia del espectáculo cinematográfico," *Contratexto* 9 (December 1995): 121–122.
41. Also an exception: three Argentine co-productions attempted to bring comedian Tulio Loza (of *Nemesio* fame) to an international audience: *Contacto en Argentina* (Contact in Argentina; Saraceni, 1980), *Abierto día y noche* (Open day and night; Ayala, 1982), and *Compre antes que se acabe* (Buy before it's gone; Galettini, 1983), none of which succeeded.
42. Durant's admission into Sundance comes less than six months after a tribute to the Sundance Film Festival made at the 2003 *elcine* (Encuentro Latinoamericano de Cine) Film Festival sponsored by Universidad Católica's cultural center; Caroline Libresco, a programmer for Sundance, represented the festival along with feature director John Cameron Mitchell (who debuted *Hedwig and the Angry Inch* in Peru at the festival) and Gail Dolgin (*Daughter from Danang*). Since then, Claudia Llosa's *Madeinusa* (2006) and Ricardo de Montreuil's *Máncora* (2008) have also competed in the feature section of the festival.
43. René Weber, "El Grupo Chaski: Una película sin 'Happy End,'" *Butaca sanmarquina* 1 (July–August–September 1998), 22–24. Weber also writes a second firsthand article about the experience of shooting and distributing *Juliana* in "La pared que habla: La fascinante experiencia de la Difución Popular del Grupo Chaski," *Butaca sanmarquina* 2 (October–December 1998), 8–9. For more information about the practices of Grupo Chaski in the 1970s and in the re-formed version in the 2000s, see Sophia McClennan's "The Theory and Practice of the Peruvian Grupo Chaski," *Jump Cut* 50 (Spring 2008), http://www.ejumpcut.org/currentissue/Chaski/text.html (accessed June 2, 2008).
44. There is a common misconception, even by Peruvian filmmakers, that D.L. 19327 was repealed at the end of 2002. José Perla Anaya's interview in Carbone's *El cine en el Perú: El cortometraje, 1972–1992* counters this argument with the explanation offered in the text (36).
45. Christian Wiener F., "Los cazadores de la ley perdida," *Contratexto* 9 (December 1995), 108.
46. The issue of governmental concern with regard to cultural exception continued

over the twelve years it would take until the UNESCO Convention on the Protection and Promotion of the Diversity of Cultural Expressions would be ratified in 2005. René Weber compiled a dossier on local concerns on the topic in *Butaca sanmarquina* 20 (June 2004), 37–43. See also the UNESCO Convention on the Protection and Promotion of the Diversity of Cultural Expressions (Paris: UNESCO, October 2005), http://unesdoc.unesco.org/images/0014/001429/142919e.pdf.

47. The Peruvian features released in 2003 are more fully detailed in chapter 7.

48. Sarah Barrow, "Peruvian Cinema and the Struggle for International Recognition: Case Study on *El destino no tiene favoritos*," in *Contemporary Latin American Cinema: Breaking into the Global Market*, ed. Deborah Shaw (Lanham, Md.: Rowman and Littlefield, 2007), 185–186. For more on the influence of Ibermedia on Latin American cinema, see Tamara Falicov, "Programa Ibermedia: Co-Production and the Cultural Politics of Constructing an Ibero-American Audiovisual Space," *Spectator* 27, no. 2 (Fall 2007), 21–30.

Chapter 2. Publication, Authority, Identity

1. "Proyecto de revista cinematográfica," Preliminary outline of journal project (Filmoteca de Lima/Museo de Arte Edubanco, Lima, Peru, (January 2, 1965), 2.

2. Marijke de Valck and Malte Hagener's fascinating edited collection *Cinephilia: Movies, Love and Memory* (Amsterdam: Amsterdam University Press, 2005) collects contemporary perspectives of cinephilia in the age of video and digital technology. In particular, Thomas Elsaesser's "Cinephilia; or, the Uses of Disenchantment" (27–44) provides brief historical context going back to France in the 1920s, though the concentration of his piece (and the rest of the volume) is on the years after the 1980s.

3. Christian Metz, *The Imaginary Signifier: Psychoanalysis and the Cinema* (Bloomington: Indiana University Press, 1997), 12.

4. Laura Mulvey, "Visual Pleasure and Narrative Cinema," in *Visual and Other Pleasures* (Bloomington: Indiana University Press, 1989). Since its original publication, Mulvey's argument on "visual pleasure" has been hotly debated and contested, with Mulvey herself stepping back from some of her most damning claims. I am making the distinction between *cinephilia* and *scopophilia* here because the latter term is still primarily used and thought of in Mulvey's context.

5. Ibid., 16.

6. Paul Willemen, *Looks and Frictions: Essays in Cultural Studies and Film Theory* (Bloomington: Indiana University Press, 1994), 232.

7. Mulvey, "Visual Pleasure and Narrative Cinema," 17.

8. Willemen, *Looks and Frictions*, 237.
9. Roland Barthes despairs of the photographic image throughout most of the second half of *Camera Lucida: Reflections on Photography* (New York: Hill and Wang, 1981). At the heart of the text (Barthes's last and written soon after his mother's death), a photograph of his mother as a young girl only reconfirms her death for him.
10. The inability to get beyond the solitary voyeur is the major problem with Norman K. Denzin's premise of *The Cinematic Society: The Voyeur's Gaze* (London: Sage, 1995), which finds the film spectators as a group doomed to individual, objectifying perversity rather than exploring the notion that those who have had the same experience might share it with one another.
11. Several publications, particularly those with an expressed international focus, like *Close-Up* in the 1920s and 1930s, did not or could not be local; such journals logically were also not concerned with questions of "national cinema," instead dealing with the medium itself. (See Anne Friedberg's dissertation on *Close-Up*.) With the advent of globzalized communities, particularly through the Internet in the 1990s, cinephilia has another opportunity to move away from its dependence on the cine-club, as evidenced by chat rooms, message boards, blogs, and webpages — all allowing multiple interactions with movies and a large potentially international community.
12. See particularly chapter 2, "Defending and Defining the Seventh Art: The Standard Version of Stylistic History," in David Bordwell's, *On the History of Film Style* (Cambridge, Mass.: Harvard University Press, 1997).
13. Interestingly, Bernadette Plot's examination of the original *Revue du cinéma* (1928–1930) does not specifically mention a particular cine-club as being instrumental to the journal's formation, though the cultural climate she describes indicates the early journal was debated among the cine-club climate. The journal was reconfigured following World War II and is seen as the primary precursor for *Cahiers du cinéma*. See Plot, *Un manifeste pour le cinéma: Les normes culturelles en question dans la première Revue du cinéma* (Paris: Editions L'Harmattan, 1996); de Baecque, "Incipit: la scène primitive," *Les Cahiers du cinéma: Histoire d'une revue* (Paris: Editions Cahiers du cinéma, 1991), 1:13–20.
14. Olivier Barrot, *L'Ecran Français, 1943–1953: Histoire d'un journal et d'une époque* (Paris: Les Edituers Français Reunis, 1979), 11–13.
15. See de Baecque, "Contre-culture cinéphilique," *Les Cahiers du cinéma: Histoire d'une revue* (Paris: Editions Cahiers du cinéma, 1991), 1:20–26; Jim Hillier, ed., introduction to *Cahiers du cinéma, The 1950s: Neo-Realism, Hollywood, New Wave* (Cambridge, Mass.: Harvard University Press, 1985), 1–5.
16. Iván Tubau, *Crítica cinematográfica española, Bazin contra Aristarco: La gran*

controversia de los años 60 (Barcelona: Publicacions Edicions Universitat de Barcelona, 1983), 33–43.

17. Mouesca, *El cine en Chile* (Santiago: Editorial Planeta, 1997), 58, 94–96.
18. Willemen, *Looks and Frictions*, 239.
19. Ibid., 233.
20. Gender is mentioned only in passing in the published interview with Nora de Izcué in issue 67 (1975). She noted that she was a housewife with no real future to speak of before coming to filmmaking: "My life, like that of so many women, was for the most part predestined. It seemed as if my future was already planned, but occasionally one can construct her own destiny" (37). Women have developed a slightly more significant presence in Peruvian film culture in the 1990s. Marianne Eyde has also emerged as a significant director, having produced three feature films in the last fifteen years. In criticism, Rafaela García Sanabria became one of the primary editors of *Hablemos de cine*'s successor *La gran illusión*, having been a critic at the large daily newspaper *El Comercio* since 1980; Monica Delgado is a younger critic now writing for *Tren de sombras*.
21. Ibid.
22. Spanish critic Iván Tubau's *Crítica cinematográfica española* gives an excellent account of the debate between the two journals, complete with numerous interviews with staff members of both magazines. *Nuestro Cine* writer and *Hablemos de cine* contributor Miguel Marías noted in an interview that he was at first "disgusted" with the idea of writing for a journal he had always detested, having affiliated himself as a reader of *Film Ideal* (263–264).
23. The *Nuestro Cine* contributors who ended up on the masthead at *Hablemos de cine* were Jesús Martínez León, Augusto M. Torres, and Vicente Molina Foix. Other collaborators included José María Carreño, José María Palá, Ramón Font, Jos Olivier, Marcelino Villegas, and Miguel Marías. Most of this last group were primary contributors to the retrospective of American cinema published between issues 39 and 46 (January–February 1968 to March–April 1969).
24. A note about the rating system at *Hablemos de cine*: according to a document written by the editors during the original planning stages of the journal ("Proyecto"), films would be reviewed and given a rating between 0 (abysmal) and 5 (extraordinary). The Peruvians based their rating system on the one established by the Spanish film journal *Film Ideal*, though they argue in this document that their system allowed a greater range.
25. Federico de Cárdenas, "La mujer de paja," *Hablemos de cine* 1 (February 15, 1965), 14.
26. "Presentación," *Hablemos de cine* 1 (February 15 1965), 1–2.

27. André Bazin, "On the *politiques des auteurs*," in *Cahiers du Cinéma*, ed. Hillier, 248.
28. Ethnomusicologist Mark Slobin coins this term in "Micromusics of the West: A Comparative Approach," *Ethnomusicology* 36, no. 1 (Winter 1992), 1–87.
29. Marsha Kinder, *Blood Cinema: The Reconstruction of National Identity in Spain* (Berkeley and Los Angeles: University of California Press, 1993), 3–4, 22–26.
30. Tubau, *Crítica cinematográfica española*, 52; emphasis in original.
31. For example, in Chile, the very first issue of *Ecran* in 1930 listed two editors-in-chief: Roberto Aldunate in Santiago and Carlos Borcosque in Hollywood, the latter of whom provided a connection with U.S. film activity during the first eight years of the publication (Mouesca, *El cine en Chile*, 58–60).
32. See Isaac León's fawning review of Corman's *Tomb of Ligeia* (1964), an adaptation of a Edgar Allan Poe story, in issue 18 (September 1, 1965), 54–56. Corman would, in fact, later co-produce a number of films in Peru directed by Luis Llosa, including *Hour of the Assassin* (1987), *Crime Zone* (1989), *Fire on the Amazon* (1991), and *800 Leagues Down the Amazon* (1993).
33. Tavernier's connection with *Hablemos de cine* ended before he achieved his own success as a director. León and de Cárdenas discuss Tavernier and other European correspondents in their published dialogue "Un oficio del siglo XX," *Contratexto* 9 (December 1995): 153–160.
34. Isaac León Frías, personal interview, November 1998. León's trip is announced in issue 42 (July–August 1968); de Cárdenas's is announced in issue 48 (July–August 1969).
35. See chapter 3 for more on the journal's Latin American identity.
36. That other French film magazines (including *Positif*, *Telcine*, and *Revue du cinéma*) also printed major articles with a similar politics at this time seems to imply that the self-assessment of *Cahiers* concerning its readership was accurate.
37. Federico de Cárdenas, personal interview, July 9, 2003.
38. Though most of the photographs included in the journal appear to have been photographic stills provided by distribution companies, it is unclear precisely where the journal obtained their images. In addition to possibly being frame enlargements, the existence of several images from films that were not distributed in Peru — such as Pier Paolo Pasolini's *Decameron* (1971), an image from which was printed in issue 63 (January–March 1972) — indicate that some images might have literally been cut and pasted from other periodicals from abroad.
39. De Cárdenas's other major accomplishment for the journal from this festival was covering a press conference with Polish director Roman Polanski (no. 47, May–June 1969, 65–67).
40. See chapter 4 for an in-depth discussion of Viña del Mar 1969.

Chapter 3. Shaping Peruvian Taste

1. "Presentación," *Hablemos de cine* 1 (February 15, 1965), 1.
2. "Nace el cine nacional," *Hablemos de cine* 3 (March 18, 1965), 3; my emphasis.
3. For a brief overview of Argentine cinema in the first half of the 1960s, see John King, *Magical Reels: A History of Cinema in Latin America* (London: Verso, 1990), 79–84; Timothy Barnard, ed., *Argentine Cinema* (Toronto: Nightwood Editions, 1986).
4. In part because I discuss the quality of films produced from 1972 onward in later chapters, I have limited my discussion within this chapter to Peruvian films made before the Film Law of 1972.
5. Pierre Bourdieu, *Distinction* (London: Routledge, 1979), 466.
6. Christian Keathley, *Cinephilia and History; or, The Wind in the Trees* (Bloomington: Indiana University Press, 2006), 16.
7. The same may be true today. Consider that very few critical reviews and no book-length critical works on Gordon Douglas as an auteur are available in English, Spanish, or French, whereas many such works are available on Bergman.
8. Howard Thompson, "Lively, Tough Western Has Premiere Here," *New York Times*, October 29, 1964, 38.
9. I have chosen to translate *acercamiento* as "analysis," although to do so loses some of the connotation of the word. Literally, the word refers to an "approach"; hence, these analyses are not meant to be definitive treatises on these artists-impossible, given that most of these directors' films were still not viewable in Peru at the time — but rather, informed and critical analyses of directors as auteurs. While it is tempting to call these analyses "introductions" to the artists, the editors seemed to imply that their readers would have at least some referential knowledge of the directors/films. As the journal continued to move away from single-artist toward nationally oriented *acercamientos*, "analysis" functions as a more consistent translation.
10. "Acercamiento a Gordon Douglas," *Hablemos de cine* 2 (March 1, 1965), 28.
11. Ibid.
12. Isaac León Frías, "*Murallas de sangre*," *Hablemos de cine* 2 (March 1, 1965), 32.
13. "Acercamiento a Vicente Minnelli," *Hablemos de cine* 6 (May 1, 1965), 41.
14. The title refers to a slightly altered verse from Mark 10:17: "And as [Jesus] was setting out on his journey, a man came running and knelt before him and asked him, 'Teacher, what must I do to inherit eternal life?'" The passage continues with Jesus telling the man that he should sell all his possessions and give the money to the poor, at which point the man walks away troubled. Elsewhere, in France and in other Spanish-speaking countries, the film was released under the title *Como una tormenta / Comme un torrente*, translated as "Like a deluge."

In Peru, distributors inexplicably changed the title to *Dios sabe cuánto amé*, translated as "God knows how many I loved."

15. "*Some Came Running*," *Variety* (December 24, 1948). In *Variety Film Reviews*, vol. 9, *1954–1958* (New York: Bowker, 1983).
16. "The New Pictures," *Time* (January 12, 1959), 72.
17. Although nominated, MacLaine did not win the Oscar for this film in 1958. Also nominated in 1960 for *The Apartment* and 1963 for *Irma la Douce*, she did not win until 1983 for *Terms of Endearment*.
18. Percy Gibson, "*Dios Sabe Cuánto Amé*," *El Comercio* (April 24, 1965), C1.
19. Philippe Demonsablon, "Scènes de la vie de province," *Cahiers du Cinéma* 97 (July 1959), 50.
20. Ibid., 51.
21. Carlos Rodríguez Larraín, "*Some Came Running (Dios sabe cuánto amé)*," *Hablemos de cine* 6 (May 1, 1965): 52–53.
22. Ibid., 56.
23. Desiderio Blanco, "*Some Came Running (Dios sabe cuánto amé)*," *Hablemos de cine* 6 (May 1, 1965): 50.
24. Larraín, "*Some Came Running*," 53.
25. Blanco, "*Some Came Running*," 48.
26. Estudios Roselló had also produced the last major (failed) feature made in Lima, *La muerte llega al segundo show* (Death Comes to the Second Show, Roselló y Beltrán, 1958). Editorial director Fernando Samillán Cavero published a critical obituary for Radovich, "Vlado, en el recuerdo," in *Butaca sanmarquina* 3 (1998), 28–29.
27. Isaac León Frías and Federico de Cárdenas, "Armando Robles Godoy: Un director peruano," *Hablemos de cine* 4 (April 1, 1965), 15.
28. Ibid., 13.
29. Ibid., 14.
30. "*Ganarás el pan*," *Oiga* (July 16, 1965). In Ricardo Bedoya, *Un cine reencontrado: Diccionario ilustrado de las películas peruanas* (Lima: University of Lima, 1997), 169.
31. León Frías and de Cárdenas, "Armando Robles Godoy," 10.
32. Juan Bullitta, "*Ganarás el pan*," *Hablemos de cine* 11 (July 15, 1965), 38.
33. Carlos Rodríguez Larraín, "*Ganarás el pan*," *Hablemos de cine* 11 (July 15, 1965), 43.
34. Isaac León Frías, "*Ganarás el pan*," *Hablemos de cine* 11 (July 15, 1965), 44.
35. Federcio de Cárdenas, "*Ganarás el pan*," *Hablemos de cine* 11 (July 15, 1965), 45.
36. Bullitta, "*Ganarás el pan*," 42. Carlos Rodríguez Larraín began his review with "*Ganarás el pan* is a film that by virtue of its *intentions* deserves all of our

praise" and ended it with "if *Ganarás el pan*, with regards to the execution, deserves a '0' (we must be fair as much as it goes against our desires), with regards to its intentions it deserves a '5' for its sincerity with which it has tried to express an authentically national theme" (43, 44). Isaac León stated: "it must be noted that this [film] is a great effort and Robles Godoy is a true pioneer who has much more land to explore. I sincerely congratulate him and I wish him the best of luck" (44).

37. Armando Robles Godoy et al., "Cine peruano: 'En las selva no hay estrellas' en un polémico debate," *Hablemos de cine* 33 (January–February 1967), 15.

38. Ibid., 16–17.

39. *En la selva no hay estrellas* was rereleased in 2007 to considerable accolades, programmed as part of a tribute to Peruvian cinema, at the Cine-Club Cinematógrafo in Barranco. The present acceptance of the film indicates the shift in ideological perspective of the new critics in the twenty-first century.

40. The journal cited his influence only once in reference to one of his most prominent students, Nora de Izcué, and even then it was to show the progression from the Robles-oriented aesthetics of her first short, *Filmación*, to a much clearer, determined style in her second major work, the medium-length *Runan Caycu* (1974). See her entry in the short-film retrospective *HdC* 70 (April 1973), 23.

41. Alfondo Delboy, "*Intimidad de los parques*," *La Prensa* (February 21, 1965). In Ricardo Bedoya's, *Un cine reencontrado: Diccionario ilustrado de las películas peruanas* (Lima: University of Lima, 1997), 167.

42. Isaac León Frías, Juan Bullitta, Carlos Rodríguez Larraín, and Federico de Cárdenas, "*Intimidad de los parques*," *Hablemos de cine* 3 (March 18, 1965), 41, 42.

43. Ibid.

44. Ibid., 42.

45. "Nace el cine nacional," *Hablemos de cine* 3 (March 18, 1965): 4.

46. The thirteen coproductions produced and exhibited in Peru between 1962 and 1970 (listed with the country producing with Peru and alternate titles where applicable) were: *Operación Ñongos* (Operation: Kiddies), also released as *Un gallo con espolones* (A Tough Guy with Spurs), Mexico, Zacarías Gómez Urquiza, 1964; *Intimidad de los parques* (Intimacy of the Parks), Argentina, Manuel Antín, 1965; *A la sombra del sol* (In the Shadow of the Sun), Mexico, Carlos Enrique Taboada, 1966; *Taita Cristo* (Daddy Christ), also released as *La espina de Cristo* (Christ's Thorn), Argentina, Guillermo Fernández Jurado, 1967; *Mi secretaria está loca, loca, loca* (My Secretary Is Completely Crazy), Argentina, Alberto Dubois, 1967; *Seguiré tus pasos* (I Will Follow Your Footsteps), Mexico, Alfredo Crevenna, 1967; *Bromas S.A.* (Jokes, Inc.), Mexico, Alberto Mariscal, 1967; *La Venus maldita* (Damned Venus), Mexico, Alfredo

Crevenna, 1967; *El tesoro de Atahualpa* (Atahualpa's Treasure), Mexico, Vicente Oroná, 1968; *Pasión oculta* (Dark Passion), Mexico, Alfredo Crevenna, 1968; *Las sicodélicas* (The Psychodelics), Mexico, Gilberto Martínez Solares, 1968; *Annabelle Lee*, United States, Harold Daniels, 1968; *Milagro en la selva* (Miracle in the Jungle), also released as *Terror in the Jungle*, United States, Andy Jaczk, 1969. Gabriela Alemán writes about how these types of films contribute to Ecuadorian cinema of this period in "An International Conspiracy: Ecuadorian Cinema in the 1960s and 1970s," *Journal of Latin American Cultural Studies* 13, no. 1 (March 2004): 97–113.

47. Both of these reviews were placed in the section titled "En pocas palabras" (In brief). *Taita Cristo* can be found in issue 34 (March–April 1967), 61; *El tesoro de Atahualpa* in issue 39 (January–February 1968), 93. Ironically, the former appears in the same issue with the summary of the 1967 Viña del Mar film festival (see chapter 4.)
48. "Nace el cine nacional," 3.
49. This expectation was ultimately frustrated. Significant film practice would not begin elsewhere in Peru until the passing of the Film Law of 1972.
50. Notably absent from this list of directors is club founder Manuel Chambi, who was actually attending the infamous Centro Sperimentale di Cinema in Rome in 1964.
51. Chapter 1 contains a more detailed plot summary and analysis of *Kukuli.*
52. It is unclear whether cinematic equipment was brought through La Paz, Bolivia, which is easier to reach from Cuzco than is the coastal city of Lima. Both *Kukuli* and *Jarawi* were edited and the soundtrack was added in laboratories in Argentina, which was standard practice at the time for Peruvian productions.
53. Quoted in Bedoya, *100 años*, 160.
54. Juan Bullitta, "Crítica a *Jarawi*," *Hablemos de cine* 26–27 (June–July 1966), 52.
55. Ibid., 54.
56. *Serrano* refers to someone from the sierra, or mountains, in this case the Andes.
57. This is developed in greater detail in chapter 6.
58. Bullitta, "Crítica a *Jarawi*," 53.
59. Fernando Vivas Sabroso, *En vivo y en directo: Una historia de la televisión peruana* (Lima: University of Lima, 2001), 21.
60. In a scene in Marta Rodríguez and Jorge Silva's often referenced Colombian documentary *Chircales* (Brickmakers, 1972), *Simplemente María* is heard broadcast on the radio in the background. Fernando Vivas discusses both soap operas at length in *En vivo y en directo*, 128–138.
61. Florence Thomas examines the intellectual's resistence to melodrama in her study Los estragos del amor: el discurso amoroso en los medios de comunicación (Bogotá: Editorial Universidad Nacional, 1994).

62. See chapter 4 for a more detailed account of the effects of the Viña del Mar film festival of 1967 on *Hablemos de cine*.
63. A similar reaction among the popular press occurred with the 1998 release of Francisco Lombardi's *No se lo digas a nadie* (Don't Tell Anyone). Based on the novel by Jaime Bayly, the film was an exposé of the very closed, white, aristocratic class of the late 1980s and early 1990s and the hypocritical subset of gay men within that society. Film critics, while expressing solidarity with a fairly well-made Peruvian film, found it to be a step backward from the masterpiece of Lombardi's *Bajo la piel* four years earlier; other cultural critiques in the popular press, however, denounced the film as obscene and entirely untrue, refusing to acknowledge the drug- and sex-obsessed young people in the film as accurate portrayals. The gossipy plotline, combined with the attractive presence of soap-opera stars Santiago Magill and Christian Meier and Lombardi's successful campaign to open the film on Independence Day weekend (traditionally locked up by multinational films, that year by the Hollywood production of *Godzilla*), enabled the film to break box-office records.
64. "'El embajador y yo' y el cine nacional," *Hablemos de cine* 41 (May–June 1968), 4.
65. Bedoya, *Un cine reencontrado*, 186.
66. Fernando Vivas notes in *En vivo y en directo* that Loza's popularity remained relatively strong on television throughout the 1970s, but that after critiquing some later reforms administered under the Velasco administration on his show, he was routinely censored and met with considerable governmental disapproval, despite his character's obvious embracing of contemporary nationalistic ideals established by the regime (116).
67. *Nemesio*'s superficial treatment of contemporary racial divisions emphasizing urban discrimination would be much more seriously considered in the films of Grupo Chaski (*Gregorio*, 1985; *Juliana*, 1989), which used more of a neorealist/Third Cinema aesthetic to tackle issues of urban sprawl through the stories of street children.
68. "*Nemesio*," *La Prensa* (November 2, 1969). In Bedoya, *Un cine reencontrado*, 193.
69. "La farsa de *Nemesio*," *Hablemos de cine* 49 (September–October 1969), 4.
70. This particular Hani film has been notoriously difficult to locate. Neither the Filmoteca de Lima in Peru nor any of the Japanese embassies or consulates in the United States or Peru were able to locate a copy of the film. While other films have been shown at Hani retrospectives — *She and He* (1963), for example, was screened at the 1998 Telluride Film Festival for his Silver Medallion award — *Andesu no hanayame* seems to have vanished.
71. Isaac León Frías et al., "Entrevista: Primer contacto con Susumu Hani: Arte y juventud," *Hablemos de cine* 10 (July 1, 1965), 18.

72. Ibid., 21; emphasis in original.
73. "Susumu hani retornó a Japón," *Hablemos de cine* 19 (November 15, 1965), 15.
74. See Y. Koichi, "Venise 66: Commentaires," *Cahiers du cinéma*, no. 183 (October 1966), 29–30.
75. Isaac León Frías, Juan Bullitta, and Pablo Guevara, "¿Una película peruana hecha por un japonés?: Susumu Hani y 'Amor en los Andes': Coloquio," *Hablemos de cine* 36 (July–August 1967), 20.
76. Ibid.
77. See chapter 5 for an examination of short films.

Chapter 4. Latin American Dis/Connections

1. There is some irony here that the *hablemistas* fully recognized and embraced genre films such as the melodrama in Hollywood filmmaking, yet routinely dismissed Mexican melodramas as substandard, perhaps once again demonstrating the influence of already published European criticism on genre.
2. Several broader Latin American film histories document the importance of the 1967 Viña del Mar film festival. See Alberto Elena and Marina Díaz López, eds., *The Cinema of Latin America: 24 Frames* (London: Wallflower Press, 2003), 6; Marina Díaz López and Alberto Elena, eds., *Tierra en trance: El cine latinoamericano en 100 películas* (Madrid: Alianza Editorial, 1999), 153; Zuzana Pick, *The New Latin American Cinema: A Continental Project* (Austin: University of Texas Press, 1993), 1; John King, *Magical Reels: A History of Cinema in Latin America* (London: Verso, 1990), 70-71.
3. "Festival de Rio de Janeiro: Declara Andrés Ruszkowski a *Hablemos de cine*," *Hablemos de cine* 17 (October 15, 1965), 5–8; Mariano Silva, "Crónica del Festival de Mar de la Plata," *Hablemos de cine* 25 (May 1966), 12–16; Augusto M. Torres, "Cannes 66: El festival de escándalo," *Hablemos de cine* 26–27 (June–July 1966), 5–15; Jesús Martínez León, "XI Semana Internacional de Cine Religioso y de Valores Humanos de Villadolid," *Hablemos de cine* 26–27 (June–July 1966), 16–23; Martínez León, "Reseña: Festival de San Sebastián," *Hablemos de cine* 28 (August 1966), 5–15; Torres, "Venecia 99: ¿Crisis?" *Hablemos de cine* 30–31 (October–November 1966), 5–12; Torres, "IX Gran Premio de Bergamo," *Hablemos de cine* 33 (January–February 1967), 24-27; Vincente Molina Foix, "8th semana de cine en color (Barcelona)," *Hablemos de cine* 33 (January-February 1967), 28–31.
4. "Primer festival de cine peruano de 16mm," *Hablemos de cine* 12 (July 31, 1965): 3–10.
5. The best source of information on the Viña del Mar festivals can be found from the accounts written by its primary organizer, Chilean director Aldo Francia.

See his *Nuevo cine latinoamericano en Viña del Mar* (Santiago: CESOC Ediciones ChileAmérica, 1990).

6. For a study devoted to the domination of the North American majors on the Latin American markets, see Gaizka S. de Usabel's *The High Noon of American Films in Latin America* (Ann Arbor: UMI Research Press, 1982), Jorge A. Schnitman's *Film Industries in Latin America: Dependency and Development* (Norwood, N.J.: Ablex, 1984), and Octavio Getino's *Cine y televisión en América Latina: Producción y mercados* (Santiago: LOM Ediciones, 1998).
7. Isaac León Frías, "Festival de Viña del Mar: Introducción," *Hablemos de cine* 34 (March–April 1967), 5.
8. The first part of Ricardo Bedoya's *El cine en el Perú* (Lima: University of Lima, 1996) features a detailed history on pre–World War II Peruvian filmmaking.
9. The only recently made feature films would have been *La muerte llega al segundo show* (Death Comes to the Second Show, Roselló, 1958), *Kukuli* (Nishiyama/Figueroa/Chambi, 1961), *Ganarás el pan* (You Will Earn the Bread, Robles Godoy, 1965), and the Argentine co-production *Intimidad de los parques* (Intimacy of the Parks, Antín, 1965). Since *Hablemos de cine* started publication in February 1965, Antín's and Robles Godoy's films were both reviewed — and soundly panned — by the journal in issues 3 (March 4, 1965) and 11 (July 15, 1965) respectively. In both cases, these negative reviews were primarily concerned with how Peruvian national cinema might be interpreted if either film was used as an example.
10. Pick, *The New Latin American Cinema.*
11. Federico de Cárdenas, "Chile," *Hablemos de cine* 34 (March–April 1967), 10.
12. Michael Chanan, *Chilean Cinema* (London: BFI, 1976).
13. See chapter 5 on short film and more about the short-film contest.
14. *Estampas del Carnaval de Kanas* (*Scenes from the Kanas Carnival*) was actually co-directed by Eulogio Nishiyama. Both Nishiyama and Chambi were principal members of the Cine-Club de Cuzco and also produced the feature-length films *Kukuli* (1961) and *Jarawi* (1966).
15. "Primer festival de cine peruano de 16mm," 8–9.
16. Juan Bullitta, "El autor y el film: Jorge Volkert, Segundo premio del I festival de cine peruano, habla de cine," *Hablemos de cine* 12 (July 31, 1965), 11.
17. The other critics and publications represented were Alfredo Guevara, director of *Cine cubano*, Brazilian film historian and critic Alex Viany, Argentine *Confirmado* critic José Augustín Mahieu, Uruguayan *Marcha* critic José Wainer, and Chileans Joaquín Olalla and Juan Ehrman from *PEC* and *Ercilla*, respectively. Except for Olalla, all of the above critics also acted as judges for the festival, along with Chileans Aldo Francia and Patricio Kaulen. For the complete list of

ratings for all the films shown at the festival, see "Viña del Mar en números," *Hablemos de cine* 34 (March–April 1967), 13–14.

18. Federico de Cárdenas, "Otros paises," *Hablemos de cine* 34 (March–April 1967), 11.

19. The Chilean *Revista Ecran*, referring to *Forjadores de mañana* as well as *Paixao* (*Passion*, Brazil, Santeiro, 1966?), called the selection committee "overly kind, [who] included some films that could only be called 'delirious cinema'" (quoted in Francia, *Nuevo cine latinoamericano*, 139–140).

20. Though one film each was shown from Bolivia and Mexico, neither country was represented with an actual person attending the filmmakers meeting.

21. Isaac León Frías, "El encuentro de cineastas latinoamericanos," *Hablemos de cine* 34 (March–April 1967), 16.

22. Ricardo Bedoya, *100 años de cine en el Perú* (Lima: University of Lima, 1996), 164.

23. "En torno al cine latinoamericano," *Hablemos de cine* 35 (May–June 1967), 4.

24. Ibid.

25. Ibid.

26. Augusto M. Torres conducted rare interviews with Colombian author and screenwriter Gabriel García Márquez (vol. 47, May–June 1969, 56–58) and Mexican author Carlos Fuentes (vol. 49, September–October 1969, 23–31). Peruvians Isaac León Frias, Juan M. Bullitta, Marino Molina, and J. G. Guevara Torres interviewed compatriot novelist Mario Vargas Llosa for no. 52 (March–April 1970), 30–35. For a discussion of these articles, see Julianne Burton, "Learning to Write at the Movies: Film and the Fiction Writer in Latin America," *Texas Quarterly* 18, no. 1 (Spring 1975), 92–103.

27. Antonio González Norris, "La violencia y la liberación: Entrevista con Fernando Solanas," *Hablemos de cine* 46 (March–April 1969): 5.

28. The encounter at Mérida took place in September 1968. According to Solanas and Getino's collected works entitled *Cine, cultura y descolonialización* (Mexico City: Siglo Veintiuno Editores, 1973), only two major articles had been published up until this point: the first declaration of Cine Liberación in May 1968 and an interview done in Pesaro the following month. The publication of the widely reprinted treatise "Hacia un tercer cine" ("Toward a Third Cinema") in *Tricontinental* would not be published until October 1969, at least six months following the publication of González Norris's interview. Thus, it is logical to say that even informed film enthusiasts in Peru knew little about the film or its directors when the article was published.

29. González, "La violencia y la liberación," 5.

30. The essay "Toward a Third Cinema" would be published by *Hablemos de cine* in issue 53 (May–June 1970), 25–29.

31. González, "La violencia y la liberación," 7.

32. Louis Marcorelles, "L'épreuve du direct," *Cahiers du cinéma* 210 (March 1969), 39.
33. Ibid., 40.
34. González, "La violencia y la liberación," 10.
35. The full-length, three-part completed version of *La hora de los hornos*, running four and a half hours, would premiere at the Viña del Mar festival in 1969. See below.
36. González, "La violencia y la liberación," 10.
37. Pick, *The New Latin American Cinema*, 22.
38. González, "La violencia y la liberación," 11.
39. Ibid., 12.
40. Ibid., 11.
41. Isaac León Frías, "Colombia: Entrevista con Carlos Álvarez," *Hablemos de cine* 53 (May–June 1970), 22. Appropriately, this same issue contained the text of Solanas's manifesto "Toward a Third Cinema" ("Hacia un tercer cine"), originally published in *Tricontinental.*
42. *Hablemos de cine* was loath to call the emergence of these films a "movement" along the lines of Brazilian Cinema Nôvo, but reviewer Antonio González Norris noted that Chile produced by this point "a national cinema that has quickly reached a self-sufficient professional level" (vol. 50–51, November 1969–February 1970, 32).
43. Hans Ehrmann, *Ercilla* no. 1788 (1968), quoted in Francia, *Nuevo cine latinoamericano*, 168.
44. Because the large Argentine contingency was to a large extent responsible for the political leanings of the encounter, Uruguayan director José Wainer called the incident "the first Chilean-Argentine border dispute" of the festival (quoted in Francia, *Nuevo cine latinoamericano*, 168).
45. Francisco Lombardi, "Reseña: Viña 69: Argentina: Entre el grito y el silencio," *Hablemos de cine* 50–51 (November 1969–February 1970), 27.
46. Antonio González Norris, "Reseña: Viña 69: Cuba: Una cultura en Revolución," *Hablemos de cine* 50–51 (November 1969–February 1970), 30.
47. Francisco Lombardi, "Reseña: Viña 69: Bolivia: Los peligros de la demagogia," *Hablemos de cine* 50–51 (November 1969–February 1970), 29.
48. Isaac León Frías, "Reseña: Viña 69: Memorias dragones y tigres en los hornos del subdesarrollo," *Hablemos de cine* 50–51 (November 1969–February 1970), 26; emphasis in original.
49. Isaac León Frías, "El cine latinoamericano en la hora de la verdad," *Hablemos de cine* 50–51 (November 1969–February 1970), 35.
50. Mexican cinema was the only other Latin American cinematic tradition that did not largely embrace the New Latin American Cinema as a movement, yet this is perhaps expected, given that Mexican cinema largely operated under its own

form as an actual industry bolstered by significant state support. Peru had none of this in place and therefore would have shared similar filming conditions to those in Chile and Bolivia.

51. Ibid.
52. Margarita de la Vega-Hurtado, interview by the author, Ann Arbor, Michigan, June 9, 2001.
53. See chapter 3 for more information on the failure of *Jarawi.*
54. See chapter 7.
55. Francia, *Nuevo cine latinoamericano*, 172–173.
56. *Hablemos de cine* reviewed *Miss Universo en el Perú* favorably in its final issue, number 77 (March 1984), 34.
57. Isaac León Frías, "¡El cine paraguayo existe!" *Hablemos de cine* 63 (1972), 45–46.
58. Isaac León Frías and Federico de Cárdenas, "Entrevista con Alfredo Guevara," *Hablemos de cine* 34 (March–April 1967), 20.
59. Unlike *Hablemos de cine* and most other Latin American film journals that began publication in the 1960s, *Cine cubano* is still published as of 2007.
60. Gabriel García Márquez, "Declaraciones de Gabriel García Márquez," *Cine cubano* 103 (1982): 18; Daniel Díaz Torres, "La pantalla conflictiva," ibid., 46–60; Ambrosio Fornet, "¿Se repite el nuevo cine?" ibid., 38–42.
61. Frías and de Cárdenas, "Entrevista con Alfredo Guevara," 21.
62. "Cine cubano: 10 años de cine en 10 años de revolución," *Hablemos de cine* 54 (July–August 1970), 14.
63. Isaac León Frías, "*Lucía* (H. Solás)," *Hablemos de cine* 54 (July–August 1970), 25.
64. Nelson García, "*La odisea del General José* (J. Fraga)," *Hablemos de cine* 54 (July–August 1970), 29.
65. Nelson García, "*Por 1ra vez/Acerca de un personaje . . . /Al sur de Maniadero* (O. Coratázar)," *Hablemos de cine* 54 (July–August 1970), 46.
66. Desiderio Blanco, "*La primera carga al machete* (M. O. Gómez) / *David* (E. P. Barnet)," *Hablemos de cine* 54 (July–August 1970), 38; emphasis in original.
67. The change was announced in an editorial entitled "Changes in *Cahiers*" in August 1968 (no. 203), translated and reprinted in Hillier's *Cahiers du cinéma, 1960–1968: New Wave, New Cinema, Reevaluating Hollywood*," 311–312), and was a harbinger of that journal's major format change.
68. For more on the international scuffle caused by the National Society of Film Critics' award in 1974, see Michael Chanan's introduction, "Lessons of Experience" (3–14), as well as the section titled "Aftermath: Politics and Cinema" (177–184) in the published English translation of Eduardo Desnoes's filmscript, in *Memories of Underdevelopment and Inconsolable Memories* (New Brunswick, N.J.: Rutgers University Press, 1990).

69. Juan Bullitta, "*Memorias del subdesarrollo* (T. G. Alea)," *Hablemos de cine* 54 (July–August 1970), 20.
70. Isaac León Frías, "Notas sobre la muestra de cine cubano," *Hablemos de cine* 75 (May 1982), 35.
71. Ibid.
72. Federico de Cárdenas, "Entrevista con Manuel Octavio Gómez," *Hablemos de cine* 54 (July–August 1970), 31.
73. The journal had a short interview with Manuel Pérez in vol. 70 (April 1979: 41–43).
74. Isaac León Frías and Federcio de Cárdenas, "Reencuentro con Manuel Octavio Gómez," *Hablemos de cine* 75 (May 1982), 32.
75. See chapter 5 for a comparison of Colombian and Peruvian short-film production, as well as an expanded discussion of the Peruvian short-film industry generated by the Film Law of 1972.
76. Frías and de Cárdenas, "Reencuentro con Manuel Octavio Gómez," 34.
77. Michael Chanan, *Cuban Cinema* (Minneapolis: University of Minnesota Press, 2004), 383.

Chapter 5. For a Few Minutes

1. See Michael Quinn's "Distribution, the Transient Audience, and the Transition to the Feature Film," *Cinema Journal* 40, no. 2 (Winter 2001), 35–56.
2. For a good theoretical background to short fiction, see the periodical *Short Fiction*; *Re-reading the Short Story*, ed. Clare Hanson (London: Macmillan, 1989), whose introduction provides a nice overview of short-story studies, including a brief discussion of the relation between the development of the short story as a format and of cinema as a medium in the early twentieth century; and Mary Louise Pratt's "The Short Story: The Long and the Short of It," in Charles M. May's collection *The New Short Story Theories* (Athens: Ohio University Press, 1994), which starts with the note that when pairs of literature dissimilar by length "may be separate but equal, one may be derived from the other, one may be 'marked' with respect to the other (as long poem is to poem), they may be related as 'major' to 'minor' or as 'greater' to 'lesser'" (91).
3. The significant exception to this rule is Eileen Elsey and Andrew Kelly's *In Short: A Guide to Short Film-making in the Digital Age* (London: BFI, 2002), which features a very brief history of short filmmaking and conversations with eleven short-film directors (including a few who have become prominent feature directors, such as Anthony Minghella (*The English Patient*, 1996; *The Talented Mr. Ripley*, 1999) and Nick Park (*Chicken Run*, 2002; *Wallace and Gromit*, 2005). The book focuses exclusively on the British fiction short and does not

provide a guide to critical analysis of short films; nonetheless, it recognizes that the form is important because it provides an "opportunity [for] film-makers to practice their art outside the pressures of feature film and television production" (3). The Internet created a new space for the viewing of short films (AtomFilms, iFilms, etc.) and gained a large amount of popular attention in the late 1990s, but the collapse of the Internet market in early 2000 means that critical interest in shorts has faded considerably.

4. Douglas Gomery, "Hollywood as Industry," in *The Oxford Guide to Film Studies*, ed. John Hill and Pamela Church Gibson (Oxford: Oxford University Press, 1998), 245.

5. For the purposes of this study, I am defining short film as anything under ten minutes, which is how the Peruvian government defined *cortometraje* for exhibition in theaters. Other definitions of "short films" exist: Ana López notes in a footnote in "The Long Life of Short Film: Brazil and Colombia Compared" that the "standard definition" is any length under one hour, while a feature-length film runs more than an hour; Elsey and Kelly in their analysis label shorts as being under a half-hour. The Peruvian government used "medium-length film," or *mediometraje*, to refer to films falling between ten and sixty minutes.

6. "1er festival de cine peruano en 16mm," *Hablemos de cine* 12 (July 31, 1965), 7.

7. Ibid., 10.

8. None of the articles pertaining to the festival are given a specific byline, and therefore the authors of the articles must be considered as the entire group of four.

9. "*Hablemos de cine* presente," *Hablemos de cine* 12 (July 31, 1965), 3.

10. "1er festival de cine peruano en 16mm," 5; emphasis in original.

11. Ibid., 5–6.

12. Personal interviews with the surviving *hablemistas* in 1998 and 2003 indicate that this interview is now lost.

13. Isaac León et al., "El autór y el film: (entrevista con) Jorge Volkert, 2do premio del I Festival de cine peruano," *Hablemos de cine* 12 (July 31, 1965), 11.

14. A fuller discussion of the reaction to *Forjadores de mañana* at the Viña del Mar Film Festival can be found in chapter 3.

15. Bullitta recounts that *Semilla* is actually one of three films being made at the same time: the first two, both in black-and-white, are documentaries of shorter lengths, while *Semilla*, the most complex of the three, is filmed in color; see his "Crónica de rodaje — 1,000,000 de ojos (hombres del lago)," *Hablemos de cine* 38 (November–December 1967), 11–12. The titles of the other two films are not offered in the piece.

16. Upper-middle-class and upper-class Peruvians from the capital would have tended more to travel to international locations rather than to other national destinations. This preference would have partially stemmed from the poor state

of infrastructure within Peru, but also to the snobbish attitude of the elite to all things Peruvian and their favoring of all things foreign.

17. Bullitta, "Crónica de rodaje," 5.
18. Ibid., 13.
19. Federico de Cárdenas, Isaac León Frías, and Nelson García, "Cine peruano y colombiano: Tientos y diferencias: Carlos Mayolo en Lima," *Hablemos de cine* 72 (November 1980), 17.
20. Bullitta, "Crónica de rodaje," 7.
21. César Linares, "En pocas palabras: *Semilla*," *Hablemos de cine* 45 (January–February 1969), 82.
22. See chapter 3 for a discussion of all of these films as examples of "poor-quality cinema" in the eyes of *Hablemos de cine*.
23. Guevara's ideas about national cinema changed significantly and often ran counter to those of *Hablemos de cine*. A later interview with Guevara indicates bitter resentment toward the journal, accusing them of "stunting Peruvian national cinema." This resentment is discussed in chapter 6; see also "La encrucijada del Cine Peruano," *Hablemos de cine* 67 (1975), 15–22; Carbone, "Pablo Guevara," in *El cine en el Perú, 1950–1972: Testimonios* (Lima: University of Lima, 1991): 191–212.
24. Chapter 3 features a more detailed analysis of the reaction to Peruvian popular comedies.
25. See chapter 1 for a translation of the relevant portions of the Film Law of 1972, found in articles 13 and 14.
26. Ricardo Bedoya and Juan Bullitta, "Nelson García: 'Al interesarme por el cine y abandonar todo por él, siento que inicio una especie de retorno a los orígenes,'" *Hablemos de cine* 67 (1975), 24.
27. José Carlos Huayhuaca et al., "Francisco Lombardi: 'Hacer cine en el Perú es para mi poner los pies en tierra,'" *Hablemos de cine* 67 (1975), 30.
28. Nelson García et al., "Nora de Izcué: 'Creo que el cine nacional se dará cuando esta mayoría peruana se exprese y se vea reflejada en las pantallas, no nuestros cuatro o cinco cineastas,'" *Hablemos de cine* 67 (1975), 41.
29. The *Hablemos de cine* encyclopedia is, as far as I can determine, the only written record of any short-film production from this period, though some material can be found about other Latin American short-film production. Most significant, filmmaker Carlos Álvarez's *Una decada de cortometraje colombiano, 1970–1980* (Bogotá: Borradores de cine, 1982) describes his frustration at working within "cine de sobreprecio." See below for *Hablemos de cine*'s reaction to the situation in Colombia. The published curatorial notes, *Short Films from Latin America: A Film Exhibition Organized by the American Federation of Arts* (New York: American Federation of Arts, 1992), edited by curator Julianne

Burton-Carvajal, are also great resources detailing the histories of short films throughout the region.

30. "Diccionario del cortometraje peruano," *Hablemos de cine* 70 (April 1979), 19.
31. Isaac León Frías et al., "El cine peruano entre realidad y deseo (mesa redonda, 1ra parte)," *Hablemos de cine* 73–74 (June 1981), 18.
32. What follows is the complete listing of directors in the "Diccionario del cortometraje peruano," with the abbreviation of the respective reviewer in parentheses. The eight reviewers were Ricardo Bedoya (RB), Juan Bullitta (JB), Constantino Carvallo (CC), Federico de Cárdenas (FdC), Nelson García (NG), Guillermo Niño de Guzmán (GNG), Juan Carlos Huayhuaca (JCH), and Isaac León (IL): (1) vol. 70 (April 1979): Mario Acha (FdC), Juan Bullitta (FdC), Juan A. Caycho (JB), Alberto Durant (FdC), Luis Figueroa (RB), Fernando Gagliuffi (NG), Nelson García (JB), Pablo Guevara (IL), Rafael Hastings (FdC), José Carlos Huayhuaca (JB), Nora de Izcué (IL), Flavio López (FdC), Luis Llosa (JCH), Pedro Morote (CC), Emilio Moscoso (JB), Alberto Nuñez Herrera (FdC), Francisco Otiniano (IL), José Antontio Portugal (RB), Mario Pozzi-Escot (CC), José Luis Rouillón (NG), Arturo Sinclair (IL), Ernesto Sprinckmoller (RB), Jorge Vignati (JCH), Jorge Volkert (NG), Leonidas Zegarra (RB); (2) vol. 71 (April 1980): Rodolfo Bedoya (?), Grupo Bruma (NG), CETUC (Centro de Tele-educación de la Universidad Católica) (FdC), Federico de Cárdenas (GNG), Felipe Degregori (JB), Fausto Espinoza (NG), Ricardo Fleiss (NG), Federico García (FdC), Reynaldo Ledgard (NG), Grupo Liberación Sin Rodeos (JB), Francisco Lombardi (JCH), Grupo Marcha (FdC), Alejandro Miró Quesada (FdC), W.S. Palacios (IL), María Esther Pallant (JB), Miguel Ramón (RB), Jorge Reyes (NG/FdC), Armando Robles Godoy (only shorts directed after 1972, RB), Ricardo Roca Rey (FdC), Kurt and Christine Rosenthal (JB), Jorge Sánchez Pauli (FdC), Jorge Suárez (JCH), Augusto Tamayo San Ramón (IL), Mario Tejada (NG), Franklin Urteaga (FdC).
33. Ricardo Bedoya, "Diccionario del cortometraje peruano (II): Armando Robles Godoy," *Hablemos de cine* 71 (April 1980), 22.
34. Juan Bullitta, "Diccionario del cortometraje peruano (I): Juan A. Caycho," *Hablemos de cine* 70 (April 1979), 20.
35. Isaac León Frías, "Diccionario del cortometraje peruano (II): W. S. Palacios," *Hablemos de cine* 71 (April 1980), 21.
36. Ricardo Bedoya, "Diccionario del cortometraje peruano (I): Ernesto Sprinckmoller," *Hablemos de cine* 70 (April 1979), 27–28.
37. Isaac León Frías, "Diccionario del cortometraje peruano (I): Nora de Izcué," *Hablemos de cine* 70 (April 1979), 23.
38. Nelson García, "Diccionario del cortometraje peruano (I): Fernando Gagliuffi," *Hablemos de cine* 70 (April 1979), 21.

39. A more complete article on the history of Peruvian animation, "Del dibujo animado . . . en el Perú," was written many years later by Benicio Vicente and Oscar Páz Soldán Pinto for *Butaca sanmarquina* 6 (April 2000), 14–16.
40. Federico de Cárdenas et al., "Cine peruano y colombiano," 17.
41. Isaac León Frías, "El cine colombiano hoy: Marta Rodríguez y Jorge Silva," *Hablemos de cine* 71 (April 1980), 29.
42. Ibid., 30.
43. Francisco Lombardi, "El cine colombiano hoy: Diálogo complementario con Luis Ospina," *Hablemos de cine* 71 (April 1980), 34.
44. In "Film History, Film Genre, and Their Discontents: The Case of the Omnibus Film," Marc Betz provides a comprehensive history of the omnibus film and the difficulty of establishing consistency for terminology surrounding this type of film, which has been referred to as compilation, episode, composite, portmanteau, and so forth. The films discussed fit ideally into Betz's taxonomy as omnibus films: "Omnibus and episode films are frequently conflated, but a crucial distinction between the two entails their wholly different textual reception and analysis in film studies. An episode film is directed by a single person and comprises two or more episodes or sketches (i.e., short films), the combination of which brings the package to feature length. An omnibus film is similarly episodic but is directed by more than one person, with each directing his or her own segment(s). In both episode and omnibus films, the separate sections may or may not carry over characters or cast members from segment to segment, and the dramatic presentations may or may not be connected by a framing or linking decide, character, or narrative. In both cases as well the episodes are not linked in a linear narrative fashion, i.e., each segment does not build upon the previous one to establish a clear line of narrative cause and effect from episode to episode" (74–75).
45. Constantín Caravallo, "*Cuentos inmorales: Intriga familiar*," *Hablemos de cine* 70 (April 1979), 30.
46. Ricardo Bedoya, "*Cuentos inmorales: Los amigos*," *Hablemos de cine* 70 (April 1979), 33.
47. Huayhuaca never completed this film. His first feature was titled *Profesión: Detective* (Profession: Detective), made in 1986.
48. Caravallo, "*Cuentos inmorales*," 31.
49. Juan Bullitta, "*Aventuras prohibidas* de Tamayo, Huayhuaca y Llosa," *Hablemos de cine* 72 (November 1980), 20–21.
50. Juan Bullitta, "*Historia de Fiorela y el Hombre Araña* de J. C. Huayhuaca," *Hablemos de cine* 72 (November 1980), 22.
51. Reynaldo Ledgard, "*Una raya más al tigre*," *Hablemos de cine* 76 (February 1983), 23.

52. Giancarlo Carbone's latest volume of collected interviews focuses on short-film directors in *El cine en el Perú: El cortometraje, 1972–1992* (Lima: University of Lima, 2007).

Chapter 6. Creating the "Lombardi Generation"

1. "'Hablemos de cine' presente," *Hablemos de cine* 12 (July 31, 1965), 3.
2. Ethnic studies in Peru are extremely complicated, in large part due to the Peruvian government's de-emphasis of race as a marker in most twentieth-century census questionnaires. Historical and sociological data suggest that even at the start of the twenty-first century a correlation exists between ethnic markers and place of origin, particularly where the white population is concerned. A simplified matrix of Peruvian ethnicities indicates indigenous populations dominating rural areas and white populations predominating only in the residential districts of Lima; *mestizos*, the mix of the two identities, abound throughout the country. See Adolfo Figueroa and Manuel Barrón, "Inequality, Ethnicity and Social Disorder in Peru," CRISE Working Paper No. 8 (Oxford: CRISE, 2005), 9.
3. See Sonia Ascué and Rosa Esquivel's cross-generational ethnographic study of a family in Lima in "Aculturación o mestizaje: una perspectiva generacional" in the TEMPO collective publication *Los nuevos limeños: Sueños, fervores y caminos en el mundo popular* (Lima: SUR Casa de Estudios del Socialismo, 1993), 377–399.
4. In his cultural critique *The Country and the City*, Raymond Williams articulates the emotional divisions from each side that permeate civilized societies in general: "On the actual settlements, which in the real history have been astonishingly varied, powerful feelings have gathered and have been generalised. On the country has gathered the idea of a natural way of life: of peace, innocence, and simple virtue. On the city has gathered the idea of an achieved centre: of learning, communication, light. Powerful hostile associations have also developed: on the city as a place of noise, worldliness and ambition; on the country as a place of backwardness, ignorance, limitation. A contrast between country and city, as fundamental ways of life, reaches back into classical times." Raymond Williams, *The Country and the City* (New York: Oxford University Press, 1973), 1.
5. James D. Rudolph, *Peru: The Evolution of a Crisis* (Westport, Conn.: Praeger, 1993), 54.
6. See chapter 5 for more on *Semilla*.
7. See Carlos Parodi Trece, *Perú, 1980–2000: Políticas Económicas y sociales en entornos cambiantes* (Lima: Universidad del Pacífico, 2002), 108.
8. Ricardo Bedoya, Federico de Cárdenas, Pablo Guevara, and Isaac León Frías, "La enrucijada del cine peruano," *Hablemos de cine* 67 (1975), 17.

9. SINAMOS also sponsored Nora de Izcué's medium-length film *Runan Caycu* (1973).
10. Isaac León Frías, "La búsqueda de una voz propria en el largometraje peruano," *Hablemos de cine* 69 (1977–78), 18.
11. Ibid.
12. Octavio Getino, *Cine y televisión en América Latina* (Santiago, Chile: LOM Ediciones, 1998), 139–140.
13. Ibid., 17.
14. Juan Bullitta, "En el sendero de un cine campesino," *Hablemos de cine* 69 (1977–78), 12.
15. Ricardo Bedoya et al., "Encuentro con Federico García," *Hablemos de cine* 75 (May 1982), 17.
16. Interestingly, neither film was censored by the Peruvian government. Of course, by 1980, Morales Bermúdez was under increased international pressure to restore democratic elections and the censorship of either film might have undermined such a process. In 1980, Fernando Belaúnde Terry was reelected president after having been deposed by Velasco's coup in 1968.
17. Isaac León Frías et al., "El cine peruano entre realidad y deseo (mesa redonda, 1ra parte)," *Hablemos de cine* 73–74 (June 1981), 17.
18. Ibid., 19.
19. In fact, though he remained on the masthead as a collaborator until volume 73–74 (June 1981), Guevara had not made a significant contribution to the journal since his input in the debate published in volume 67 (1975). His absence from these later debates confirms somewhat his disgust and resentment toward *Hablemos de cine* as a whole. See Carbone, "Pablo Guevara," *El cine en el Perú, 1950–1972: Testimonios* (Lima: Universidad de Lima, 1991), 191–212.
20. José Carlos Huayhuaca, "El dilemma del lenguaje o el compromise: el cine de Federico García," *Hablemos de cine* 75 (May 1982), 26.
21. Bedoya et al., "Encuentro con Federico García," 18.
22. As seen in the passage quoted previously, the interviewers had not made the original reference to Sanjinés; rather, García had done so himself.
23. Bedoya et al., "Encuentro con Federico García," 24.
24. Ibid., 25.
25. Julio García Espinosa, "For an Imperfect Cinema" (trans. Julianne Burton), in *New Latin American Cinema*, vol. 1: *Theory, Practices and Transcontinental Articulations*, ed. Michael Martin (Detroit, Mich.: Wayne State University Press, 1997), 82.
26. "Cine peruano: Introducción," *Hablemos de cine* 77 (March 1984), 16.
27. Patricia R. Zimmerman, personal interview, April 20, 2007.

28. Isaac León Frías, "¿Predicando en el desierto?" *Hablemos de cine* 77 (March 1984), 17.
29. Ibid., 17–18.
30. Bedoya et al., "Encuentro con Federico García," 24.
31. See chapter 7 for more on the reading of Spaniards in Lombardi's films of the 1990s.
32. Fascinating to read in this respect is César Arróspide de la Flor's *Reflexiones sobre el cambio cultural en el Perú* (Lima: C.E.P., 1985), which privileged Velasco's ideals many years after the fall of his regime.
33. Ricardo Bedoya et al., "Encuentro con Federico García," 16.
34. "El cine peruano entre realidad y deseo (II): Introducción," *Hablemos de cine* 75 (May 1982), 15; my emphasis.
35. The political leanings of each of these governments were: Velasco, military leftist; Morales Bermúdez, military reactionary; Belaúnde, democratic rightist (PPC, Partido Popular Cristiano); García, democratic leftist (APRA); Fujimori, democratic centrist (Cambio 90).
36. In 2008, Italian authorities uncovered classified documents concerning Operation Condor that implicated Peru along with six other Latin American countries for quashing leftist political dissent through violence and death squads, naming former president Morales Bermúdez as a primary figure. See Alexei Barrionuebo, "Italy Follows Trail of Sexret South American Abductions," *New York Times*, February 22, 2008, A12.
37. Ricardo Bedoya, *100 años de cine en el Perú* (Lima: University of Lima, 1996), 257.
38. Javier Proetzel, "Grandez y decandencia del espectáculo cinematográfico," *Contratexto* 9 (December 1995), 121–122.
39. See chapter 7 for more on *Butaca sanmarquina* and other Peruvian film journals of the 2000s.
40. George D. E. Philip relates a detailed account of the nationalization of the press and its impact on the remainder of Velasco's rule in *The Rise and Fall of the Peruvian Military Radicals, 1968–1976* (London: Athlone Press, 1978), 136–140.
41. Ricardo Bedoya, Federico de Cárdenas, Pablo Guevara, and Isaac León Frías, "La encrucijada del cine peruano," *Hablemos de cine* 67 (1975), 16.
42. Ibid., 17.
43. Ibid., 16.
44. Ibid., 18.
45. Ibid., 19.
46. Mariátegui's articles, originally published in *Amauta*, the journal he published in the 1930s, are minor pieces on Charlie Chaplin and short films of the period. They are reprinted in volume 61–62 (September–December 1971), 19–23.

47. "Cine de aquí y de allá," *Hablemos de cine* 28 (August 1966), 27.
48. Working with screenwriter José Watanabe, Lombardi streamlined the novel's plot to the basic conflict in a Peruvian military academy between three cadets: "Poet," the hero, the upper-class kid with a conscience who writes dirty stories to garner favor with his classmates; "Slave," the victim, who is eternally ostracized and ridiculed and betrays his comrades for his own benefit; and "Jaguar," the antagonist, the lower-class street kid who is respected out of fear by his classmates and who may or may not have killed the Slave out of revenge.

Chapter 7. The Changing of the Guard

1. Though they were both short-lived exercises, at least two foreign journals—*Primer plano* in Chile and *Ojo al cine* in Colombia (the latter the work of *Hablemos* correspondent Andrés Caicedo)—used the style of *Hablemos de cine* as a model for their own local publications.
2. While the English translation of the film's original Portuguese title is appropriate, the phrase "tierra en trance" has some additional interpretations. The Spanish word "trance" may be interpreted as both "a bad patch" or "a critical moment" as well as the English homonym.
3. "Tierra en trance," *La gran ilusión* 1 (1993), 67.
4. Javier Proetzel, "El cortometraje: explorando su aceptación," *La gran ilusión* 1 (1993), 75–83. Though Proetzel's study also examines the data in terms of age, levels of education, and frequency of cinema attendance, his essay does not specify the location of his sample of some four hundred filmgoers—an important consideration given the wide variety of Peruvian theatrical standards. For example, what part of Lima were the filmgoers in? What film were they going to see when given the survey? Most important, was the film distributed at general public screenings or at cine-clubs?
5. José Perla Anaya, "El cine y su derecho: El rol de lo legal en el nacimiento de una cinematografía," *La gran ilusión* 1 (1993), 84–93. The article is a condensed, updated version of a chapter in his 1991 published study *Censura y promoción en el cine* (Lima: University of Lima, 1991).
6. "Corto peruano: ¿el fin del juego? Conversación con tres realizadores de cortometrajes," *La gran ilusión* 1 (1993): 95.
7. Ibid.
8. Ibid., 96.
9. Ibid.
10. Aldo Salvini nevertheless said during this discussion: "I am interested in features, but I have never seen the short as only a preparatory step for the feature. They

are different genres" (97). Álvarez and Cabada agreed that they wished to use the short as a bridge to the feature.

11. One of the later editors at *Hablemos de cine*, Melvin Ledgard is one of the very few of the group of staff writers to continue in an academic trajectory; he earned a doctorate from the University of Texas in literature. (While Bedoya, León, and Tamayo all teach at the University of Lima, none has a doctorate; Bedoya, the country's pre-eminent film historian, has a law degree.) Unique therefore among the *hablemistas*, Ledgard teaches at Universidad Católica. Although he has published a monograph on literature titled *Amores adversos y apasionados: La evolución del tema del amor en cinco novellas latinoamericanas* (Lima: Fondo Editorial PUCP, 2002), he has since become an expert on Peruvian comic books, curating a 2004 exhibition at ICPNA, "De Supercholo a Teodosio."
12. Naturally, the exception was the cine-club at the Universidad de Lima itself. Called "La Ventana Indiscreta" (Rear window), the cine-club functions as the cultural arm of the school's communications program and continues to program a mixture of classic and art-house films.
13. ["¿Una revista de cine?"], *La gran ilusión* 1 (1993), 1.
14. Programa Ibermedia was founded in 1997 to provide economic stimulation and coproduction arrangements between participating Iberoamerican nations, each of which contributes a sum that is then redistributed among projects from around the region selected by competition. (Member states as of 2007 included Argentina, Bolivia, Brazil, Colombia, Chile, Cuba, Mexico, Panama, Peru, Portugal, Puerto Rico, Spain, Uruguay, and Venezuela.) In "Programa Ibermedia: Co-production and the Cultural Politics of Constructing an Ibero-American Audiovisual Space" (*Spectator* 27, no. 2 [Fall 2007]), Tamara L. Falicov identifies how other directors' uses of the Spaniard in Ibermedia-funded projects have altered the script. She also identifies "types" of Spaniards in these films: the sympathetic Spaniard, the Spanish anarchist, the evil or racist Spaniard, and the Spanish tourist (24–26). Her examples do not include Lombardi's films and his use of Spanish funding and actresses (not male actors) predated the founding of Ibermedia.
15. Velarde's short films made for his U.S. program, "98 Thompson" (1994), "C. Lloyd, un cuento de crimen y castigo" (C. Lloyd, a story of crime and punishment, 1996), and "Roces" (1998) all won top prizes for short filmmaking in Peru at the national level sponsored by CONACINE.
16. "La regla del juego," *La gran ilusión* 13 (2003), 1.
17. In an interesting coincidence, an online film journal was founded in Spain almost at the same time, with its first issue released in January 2004. The Spanish e-journal (http://www.trendesombras.com) and the Peruvian print journal seemingly have nothing in common other than the name.

18. "Editorial," *Tren de sombras* 1 (March 2004), 2.
19. Isaac León Frías, "El crítico frente al cine peruano," *Tren de sombras* 2 (August 2004), 19.
20. "Nace el cine nacional," *Hablemos de cine* 3 (March 18, 1965), 5.
21. León, "El crítico frente al cine peruano," 20.
22. Susan Sontag, "The Decay of Cinema," *New York Times Magazine* (February 15, 1996), 61.
23. J. Hoberman, "The Film Critic of Tomorrow, Today," in *The Crisis of Criticism*, ed. Maurice Berger (New York: New Press, 1998), 83, 85.
24. This point concerning the co-opting of objects by cinephilia is central to an argument presented in Patricia R. Zimmerman and Dale Hudon's talk, "Trafficking in the Archives: Remixing across, between and through nations" (ACLA Conference, Puebla, Mexico, April 20, 2007).
25. Jonathan Rosenbaum's *Movie Mutations: The Changing Face of World Cinephilia* (London: BFI, 2003) documents a novel use of the Internet to create dialogues among cinephiles from around the world. For example, one chapter collects a series of "letters" as they move from Argentine Quintín to Canadian Mark Peranson, followed successively by Nicole Brenez from France, Adrian Martin from Australia, and Rosenbaum from the United States. See also his chapter 2 for a more detailed discussion concerning Willemenian cinephilia.
26. "Peru Internet Usage and Telecom Marketing Reports," Internet World Stats: Usage and Population Statistics, Miniwatts Marketing Group, http://www.internetworldstats.com/sa/pe.htm (accessed April 15, 2007). Source for 2000 data: International Telecommunication Union; for 2005 data: Computer Industry Almanac.
27. For an exhaustive examination of Internet usage focusing particularly on Lima that also serves as a historical resource for use in Lima in 1999, see Ana María Fernández-Maldonado, "The Diffusion and Use of Information and Communications Technologies in Lima, Peru," *Journal of Urban Technology* 8, no. 3 (2001), 21–43.
28. Eduardo Villanueva Mansilla, "Internet availability and politics in Peru: A preliminary report on an apparent Paradox," Presentation at PISTA (Politics and Information Systems: Technologies and Applications) Conference 2004, published online at author's Web site, http://macareo.pucp.edu.pe/evillan/Eduardo%20Villanueva%20Mansilla/Escritos_files/PISTA-EVM-P025SV.pdf (accessed April 15, 2007).
29. It is somewhat unclear why none of these publications (as of 2007) has made any attempts at publishing content online, except for the fact that by selling magazines the publishers are sure to get paid for their work, as opposed to the "free" nature of Internet postings. The same holds true for other local publi-

cations, such as Argentina's leading film magazine *El Amante*, whose online content is very limited compared to what is in the paper version. In lieu of online versions of the printed magazines, however, a plethora of blogs written by Peruvian critics provide immediate outlets for many of the same people who write for the print versions. Although only *Butaca* officially has an affiliated blog (started in mid-2007; http://butacaenlinea.blogspot.com) Ricardo Bedoya writes "Páginas del diario de Satán" (Pages from Satan's diary) (http://paginasdeldiariodesatan.blogspot.com/); Mario Castro Cobos contributes to "La cinefilia no es patriota" (Cinephilia is not patriotic) (http://lacinefilianoespatriota.blogspot.com/). As of this writing, the primary blog for information and opinions on Peruvian cinema and cinephilia — including previews of the release of all the current film journals — can be found at "Cinencuentro" (CinEncounter) (http://www.cinencuentro.com/).

30. "Godard 2, aquí vamos," *godard!* 1, no. 2 (September 2001), 2.
31. Francisco Ángeles, "El crítico de cine no puede ser un perdonavidas: Entrevista a Claudio Cordero, Director de *godard!*" *Bitácora de el Hablador* (March 11, 2007), http://elhablador.com/blog/2007/03/11/entrevista-a-claudio-cordero-director-de-godard/.
32. Of the other awards distributed at the 2001 *elcine*, *Nueve reinas* won the audience award (Premio *elcine*) and *25 Watts* won two awards, for best screenplay and for best film as determined specifically by the magazine *La gran ilusión*. Lombardi's *Tinta roja* won second place for the audience award.
33. Claudio Cordero, "Latinoamérica va al cine," *godard!* 1, no. 2 (September 2001), 20.
34. Jaime Luna Victoria, quoted in José Tsang, "Escorpiones, arañas y chanchitos," *godard!* 1, no. 2 (September 2001), 23.
35. Ibid.
36. Sebastián Pimentel, "El enigma de la crítica, o el problema de pensar y hacer cine en el Perú," *godard!* 1, no. 2 (September 2001), 24.
37. Ibid., 26.
38. Christian Wiener, "Crítica de la crítica," *Butaca sanmarquina* 13 (October 2002), 19.
39. Ángeles, "El crítico de cine no puede ser un perdonavidas."
40. "Editorial," *Abre los ojos* 1 (June 2002), 3.
41. Mario Castro Cobos, "Dossier 2001: *El bien esquivo*," *Abre los ojos* 1 (June 2002), 16.
42. Founded in 1551, Universidad Nacional Mayor de San Marcos (referred to in the rest of this book through its more common abbreviated form, Universidad de San Marcos) is the oldest institute of higher learning in the Americas and the top public institution in Peru.

43. Fernando Samillán Cavero, "Primeras palabras . . . ," *Butaca sanmarquina* 1 (July–September 1998), 3.
44. Marco Avilés, "El rincón de los Cinéfilos: *El Amauta*," *Butaca sanmarquina* 4 (1999), 4.
45. Ibid., 5.
46. Ibid., 6.
47. Federico García, personal interview, Lima, Peru, July 12, 2003.
48. Fernando Samillán [and René Weber], "Al cierre," *Butaca sanmarquina* 7 (September 2000): 3.
49. René Weber, "Editorial," *Butaca sanmarquina* 11 (April 2002), 1.
50. Claudia Ugarte, "Butacas interactivas: Cine en discussion," *Butaca* 20 (June 2004), 31.
51. Wiener, "Crítica de la crítica," 18.
52. René Weber, "Editorial," *Butaca* 20 (June 2004), 4.

BIBLIOGRAPHY

Articles from Peruvian Film Journals

"Acercamiento a Gordon Douglas." *Hablemos de cine* 2 (March 1, 1965): 28.

"Acercamiento a Vicente Minnelli." *Hablemos de cine* 6 (May 1, 1965): 41.

Avilés, Marco. "El rincón de los Cinéfilos: *El Amauta*." *Butaca sanmarquina* 4 (1999): 4–6.

Bedoya, Ricardo. "*Cuentos inmorales: Los amigos*." *Hablemos de cine* 70 (April 1979): 33.

———. "Diccionario del cortometraje peruano (I): Ernesto Sprinckmoller." *Hablemos de cine* 70 (April 1979): 27–28.

———. "Diccionario del cortometraje peruano (II): Armando Robles Godoy." *Hablemos de cine* 71 (April 1980): 22.

———. "La formación del público cinematográfico en el Perú: El cine de los señores." *Contratexto* 9 (December 1995): 57–70.

Bedoya, Ricardo, and Juan Bullitta. "Nelson García: 'Al interesarme por el cine y abandonar todo por él, siento que inicio una especie de retorno a los orígenes.'" *Hablemos de cine* 67 (1975): 23–27.

Bedoya, Ricardo, et al. "Encuentro con Federico García." *Hablemos de cine* 75 (May 1982): 16–25.

Bedoya, Ricardo, et al. "La enrucijada del cine peruano." *Hablemos de cine* 67 (1975): 16–23.

Blanco, Desiderio. "*La primera carga al machete* (M. O. Gómez) / *David* (E. P. Barnet)." *Hablemos de cine* 54 (July–August 1970): 37–38.

———. "*Some Came Running (Dios sabe cuánto amé)*." *Hablemos de cine* 6 (May 1, 1965): 47–51.

Bullitta, Juan. "El autor y el film: Jorge Volkert, Segundo premio del I festival de cine peruano, habla de cine." *Hablemos de cine* 12 (July 31, 1965): 11–18.

———. "*Aventuras prohibidas* de Tamayo, Huayhuaca y Llosa." *Hablemos de cine* 72 (November 1980): 20–21.

———. "Crítica a *Jarawi*." *Hablemos de cine* 26–27 (June–July 1966): 52–54.

———. "Crónica de rodaje—1,000,000 de ojos (hombres del lago)." *Hablemos de cine* 38 (November–December 1967): 5–17.

———. "Diccionario del cortometraje peruano (I): Juan A. Caycho." *Hablemos de cine* 70 (April 1979): 20.

———. "En el sendero de un cine campesino." *Hablemos de cine* 69 (1977–78): 12–13.

———. "*Ganarás el pan*." *Hablemos de cine* 11 (July 15, 1965): 37–42.

———. "*Historia de Fiorela y el Hombre Araña* de J. C. Huayhuaca." *Hablemos de cine* 72 (November 1980): 22.

———. "*Memorias del subdesarrollo* (T. G. Alea)." *Hablemos de cine* 54 (July–August 1970): 20–21.

———. "El otro lado del espejo." *Hablemos de cine* 52 (March–April 1970), 6–7.

Carbone, Giancarlo. "En busca de un cine peruano." *Contratexto* 9 (December 1995): 79–86.

Caravallo, Constantín. "*Cuentos inmorales: Intriga familiar*." *Hablemos de cine* 70 (April 1979): 30.

Castro Cobos, Mario. "Dossier 2001: *El bien esquivo*." *Abre los ojos* 1 (June 2002): 16.

"5, 50: Activos y en Forma." *Hablemos de cine* 50–51 (November 1969–February 1970): 7–8.

"Cine cubano: 10 años de cine en 10 años de revolución." *Hablemos de cine* 54 (July–August 1970): 14–15.

"Cine de aquí y de allá." *Hablemos de cine* 28 (August 1966): 27.

"El cine peruano entre realidad y deseo (Mesa redonda, primera parte)." *Hablemos de cine* 73–74 (June 1981): 17–21.

"El cine peruano entre realidad y deseo (II): Introducción." *Hablemos de cine* 75 (May 1982): 15.

"Cine peruano: Introducción." *Hablemos de cine* 77 (March 1984): 16.

Cordero, Claudio. "Latinoamérica va al cine." *godard!* 1, no. 2 (September 2001): 18–20.

"Corto peruano: ¿el fin del juego? Conversación con tres realizadores de cortometrajes." *La gran ilusión* 1 (1993): 94–106.

De Cárdenas, Federico. "Chile." *Hablemos de cine* 34 (March–April 1967): 10.

———. "Una constación y una repuesta." *Hablemos de cine* 69 (1977–78): 21.

———. "Entrevista con Manuel Octavio Gómez." *Hablemos de cine* 54 (July–August 1970): 31–32.

———. "*Ganarás el pan.*" *Hablemos de cine* 11 (July 15, 1965): 45.
———. "Hombres de Cine: Roman Polanski: Conferencia de prensa en Rio." *Hablemos de cine* 47 (May–June 1969): 65–67.
———. "*La mujer de paja.*" *Hablemos de cine* 1 (February 15, 1965): 13–14.
———. "Otros paises." *Hablemos de cine* 34 (March–April 1967): 11.
———. "Roman Polanski: Conferencia de prensa en Rio." *Hablemos de cine* 47 (May–June 1969): 68–73.
———, Isaac León Frías, and Nelson García. "Cine peruano y colombiano: Tientos y diferencias: Carlos Mayolo en Lima." *Hablemos de cine* 72 (November 1980): 16–19.
"Diccionario del cortometraje peruano." *Hablemos de cine* 70 (April 1979): 19.
"Editorial." *Abre los ojos* 1 (June 2002): 3.
"Editorial." *Tren de sombras* 1 (March 2004): 2.
"'El embajador y yo' y el cine nacional." *Hablemos de cine* 41 (May–June 1968): 4.
"La encrucijada del Cine Peruano." *Hablemos de cine* 67 (1975): 15–22.
"En torno al cine latinoamericano." *Hablemos de cine* 35 (May–June 1967): 4.
"Encuesta que responde América Penichet, José Ravillon y Julio Ortega." *Hablemos de cine* 28 (August 1966): 44–45.
"La farsa de *Nemesio.*" *Hablemos de cine* 49 (September–October 1969): 4.
"Festival de Rio de Janeiro: Declara Andrés Ruszkowski a *Hablemos de cine.*" *Hablemos de cine* 17 (October 15, 1965): 5–8.
García, Nelson. "Diccionario del cortometraje peruano (I): Fernando Gagliuffi." *Hablemos de cine* 70 (April 1979): 21.
———. "*La odisea del General José* (J. Fraga)." *Hablemos de cine* 54 (July–August 1970): 29–30.
———. "*Por 1ra vez/Acerca de un personaje . . . /Al sur de Maniadero* (O. Coratázar)." *Hablemos de cine* 54 (July–August 1970): 45–46
García, Nelson, et al. "Nora de Izcué: 'Creo que el cine nacional se dará cuando esta mayoria peruana se exprese y se vea reflejada en las pantallas, no nuestros cuatro o cinco cineastas.'" *Hablemos de cine* 67 (1975): 37–43.
Gibson, Percy. "*Dios Sabe Cuánto Amé.*" *El Comercio* (April 24, 1965): C1.
"Godard 2, aquí vamos." *godard!* 1, no. 2 (September 2001): 2.
González Norris, Antonio. "Reseña: Viña 69: Cuba: Una cultura en Revolución." *Hablemos de cine* 50–51 (November 1969–February 1970): 39–42.
———. "La violencia y la liberación: Entrevista con Fernando Solanas." *Hablemos de cine* 46 (March–April 1969): 5–12.
"*Hablemos de cine* presente." *Hablemos de cine* 12 (July 31, 1965): 3–4.
Huayhuaca, José Carlos. "El dilemma del lenguaje o el compromise: el cine de Federico García." *Hablemos de cine* 75 (May 1982): 26–29.

———, et al. "Francisco Lombardi: 'Hacer cine en el Perú es para mi poner los pies en tierra.'" *Hablemos de cine* 67 (1975): 27–31.

"Información: La sociedad peruana de cinematografía." *Hablemos de cine* 34 (March–April 1967): 30–31.

Ledgard, Reynaldo. "*Miss Univero en el Perú*." *Hablemos de cine* 77 (March 1984): 34.

———. "*Una raya más al tigre*." *Hablemos de cine* 76 (February 1983): 23–24.

León Frías, Isaac. "*La boca del lobo*." *Caretas* (December 12, 1988): 70–71.

———. "La búsqueda de una voz propria en el largometraje peruano." *Hablemos de cine* 69 (1977–78): 16–18.

———. "El cine colombiano hoy: Marta Rodríguez y Jorge Silva." *Hablemos de cine* 71 (April 1980): 26–30.

———. "El cine latinoamericano en la hora de la verdad," *Hablemos de cine* 50–51 (November 1969–February 1970): 34–36.

———. "¡El cine paraguayo existe!" *Hablemos de cine* 63 (1972): 45–46.

———. "Cine peruano: La búsqueda de una voz propria en el largometraje peruano." *Hablemos de cine* 29 (1977–78): 17.

———. "Colombia: Entrevista con Carlos Álvarez." *Hablemos de cine* 53 (May–June 1970): 21–24.

———. "El crítico frente al cine peruano." *Tren de sombras* 2 (August 2004): 18–21.

———. "Diccionario del cortometraje peruano (I): Nora de Izcué." *Hablemos de cine* 70 (April 1979): 23.

———. "Diccionario del cortometraje peruano (II): W. S. Palacios." *Hablemos de cine* 71 (April 1980): 21.

———. "El encuentro de cineastas latinoameicanos." *Hablemos de cine* 34 (March–April 1967): 15–16.

———. "Entrevista con Manuel Pérez," *Hablemos de cine* 70 (April 1979): 41–43.

———. "Festival de Viña del Mar: Introducción." *Hablemos de cine* 34 (March–April 1967): 5.

———. "*Ganarás el pan*." *Hablemos de cine* 11 (July 15, 1965): 44–45.

———. "Hacia una historia del Cine Peruano." *Hablemos de cine* 50–51 (Novermber 1969–February 1970): 43–53.

———. "*Lucía* (H. Solás)." *Hablemos de cine* 54 (July–August 1970): 25–26.

———. "*Misión en los Andes*." *Caretas* (September 7, 1987): 60.

———. "*Murallas de sangre*." *Hablemos de cine* 2 (March 1, 1965): 31–32.

———. "Notas sobre la muestra de cine cubano." *Hablemos de cine* 75 (May 1982): 35–37.

———. "¿Predicando en el desierto?" *Hablemos de cine* 77 (March 1984): 17–21.

———. "Reseña: Viña 69: Memorias dragones y tigres en los hornos del subdesarrollo." *Hablemos de cine* 50–51 (November 1969–February 1970): 38–42.

———. "*La tumba de Ligeia* (R. Corman)."*Hablemos de cine* 18 (September 1, 1965): 54–56.

León Frías, Isaac and Federico de Cárdenas. "Armando Robles Godoy: Un director peruano." *Hablemos de cine* 4 (April 1, 1965): 7–17.

———. "El cine latinoamericano: El cine cubano, hoy—Entrevista con Alfredo Guevara." *Hablemos de cine* 34 (March–April 1967): 19–29.

———. "Reencuentro con Manuel Octavio Gómez." *Hablemos de cine* 75 (May 1982): 30–34.

———. "Un oficio del siglo XX." *Contratexto* 9 (December 1995): 153–160.

León Frías, Isaac, Desiderio Blanco and Francisco Lombardi. "El cine colombiano hoy: Diálogo complementario con Luis Ospina." *Hablemos de cine* 71 (April 1980): 26–34.

León Frías, Juan Bullitta, Carlos Rodríguez Larraín, and Federico de Cárdenas. "*Intimidad de los parques.*" *Hablemos de cine* 3 (March 18, 1965): 41–43.

León Frías, Isaac, Juan M. Bullitta, and Pablo Guevara. "¿Una película peruana hecha por un Japonés? Susumi Hani y *Amor en los Andes*: Coloquio." *Hablemos de cine* 36 (July–August 1967): 18–20.

León Frías, Isaac, et al. "El autór y el film: (entrevista con) Jorge Volkert, 2do premio del I Festival de cine peruano." *Hablemos de cine* 12 (July 31, 1965): 11–18.

León Frías, Isaac, et al. "Entrevista: Mario Vargas Llosa habla de cine." *Hablemos de cine* 52 (March–April 1970): 30–35.

León Frías, Isaac, et al. "Entrevista: Primer contacto con Susumu Hani: Arte y juventud." *Hablemos de cine* 10 (July 1, 1965): 16–24.

Linares, César. "En pocas palabras: *Semilla.*" *Hablemos de cine* 45 (January–February 1969): 82.

Lombardi, Francisco. "El cine colombiano hoy: Diálogo complementario con Luis Ospina." *Hablemos de cine* 71 (April 1980): 34.

———. "Reseña: Viña 69: Bolivia: Los peligros de la demagogia," *Hablemos de cine* 50–51 (November 1969–February 1970): 29.

Martínez León, Jesús. "XI Semana Internacional de Cine Religioso y de Valores Humanos de Villadolid." *Hablemos de cine* 26–27 (June–July 1966): 16–23.

———. "Reseña: Festival de San Sebastián." *Hablemos de cine* 28 (August 1966): 5–15.

Molina Foix, Vicente. "8th semana de cine en color (Barcelona)." *Hablemos de cine* 33 (January–February 1967): 28–31.

"Nace el cine nacional." *Hablemos de cine* 3 (March 18, 1965): 3.

"Un oficio del siglo XX: Federico de Cárdenas e Isaac León Frías dialogan sobre más de treinta años de ver cine." *Contratexto* 9 (December 1995): 153–160.

Perla Anaya, José. "El cine y su derecho: El rol de lo legal en el nacimiento de una cinematografía." *La gran ilusión* 1 (1993): 84–93.

Pimentel, Sebastian. "El enigma de la crítica, o el problema de pensar y hacer cine en el Perú." *godard!* 1, no. 2 (September 2001): 24–26.

"Presentación." *Hablemos de cine* 1 (February 15, 1965): 1–2.

"Primer festival de cine peruano de 16mm." *Hablemos de cine* 12 (July 31, 1965): 3–10.

Proetzel, Javier. "El cortometraje: explorando su aceptación." *La gran ilusión* 1 (1993): 75–83.

———. "Grandez y decandencia del espectáculo cinematográfico." *Contratexto* 9 (December 1995): 111–125.

"La regla del juego." *La gran ilusión* 13 (2003): 1–2.

["¿Una revista de cine?"] *La gran ilusión* 1 (1993): 1.

Robles Godoy, Armando, et al. "Cine peruano: 'En las selva no hay estrellas' en un polémico debate." *Hablemos de cine* 33 (January–February 1967): 10–18.

Rodríguez Larraín, Carlos. *Ganarás el pan*," *Hablemos de cine* 11 (July 15, 1965): 42–44.

———. "*Some Came Running (Dios sabe cuánto amé)*." *Hablemos de cine* 6 (May 1, 1965): 52–59.

Samillán Cavero, Fernando. "Primeras palabras...." *Butaca sanmarquina* 1 (July–September 1998): 3.

———. "Vlado, en el recuerdo." *Butaca sanmarquina* 3 (1998): 28–29.

Samillán, Fernando [and René Weber]. "Al cierre." *Butaca sanmarquina* 7 (September 2000): 3.

Silva, Mariano. "Crónica del Festival de Mar de la Plata." *Hablemos de cine* 25 (May 1966): 12–16.

"Susumu Hani retornó a Japón." *Hablemos de cine* 19 (November 15, 1965): 14–15.

"Tierra en trance." *La gran ilusión* 1 (1993): 67.

Torres, Augusto M. "Cannes 66: El festival de escándalo." *Hablemos de cine* 26–27 (June–July 1966): 5–15.

———. "Cine mexicano: Carlos Fuentes habla de cine y de literatura latinoamericana." *Hablemos de cine* 49 (September–October 1969): 23–31.

———. "Gabriel García Márquez y el cine." *Hablemos de cine* 47 (May–June 1969): 56–58.

———. "IX Gran Premio de Bergamo." *Hablemos de cine* 33 (January–February 1967): 24–27.

———. "Venecia 99: ¿Crisis?" *Hablemos de cine* 30–31 (October–November 1966): 5–12.

Tsang, José. "Escorpiones, arañas y chanchitos." *godard!* 1, no. 2 (September 2001): 22–23.

Ugarte, Claudia. "Butacas interactivas: Cine en discussion." *Butaca* 20 (June 2004): 31–33.

Vicente, Benicio, and Oscar Páz Soldán Pinto. "Del dibujo animado . . . en el Perú." *Butaca sanmarquina* 6 (April 2000): 14–16.

"Viña del Mar en números." *Hablemos de cine* 34 (March–April 1967): 13–14.

Weber, René. "Editorial." *Butaca* 20 (June 2004): 4.

———. "Editorial." *Butaca sanmarquina* 11 (April 2002): 1.

———. "El Grupo Chaski: Una película sin 'Happy End." *Butaca sanmarquina* 1 (July–August–September 1998): 22–24.

———. "La pared que habla: La fascinante experiencia de la Difución Popular del Grupo Chaski." *Butaca sanmarquina* 2 (October–December 1998): 8–9.

Wiener F., Christian. "Los cazadores de la ley perdida." *Contratexto* 9 (December 1995): 106–109.

———. "Crítica de la crítica." *Butaca sanmarquina* 13 (October 2002): 18–20.

Other Sources

Alemán, Gabriela. "An International Conspiracy: Ecuadorian Cinema in the 1960s and 1970s." *Journal of Latin American Cultural Studies* 13, no. 1 (March 2004): 97–113.

Álvarez, Carlos. *Una decada de cortometraje colombiano, 1970–1980*. Bogota: Borradores de cine, 1982.

Anderson, Benedict. *Imagined Communities: Reflections on the Origin and Spread of Nationalism*. London: Verso, 1983.

Angeles, Francisco. "El crítico de cine no puede ser un perdonavidas: Entrevista a Claudio Cordero, Director de *godard!*" *Bitácora de el Hablador* (March 11, 2007), http://elhablador.com/blog/2007/03/11/entrevista-a-claudio-cordero-director-de-godard/.

Arróspide de la Flor, César. *Reflexiones sobre el cambio cultural en el Perú*. Lima: C.E.P., 1985.

Ascué, Sonia, and Rosa Esquivel. "Aculturación o mestizaje: una perspectiva generacional." In *Los nuevos limeños: Sueños, fervores y caminos en el mundo popular*, by TEMPO, 377–399. Lima: SUR Casa de Estudios del Socialismo, 1993.

Barnard, Timothy, ed. *Argentine Cinema*. Toronto: Nightwood Editions, 1986.

Barrionuebo, Alexei. "Italy Follows Trail of Secret South American Abductions." *New York Times*, February 22, 2008, A12.

Barrot, Olivier. *L'Ecran Français, 1943–1953: Histoire d'un journal et d'une époque*. Paris: Les Editeurs Français Reunis, 1979.

Barrow, Sarah. "Peruvian Cinema and the Struggle for International Recognition: Case Study on *El destino no tiene favoritos*." In *Contemporary Latin American Cinema: Breaking into the Global Market*, edited by Deborah Shaw, 173–189. Lanham, MD: Rowman and Littlefield, 2007.

Barthes, Roland. *Camera Lucida: Reflections on Photography.* New York: Hill and Wang, 1981.

Bazin, André. "On the *politiques des auteurs.*" In *Cahiers du Cinéma: The 1950s: Neo-Realism, Hollywood, New Wave*, edited by Jim Hillier, 248–259. Cambridge, Mass.: Harvard University Press, 1985.

Bedoya, Ricardo. *100 años de cine en el Perú: Una historia crítica.* Lima: Universidad de Lima, 1996.

———. *Un cine reencontrado: Diccionario ilustrado de las películas peruanas.* Lima: Universidad de Lima, 1997.

———. Personal interview. November 9, 1998.

———. Personal interview. July 20, 2003.

Betz, Marc. "Film History, Film Genre, and Their Discontents: The Case of the Omnibus Film." The Moving Image: Journal of the Association of Moving Image Archivists, no. 2 (Fall 2001): 56–87.

Bordwell, David. *On the History of Film Style.* Cambridge, Mass.: Harvard University Press, 1997.

Bourdieu, Pierre. *Distinction.* London: Routledge, 1979.

———. *The Field of Cultural Production: Essays on Art and Literature.* New York: Columbia University Press, 1993.

Burton, Julianne. "Learning to Write at the Movies: Film and the Fiction Writer in Latin America." *Texas Quarterly* 18, no. 1 (Spring 1975): 92–103.

Burton-Carvajal, Julianne, ed. *Short Films from Latin America: A Film Exhibition Organized by the American Federation of Arts.* New York: American Federation of Arts, 1992.

Carbone, Giancarlo, ed. *El cine en el Perú, 1897–1950.* Lima: Universidad de Lima, 1991.

———. *El cine en el Perú: El cortometraje, 1972–1992.* Lima: Universidad de Lima, 2007.

———. *El cine en el Perú: Testimonios, 1950–1972.* Lima: Universidad de Lima, 1994.

Chanan, Michael. *Chilean Cinema.* London: BFI, 1976.

———. "New Cinemas in Latin America." In *The Oxford History of World Cinema*, edited by Geoffrey Nowell-Smith, 740–749. Oxford: Oxford University Press, 1997.

La cinefilia no es patriota. June 1, 2008, http://lacinefilianoespatriota.blogspot.com/.

Cinencuentro. June 1, 2008, http://www.cinencuentro.com/.

De Baeque, Antoine. *Les Cahiers du Cinéma: Histoire d'une revue.* Vol. 1: *A l'assaut du cinéma, 1951–1959.* Paris: Editions Caheirs du Cinéma, 1991.

De Cárdenas, Federico. Personal interview. November 10, 1998.

———. Personal interview. July 9, 2003.

De la Vega-Hurtado, Margarita. Personal interview. June 9, 2001.

De Usabel, Gaizka S. *The High Noon of American Films in Latin America*. Ann Arbor: UMI Research Press, 1982.

De Valck and Malte Hagener. *Cinephilia: Movies, Love and Memory*. Amsterdam: Amsterdam University Press, 2005.

Demonsablon, Philippe. "Scènes de la vie de province." *Cahiers du Cinéma* 97 (July 1959): 50.

Denzin, Norman K. *The Cinematic Society: The Voyeur's Gaze*. London: Sage Publications, 1995.

Díaz López, Marina, and Alberto Elena, eds. *Tierra en trance: El cine latinoamericano en 100 películas*. Madrid: Alianza, 1999.

Díaz Torres, Daniel. "La pantalla conflictive." *Cine cubano* 103 (1982): 46–60.

Elena, Alberto, and Marina Díaz López, eds. *The Cinema of Latin America: 24 Frames*. London: Wallflower Press, 2003.

Elsey, Eileen, and Andrew Kelly. *In Short: A Guide to Short Film-making in the Digital Age*. London: BFI, 2002.

Everett, Anna. *Returning the Gaze: A Genealogy of Black Film Content, 1909–1949*. Durham, N.C.: Duke University Press.

Falicov, Tamara L. "Programa Ibermedia: Co-Production and the Cultural Politics of Constructing an Ibero-American Audiovisual Space." *Spectator: The University of Southern California Journal of Film & Television* 27, no. 2 (Fall 2007): 21–30.

Fernández-Maldonado, Ana María. "The Diffusion and Use of Information and Communications Technologies in Lima, Peru." *Journal of Urban Technology* 8, no. 3 (2001): 21–43.

Figueroa, Adolfo and Manuel Barrón. "Inequality, Ethnicity and Social Disorder in Peru." CRISE Working Paper No. 8. Oxford: CRISE, 2005.

Fornet, Ambrosio. "¿Se repite el nuevo cine?" *Cine cubano* 103 (1982): 38–42.

Francia, Aldo. *Nuevo cine latinoamericano en Viña del Mar*. Santiago de Chile: CESOC Ediciones ChileAmérica, 1990.

Friedberg, Anne. "Writing About Cinema: 'Close Up,' 1927–1933." Ph.D. diss., New York University, 1986. Ann Arbor: UMI, 1986; 8405770.

García, Federico. Personal interview. July 12, 2003.

García Márquez, Gabriel. "Declaraciones de Gabriel García Márquez." *Cine cubano* 103 (1982): 18.

García Riera, Emilio. *Breve historia del cine mexicano: Primer siglo, 1897–1997*. Mexico City: Instituto Mexicano de Cinematografía, 1998.

Getino, Octavio. *Cine y televisión en América Latina: Producción y mercados*. Santiago, Chile: LOM Ediciones, 1998.

Gomery, Douglas. "Hollywood as Industry." In *The Oxford Guide to Film Studies*, edited by John Hill and Pamela Church Gibson, 245–255. Oxford: Oxford University Press, 1998.

Gutiérrez Alea, Tomás, and Edmundo Desnoes. *Memories of Underdevelopment and Inconsolable Memories*. New Brunswick, N.J.: Rutgers University Press, 1990.

Hanson, Claire, ed. *Re-reading the Short Story*. London: Macmillan Press, 1989.

Hill, John, and Pamela Church Gibson, eds. *The Oxford Guide to Film Studies*. Oxford: Oxford University Press, 1998.

Hillier, Jim, ed. *Cahiers du cinéma, The 1950s: Neo-Realism, Hollywood, New Wave*. Cambridge, Mass.: Harvard University Press, 1985.

———. *Cahiers du Cinéma: 1960–1968, New Wave, New Cinema, Reevaluating Hollywood*. Cambridge, Mass.: Harvard University Press, 1986.

Hoberman, J. "The Film Critic of Tomorrow, Today." In *The Crisis of Criticism*, ed. Maurice Berger, 71–89. New York: New Press, 1998.

Keathley, Christian. *Cinephilia and History; or, The Wind in the Trees*. Bloomington: Indiana University Press, 2006.

Kinder, Marsha. *Blood Cinema: The Reconstruction of National Identity in Spain*. Berkeley and Los Angeles: University of California Press, 1993.

King, John. *Magical Reels: A History of Cinema in Latin America*. London: Verso, 1990.

Koichi, Y. "Venise 66: Commentaires." *Cahiers du cinéma*, no. 183 (October 1966): 29–30.

Ledgard, Melvin. *Amores adversos y apasionados: La evolución del tema del amor en cinco novellas latinoamericanas*. Lima: Fondo Editorial PUCP, 2002.

León Frías, Isaac. "Carta de Isaac León Frías." *Nuevo Texto Critico* 21/22 (January–December 1998): 345–346.

———. "Pérou." *Les Cinémas de l'Amérique latine: pays par pays, l'histoire, l'économie, les structuresm les auteurs, les oeuvres*, edited by Guy Hennebelle and Alfonso Gumucio Dagrón, 423–437. Paris: Lherminier, 1981.

———. Personal interview. November 17, 1998.

———. Personal interview. July 23, 2003.

Lombardi, Francisco. Personal interview. November 5, 1998.

López, Ana. "Early Cinema and Modernity in Latin America." *Cinema Journal* 40, no. 1 (Fall 2000): 48–78.

———. "The Long Life of Short Film: Brazil and Colombia Compared." In *Short Films from Latin America: A Film Exhibition Organized and Circulated by the American Federation of Arts*, edited by Julianne Burton-Carvajal, 33–39. New York: American Federation of Arts, 1992.

Luis, Mikel. "*La boca del lobo*." In *Tierra en trance: El cine latinoamericano en 100 películas*, edited by Alberto Elena y Marina Díaz López, 365–360. Madrid: Alianza, 1999.

Lunders, L. "Office Catholique International du Cinéma." In *The New Catholic Encyclopedia*. Vol. 10: *Mos to Pat*, 655–656. New York: McGraw-Hill, 1967.

MacDonald, Scott. *Cinema 16: Documents Toward a History of the Film Society*. Philadelphia: Temple University Press, 2002.

Man, Glenn. *Radical Visions: American Film Renaissance, 1967–1976*. Westport, Conn.: Greenwood Press, 1994.

Manwell, Roger. *New Cinema in the USA: The Feature Film Since 1946*. London: Studio Vista/Dutton Pictureback, 1968.

Marcorelles, Louis. "L'épreuve du direct." *Cahiers du cinéma* 210 (March 1969): 39–45, 58–64.

Mariategui, José Carlos. *Siete ensayos de interpretación de la realidad peruana*. Barcelona: Linkgua, 2006.

Martin, Michael T., ed. *New Latin American Cinema*. Vol. 1: *Theory, Practices and Transcontinental Articulations*. Detroit, Mich.: Wayne State University Press, 1997.

May, Charles M., ed. *The New Short Story Theories*. Athens: Ohio University Press, 1994.

McClennen, Sophia A. "The Theory and Practice of the Peruvian Grupo Chaski." *Jump Cut* 50 (Spring 2008), http://www.ejumpcut.org/currentissue/Chaski/text.html (accessed June 2, 2008).

Metz, Christian. *The Imaginary Signifier: Psychoanalysis and the Cinema*. Bloomington: Indiana University Press, 1997.

Mouesca, Jacqueline. *El cine en Chile: Crónica en tres tiempos*. Santiago de Chile: Editorial Planeta, 1997.

Mulvey, Laura. "Visual Pleasure and Narrative Cinema." 1973, 1975. In *Visual and Other Pleasures*, 14–26. Bloomington: Indiana University Press, 1989.

Neale, Steve. "Art Cinema as Institution." *Screen* 22, no. 1 (1981): 11–40.

"The New Pictures." *Time* (January 12, 1959).

Nowell-Smith, Geoffrey, ed. *The Oxford History of World Cinema*. Oxford: Oxford University Press, 1997.

Páginas del diario de Satán. June 1, 2008, http://paginasdeldiariodesatan.blogspot.com/.

Paranaguá, Paulo Antonio. "América latina busca su imágen." In *Historia general del cine*, edited by Carlos F. Heredero and Casimiro Torreiro. Madrid: Cátedra, 1996. 205–393.

———. *Le cinéma en Amérique Latine: le miroir éclaté*. Paris: L'Harmattan, 2000.

———. "Of Periodizations and Paradigms: The Fifties in Comparative Perspective." *Nuevo Texto Critico* 21/22 (January–December 1998): 31–44.

Parodi Trece, Carlos. *Perú, 1980–2000: Políticas Económicas y sociales en entornos cambiantes*. Lima: Universidad del Pacífico, 2002.

Perla Anaya, José. *Censura y promoción en el cine*. Lima: Universidad de Lima, 1991.

"Peru Internet Usage and Telecom Marketing Reports." Internet World Stats: Usage and Population Statistics. Miniwatts Marketing Group. April 15, 2007, http://www.internetworldstats.com/sa/pe.htm.

Philip, George D. E. *The Rise and Fall of the Peruvian Military Radicals, 1968–1976*. London: Athlone Press, 1978.

Pick, Zuzana M. *The New Latin American Cinema: A Continential Project*. Austin: University of Texas Press, 1993.

Pius XI. "Vigilanti Cura." In *The Papal Encyclicals, 1903–1939*, compiled by Claudia Carlen, 517–523. Wilmington, N.C.: McGrath Publishing, 1981.

Pius XII. "Miranda Prorsus." In *The Papal Encyclicals, 1939–1958*, compiled by Claudia Carlen, 347–364. Wilmington, N.C.: McGrath Publishing, 1981.

Plot, Bernadette. *Un manifeste pour le cinéma: Les normes culturelles en question dans la première Revue du cinéma*. Paris: Editions L'Harmattan, 1996.

Pratt, Mary Louise. "The Short Story: The Long and the Short of It." In *The New Short Story Theories*, edited by Charles M. May, 91–113. Athens: Ohio University Press, 1994.

"Proyecto de revista cinematográfica." Preliminary outline of journal project. Filmoteca de Lima/Museo de Arte, Lima, Peru, January 2, 1965.

Quinn, Michael. "Distribution, the Transient Audience, and the Transition to the Feature Film." *Cinema Journal* 40, no. 2 (Winter 2001): 35–56.

Rama, Ángel. *The Lettered City*. Translated by John Chasteen. Durham, N.C.: Duke University Press, 1996.

Rosenbaum, Jonathan. *Movie Mutations: The Changing Face of World Cinephilia*. London: BFI, 2003.

Rudolph, James D. *Peru: The Evolution of a Crisis*. Westport, Conn.: Praeger, 1993.

Sarmiento, Domingo Faustino. *Facundo: Civilization and Barbarism*. Translated by Kathleen Ross. With an introduction by Roberto González Echevarría. Berkeley and Los Angeles: University of California Press, 2004

Schnitman, Jorge. *Film Industries in Latin America: Dependency and Development*. Norwood, N.J.: Ablex, 1984.

Slobin, Mark. "Micromusics of the West: A Comparative Approach." *Ethnomusicology* 36, no. 1 (Winter 1992): 1–87.

Smith, Ian Hayden, ed. *TCM International Film Guide 2008: The Definitive Annual Review of World Cinema*. London: Wallflower Press, 2008.

Solanas, Fernando E. and Octavio Getino. "Towards a Third Cinema." In *New Latin American Cinema*. Vol 1: *Theory, Practices and Transcontinental Articulations*, edited by Michael T. Martin, 33–58. Detroit, Mich.: Wayne State University Press, 1997.

"*Some Came Running*," *Variety* (December 24, 1948). In *Variety Film Reviews*, vol. 9, *1954–1958*. New York: Bowker, 1983.

Sontag, Susan. "The Decay of Cinema." *New York Times*, February 25, 1996.

TEMPO [Taller de Estudios de las Mentalidades Populares]. *Los nuevos limeños: Sueños, fervores y caminos en el mundo popular*. Lima: SUR Casa de Estudios del Socialismo, 1993.

Thomas, Florence. *Los estragos del amor: el discurso amoroso en los medios de comunicación*. Bogotá: Editorial Universidad Nacional, 1994.

Thompson, Howard. "Lively, Tough Western Has Premiere Here." *New York Times*, October 29, 1964.

Triana-Toribio, Núria. *Spanish National Cinema*. London: Routledge, 2003.

Tubau, Iván. *Crítica cinematográfica española, Bazin contra Aristarco: La gran controversia de los años 60*. Barcelona: Publicacions Edicions Universitat de Barcelona, 1983.

UNESCO Convention on the Protection and Promotion of the Diversity of Cultural Expressions. Paris: UNESCO (October 2005), http://unesdoc.unesco.org/images/0014/001429/142919e.pdf.

Villanueva Mansilla, Eduardo. "Internet availability and politics in Peru: A preliminary report on an apparent paradox." Presentation at PISTA (Politics and Information Systems: Technologies and Applications) Conference, 2004. Published online at author's Web site, http://macareo.pucp.edu.pe/evillan/Eduardo%20Villanueva%20Mansilla/Escritos_files/PISTA-EVM-P025SV.pdf (accessed April 15, 2007).

Vivas Sabroso, Fernando. *En vivo y en directo: Una historia de la television peruana*. Lima: University of Lima, 2001.

Willemen, Paul. *Looks and Frictions: Essays in Cultural Studies and Film Theory*. Bloomington: Indiana University Press, 1994.

Williams, Raymond. *The Country and the City*. New York: Oxford University Press, 1973.

Zimmerman, Patricia R. Personal interview. April 20, 2007.

———, and Dale Hudson. "Trafficking in the Archives: Remixing Across, Between and Through Nations." Trans/National Cinephilias. American Comparative Literature Association annual meeting, Puebla, Mexico, April 20, 2007.

INDEX

Page numbers in italics refer to illustrations.